Praise for **BOOK LUST** and Nancy Pe

"Readers who travel the pages of *Book Lust* will be astonished at th and depth of Pearl's reading experience. It's a book best read twice; on through, then kept as a reference that will forever forestall the questi should I read next?'"

—*The Seattle Times*

"She's the talk of librarian circles." —*The New York Times*

"A tour de force that would thrill any listmaker.... This is one lusty librarian!"

—*The Los Angeles Times*

"With their own action figurines, 'zines, and websites, a new breed of librarian is closing the book on a stodgy old stereotype . . . [Nancy Pearl] has become pretty much the librarian version of a rock star." —*Bust* magazine

"The country's most famous librarian (and there are no candidates for second place) . . . Pearl is cherished by bibliophile strangers who consider her a trusted friend."

—*The Seattle Post-Intelligencer*

"Looking for a good book? Naturally Nancy Pearl has a few recommendations."

—*Sunset* magazine

"Perhaps the librarian best known in popular culture . . ." —*Library Journal*

"Just as I was ready to put the last nail in the coffin of reader's advisory services, up pops the best book ever written on the subject. In fact, this may be the best book ever written by a librarian." —*American Libraries Magazine*

"*Book Lust* should be a hit with book clubs looking for all manner of reading."

—*Bloomsbury Review*

MORE BOOK LUST

MORE
BOOK
LUST

NANCY PEARL

RECOMMENDED READING FOR EVERY
MOOD, MOMENT, AND REASON

SASQUATCH BOOKS
SEATTLE

Printed in the United States of America
Published by Sasquatch Books
Distributed by Publishers Group West
10 09 08 07 06 05   8 7 6 5 4 3 2

Cover photograph: Jason Koski
Select icon illustrations: Bob Suh
Cover design: Rowan Moore/DoubleMRanch
Interior design: Rowan Moore
Interior composition: Stewart A. Williams

Library of Congress Cataloging-in-Publication Data
Pearl, Nancy.
  More book lust : recommended reading for every mood, moment, and reason / by Nancy Pearl.
    p. cm.
  Includes index.
  ISBN 1-57061-435-0
  1. Best books. 2. Books and reading—United States. I. Title.

  Z1035.9.P38 2005
  011'.73—dc22

                                                                              2004066292

Sasquatch Books
119 South Main Street, Suite 400
Seattle, WA 98104
(206) 467-4300
www.sasquatchbooks.com
custserv@sasquatchbooks.com

Contents

INTRODUCTION

If we were at a twelve-step meeting together, I would have to stand up and say, "Hi, I'm Nancy P., and I'm a readaholic." As I explained in the introduction to *Book Lust*, my addiction to reading (and my career as a librarian) grew out of a childhood that was rescued from despair by books, libraries, and librarians. I discovered at a young age that books—paradoxically—allowed me both to find and to escape myself. I was enthralled with the sheer glory of the written word when I read (or had read to me), for example, Robert McCloskey's **One Morning in Maine** and **A Child's Garden of Verses** by Robert Louis Stevenson as a child, and I've never looked back. Recently a friend reminded me of what Francis Spufford says in **The Child That Books Built: A Life in Reading:** "The books you read as a child brought you signs you hadn't seen yourself, scents you hadn't smelled, sounds you hadn't heard. They introduced you to people you hadn't met, and helped you to sample ways of being that would never have occurred to you." As a child, I lived those words, and continue to do so as an adult reader.

I live now in a small condominium whose four rooms are piled high with books that have spilled off the bookcases that line all the available wall space, and which themselves are already double-shelved with books. (It perhaps sounds messier than it is.)

In addition to being an addicted reader, I have to confess that I am a promiscuous reader as well. I basically read anything, as long as it's well written and has interesting characters. And there's no subject in which you won't find books that meet those criteria. As I write this, stacked next to my bed are these books, waiting patiently for me to read or reread them: **Collected Poems** by Donald Justice; Robert Byron's classic travel book, **The Road to Oxiana;** James Muirden's **Shakespeare Well-Versed: A Rhyming Guide to All His Plays; Why Didn't They Ask Evans?** by Agatha Christie; Francine Prose's

A Changed Man; Boys and Girls Together by William Goldman; Sheila Levine Is Dead and Living in New York by Gail Parent; The Children's Blizzard by David Laskin; Vanity Fair by William Makepeace Thackeray; Mantrapped by Fay Weldon; Mrs. Daffodil by Gladys Taber; and The Saturdays by Elizabeth Enright. A frighteningly eclectic list, to be sure.

Any life devoted to reading is extraordinarily rich and rewarding, but it can certainly become an unbalanced life. Because of all the time I spend devoted to reading, here are some things that I've, perforce, given up: gardening, cooking, Rollerblading, and cleaning house. But in return I've gotten so much gratification from the life that reading has allowed me to live. I've gotten enormous pleasure from writing *Book Lust* and now *More Book Lust*. Writing these two books has given me a chance to select from the huge assortment of books that are available at bookstores and libraries a group of books that I've read and enjoyed—fiction, nonfiction, old, new, happy books, dark books, books for children, teens, and adults—and that I believe that other readers will enjoy too.

I very much wanted to call this new book *Book Lust II: The Morning After* because of all that happened after I finished writing *Book Lust*. For about a week after I turned in the final manuscript of *Book Lust: Recommended Reading for Every Mood, Moment, and Reason*, I was elated. I had done it! Here, I thought, in one manuscript were all the books I've ever read and loved. And then, nearly a week to the day—when everything was out of my hands and no more changes were possible—I began sitting bolt upright in the middle of the night and saying, "Oh no, did I include Marge Piercy's *Vida* in the 'Pawns of History' section?" (Answering that question entailed getting out of bed, turning on the computer, opening up the manuscript, and discovering to my horror that I had not.) And on and on it went—how on earth had I left out the first line of Anita Brookner's debut novel, The Debut? Where was Dorothy Dunnett?

Why, oh why, had I omitted Jerome K. Jerome's **Three Men in a Boat?** Why did I include so little poetry when poetry is one of my great loves? The regrets were beginning to outweigh the joy.

And then—because I had included my email address in the introduction to *Book Lust*—I started hearing from readers from Florida to Massachusetts, from Washington State to Washington, D.C., from Michigan to Texas, asking me the same sorts of questions—had I ever read Elizabeth Goudge's **Green Dolphin Street?** (Yes.) What about **Nervous Conditions** by Tsitsi Dangarembga for another good first line? (Yes, definitely.) Had I thought about including Simon Singh's **The Code Book**, or had I not read it or not liked it? (Hadn't read it but would.) Many of the books that were recommended I had read, and had either forgotten or not enjoyed as much as the sender did; but others were completely new to me. I made reading lists of the books that sounded good to me, checked them out from the library, searched my local bookstores, scoured the Internet, and made heavy use of The Seattle Public Library's Interlibrary Loan department.

When Sasquatch Books asked me if I was interested in writing another book about good reads, I was overjoyed. It gave me a chance to make up for my previous omissions, add books that had just been published, and come up with new categories to fit these books into. (For various reasons—you'll have to ask them—the folks at Sasquatch decided that it would be better to call the book *More Book Lust*, and so it is.)

I think of *More Book Lust* not as a sequel to *Book Lust*, and certainly not as an updating of the first book, but rather as its true companion. I picture the two sitting on someone's bookshelf—not next to each other, but rather bookending rows and rows of books that have been discovered, or rediscovered, and thoroughly enjoyed, from reading *Book Lust* and *More Book Lust*. Only a few books in *Book Lust* are also in *More Book Lust*. When a book appeared only as part of a list in *Book Lust*, with no (or minimal) description, I occasionally incorporated it into *More Book Lust*, adding an annotation. But even when it made perfect sense to include a *Book Lust* book in one of the new categories I created for *More Book Lust*, I restrained myself. You won't find, for example, P. F. Kluge's **Biggest Elvis** under either "Friend Makers" or "You Can't Judge a Book by Its Cover" in *More Book Lust*, although it clearly should be in both sections, because I wrote so much about the book in *Book Lust*.

You will find that many of the books in *More Book Lust* (and in *Book Lust*, for that matter) are out of print. If that's the case, you have a couple of options. Your first stop should be your local library. If they don't own it, they can usually borrow it from another library, at little or no cost to you. You can check out your local used bookstores. You can search the Internet—I generally make www. bookfinder.com or www.abebooks.com my first stop—or you can just enter the author and title into Google and see what comes up.

Lastly, as I wrote in *Book Lust*, one of my strongest-held beliefs is that no one should ever finish a book that they're not enjoying, no matter how popular or well reviewed the book is. (Except, of course, if it's for a homework assignment or for a book group.) Believe me, nobody is going to get any points in heaven by miserably slogging their way through a book they aren't enjoying but think they ought to read. I live by what I call "the rule of fifty," which is based on the reality of the shortness of time and the immensity of the world of books. If you're fifty years old or younger, give every book about fifty pages before you decide to commit yourself to reading it, or give it up. If you're over fifty, which is when time gets even shorter, subtract your age from 100—the result is the number of pages you should read before deciding whether or not to quit. (If you're 100 or over, you get to judge the book by its cover, despite the dangers in doing so—see the section "You Can't Judge a Book by Its Cover.")

A corollary to the rule: If you care only about what happens—who the murderer is, who marries whom—well, just turn to the last page and read that. Or thumb through the last chapter. The point is, reading should be pure pleasure. You haven't failed the author by not enjoying the book. Instead, the author has, at that moment in your life, failed you. That doesn't mean that in six days, or six months, or six years, or sixty years, you won't go back to the book and find that you love it. All it means is that at that particular moment in your life, you were looking for a different sort of book.

Lawrence Clark Powell, founding dean of the School of Library Service at the University of California at Los Angeles, wrote: "I have always been reconciled to the fact that I was born a bibliomaniac, never have I sought a cure, and my dearest friends have been drawn from those likewise suffering from book madness." That's how I feel and, I suspect, so do you. So grab a pen and a pad of paper, make yourself comfortable, and start reading. And remember, I love hearing from readers—please email me with suggestions of good books I might have missed or overlooked at nancy@nancypearl.com.

Book lust forever!

ACKNOWLEDGMENTS

After *Book Lust* was published, I got hundreds of emails and letters from people who offered wonderful suggestions for books to include in *More Book Lust*, well before a second book was even a gleam in anyone's eye. Many of these emails reminded me of books I had simply forgotten, while others listed books with which I was unfamiliar. I read many of those new books, was grateful for the reminders of other titles, and want to thank the following people for recommending books that ended up in *More Book Lust*. (Let me apologize in advance if I've inadvertently omitted anyone.)

Sharon Aderman; Tom Adkins; Amy Alexander; Elinor Appel for help with the section on books for boys and girls; Nancy Bass; Martha Bayley; Victoria Beatty (for the "Living High in Cascadia" section); Terry Beck and the Reader's Advisory group at Sno-Isle Library System for the section on fishing; Linda Beeman; Carrie Bowman; Scott Bradley; David Brown; Kathleen Burgess; Pam Cahn; Elaine Camuso; Raman Chandarsekar; Nancy Bogardus Colm; Lisa Creegan; Nina Crocker; Larry Curnutt; Gretchen DeMedeiros; Clare DeVries; Doreen Disney; Rome Doherty; Anita Elder; Jane English; Mary Kay Feather; Anne Ferris; Mike Flaxman; Dan Foran; Barbara Foster; Iva Freeman for "Near Novels" and "The Immigrant Experience"; George Frein; Elizabeth Fry; Robert Gardner; Gloria Gehrman; Ann Haward; Bob Hearn; Beth Henkes; Christopher Hodgkin; Joan Hortin; Amy O'Neill Houck; Margy Hovren; Sheryl Kelsey; Walter Kephart; Judy Kessinger; Jane Kops; Kathleen Lamantia; Eloise Lamum; Carol Lord; Pam Loya; Janet Martinson; Cheryl McKeon; Joan Moritz; Jeanne Nichols; Sheila Nickerson; Susan Noonan; Davis Oldham; Angela M. Otwell; Katherine Pennavaria (for the section on British literary biographies); Elaine Pfeffer; Brian Phillips; Aimee Quinn; Nancy Randall; Barbara Reed;

B. J. Riter; Charlie Rossiter; Sue Ryan; Lindsy Serrano; Annie Sherrill; Robert Sloan; Barbara Smith; Wendy Smith; Marcia H. Snowden; Norm Solomon; Donna Stone; Jeanette Sullivan; Vicky Taylor; Kathy Waskiewicz; Celia White; Jennifer Wiegert; Alice Wilkinson; Deborah Wills; Lisa Winchester; Neal Wyatt (for the sections on horror, the Brontës, and Mary Stewart); and Yvette Zaepfel.

And to my former colleagues at The Seattle Public Library, including crackerjack young-adult librarians Amy Kennedy, Sarah Webb, Marin Younker, Lesley James, Peg Dombek, and Christiane Woten for their suggestions for good books for teenagers; Carol Edlefsen; Susan Fort for help with the "Child Prodigies," "All in the Family," and "Nagging Mothers, Crying Children" categories; and Beth de la Fuente, Misha Stone, David Wright, and Jennifer Baker, for just about everything.

And, once again, thanks to the great folks at Sasquatch Books—no one could ever wish for a better experience than I've had working with them: Gary Luke, Sarah Hanson, and Gina Johnston, especially. And special thanks to Sherri Schultz and Phyllis Hatfield for their most helpful and careful editing.

Finally, I want once again to thank my husband, Joe, who not only makes my reading life possible but who will also occasionally enjoy a book that I've suggested he read.

More Book Lust is dedicated to my two daughters, Eily and Katie, who not only love to read but (more importantly) are thoughtful, generous, and all-around wonderful women.

ADAPTING TO ADOPTION

The aftereffects of adoption are felt not just by the adopted child but also, of course, by the women who give up their babies, by the men in their lives, and by the adoptive parents. Here are some wonderful novels that explore adoption from various perspectives.

The Crossley Baby by Jacqueline Carey is the story of two sisters—a stay-at-home mom and a career-driven businesswoman—who battle for custody of their dead sister's child.

Two characters are "confined" in Carrie Brown's **Confinement**: World War II refugee Arthur Henning and Agatha, the teenage daughter of his employer. Arthur is trapped in memories of the past, while Agatha is in a home for unwed mothers where she is forced to relinquish her newborn child for adoption. As Arthur and Agatha—always friends and allies, despite the difference in their ages—secretly grow closer during Agatha's pregnancy, their relationship subtly changes, and both start to set themselves free.

In Joanna C. Scott's **The Lucky Gourd Shop**, Mi Sook, herself abandoned as a child in postwar South Korea and now in a difficult marriage, must decide whether or not to give up her three children for adoption by an American couple.

Unexpectedly made guardians of an eleven-year-old boy, Ed and Sam find their lives turned upside down, in **Breakfast with Scot** by Michael Downing.

Rose, the main character in Ann Patchett's first novel, **The Patron Saint of Liars**, abandons her young husband and winds up in a home for unwed mothers.

Trying to get over the unexpected death of her husband, Livia befriends a pregnant fifteen-year-old girl, who gives birth to a baby that Livia longs to adopt, in Ann Hood's novel **Ruby**.

When Taylor Greer leaves Kentucky for points west in order to escape the confines of small-town life, she finds an abandoned and abused Cherokee child left in her car, in Barbara Kingsolver's first novel, **The Bean Trees**.

With the love and support of the adoptive parents, sixteen-year-old Sara survives the trauma of giving up her child, but when George and Eva Rivers start worrying about Sara's constant presence in little Anne's life, she makes a decision that threatens to undo everything in **Girls in Trouble** by Caroline Leavitt.

In Susan Merrell's **A Member of the Family,** Deborah and Chris's dream of a happy family is shattered when their son, Michael (adopted from Romania when he was eighteen months old), becomes increasingly violent both at school and at home.

AFRICA: A READER'S ITINERARY

I've always found reading about Africa immensely rewarding as well as sobering. Whether it's fiction or nonfiction, whether explicitly or implicitly, all these books reveal the effects of colonialism and raise the question of how people with radically different beliefs, ethnicity, and backgrounds can possibly live together in peace.

Grace Berggren is the charming heroine of Margaret Meyers's **Swimming in the Congo**, set in the Belgian Congo (now Zaire), where she lives with her missionary parents. Her father's jungle sickness and her experiences with racism and boarding school give a picture of pre-independence Africa that I've never before seen explored from this point of view.

Bryce Courtenay's **The Power of One** tells the story of Peekay, a young English boy growing up during World War II in a racially divided South Africa, who uses his talent for boxing to overcome both the personal and social obstacles that he faces. **Tandia**, the sequel, is just as good.

Louisa Dawkins's **Natives and Strangers** takes place in 1950s Tanganyika, just as the territory is struggling for independence. Marietta Hamilton, the granddaughter of British settlers, tries to balance her relationships with blacks and the demands of white society.

Moses Isegawa's sprawling, ambitious, and autobiographical first novel, **Abyssinian Chronicles**, is set in Uganda from the 1960s to the 1980s.

The Somali Nuruddin Farah is probably the best-known African writing in English today. Exiled from his native country in 1991, Farah won the prestigious Neustadt Prize in 1998, an award that often leads to a subsequent Nobel Prize in Literature. His novel **Links** is the story of Jeebleh, a former political prisoner who returns to Somalia from New York to help find the young kidnapped daughter of a childhood friend.

In M. G. Vassanji's **The In-Between World of Vikram Lall**, we follow the lives of Vikram, his sister Deepa (who are Indians living in Africa with their parents), their native friend Njoroge, and their two British playmates, Bill and Annie, during a time and in a place of great contradictions. The story begins in colonial Kenya in 1953, when Queen Elizabeth is being inaugurated and at the same time the Mau Maus are waging their guerrilla war against British rule. It ends in contemporary Canada, where Lall has fled.

Here are three of the best nonfiction books about Africa and its peoples that I've ever encountered:

Two books about the Bushmen of the Kalahari Desert take different approaches and should be read together if one is to appreciate the basically unchanged culture of these earliest Africans. The first book is one of the classic armchair travel narratives, written by South African Laurens van der Post, the son of Dutch immigrants. **The Lost World of the Kalahari** is an account of his 1957 trek through the Kalahari Desert in search of the Bushmen, in order to study their beliefs and behavior. The second book is **The Harmless People** by Elizabeth Marshall Thomas. A few years before van der Post conducted his research into the Bushmen, Thomas went to the desert to live with them, and was one of the first Westerners to do so. She returned to Botswana and South Africa in the 1980s to study the effects of "modernization" on the culture of these people whom she so clearly appreciated.

Howard W. French spent time in the Ivory Coast with his family after finishing college and eventually became bureau chief for the *New York Times*, covering Central and West Africa in the 1990s. In **A Continent for the Taking: The Tragedy and Hope of Africa**, French writes with skill and style about the major events of the twentieth and early twenty-first centuries: the Rwandan genocide, the AIDS crisis, the tragedy of gun-toting children in the Liberian army. He includes, as well, a discussion of how the West has abused and misused Africa for its own benefit, with dire consequences for the Africans.

As for cookbooks, the two best are **The Africa News Cookbook: African Cooking for Western Kitchens** by Tami Hultman and **The African Cookbook** by Bea Sandler, which has the added benefit of drawings by Diane and Leo Dillon, the noted illustrators of children's books.

For more books about Africa, you might want to look at two *Book Lust* categories: "Africa: Today and Yesterday" and "African Colonialism: Fiction."

ALL IN THE FAMILY:
WRITER DYNASTIES

What do Benjamin Cheever, Eliza Minot, Nora Ephron, Richard Bausch, and Jenny McPhee have in common? They're all writers related to writers.

Raised apart, brothers Geoffrey and Tobias Wolff experienced dramatically different childhoods. Geoffrey relates his life with his father, the dissolute and charming Duke, in **The Duke of Deception**, while Tobias chronicles his difficult childhood with an abusive stepfather in **This Boy's Life**.

Susan Minot in **Monkeys**, Eliza Minot in **The Tiny One**, and George Minot in **The Blue Bowl** each offer their own fictional perspective on growing up as siblings in a large, dysfunctional New England Catholic family irredeemably scarred by their father's alcoholism and their mother's sudden and untimely death.

I suppose that if you're the child of a famous author you face an almost irresistible temptation to write about that experience, whether in fiction or in memoir, either directly or obliquely. John Cheever's children, Susan and Benjamin, have done both: Benjamin has written the novels **The Plagiarist** and **The Partisan**, and Susan has written **Home Before Dark** (which won the National Book Critics Circle Award for biography/autobiography) and **Treetops: A Family Memoir**.

Although their father, John McPhee, sticks to nonfiction, two of his daughters, Jenny and Martha, have both become novelists. Jenny McPhee's delightful novel **No Ordinary Matter** features two sisters, an engineered pregnancy, detectives, incest, and other soap opera staples, while Martha McPhee's **Bright Angel Time** captures much of the McPhee sisters' own unique childhood experiences in a tale of marriages breaking up, blended families, and a charismatic stepfather.

The Ephron sisters, Amy, Delia, and Nora, offspring of writers Phoebe and Henry, all have an ironically humorous view of the contemporary world. **Hanging Up** by Delia may be the most autobiographical; it's a poignant description of three sisters coping with a parent's senility and death. Amy Ephron's novels include the seemingly autobiographical **Biodegradable Soap** and **Bruised Fruit**, while Nora is best known for her novel **Heartburn**.

Frederick and Steve Barthelme are both college professors and gamblers—as described in their autobiographical memoir, **Double Down: Reflections on Gambling and Loss**—and their deceased older brother, Donald, was a prolific writer who explored existential and postmodern themes in such books as **The Dead Father** and **Sixty Stories**.

You wouldn't know that Margaret Drabble and A. S. Byatt were sisters unless you happened to stumble across that bit of information, since the two seem to prefer to keep their relationship under wraps. Still, both of them write with a searching intelligence and an enviable prose style. Although **Possession** is probably Byatt's best-known novel, my favorite has always been **The Virgin in the Garden**, the first of a quartet that includes **Still Life**, **Babel Tower**, and **A Whistling Woman**. As for Drabble, I've never forgotten **The Millstone**, a novel set in London in the 1960s, but I also thoroughly enjoyed two of her more recent novels, **The Seven Sisters** and **The Red Queen**.

Twin brothers Richard and Robert Bausch have each produced a significant body of good fiction, including Robert's **A Hole in the Earth** and Richard's **Wives & Lovers: Three Short Novels and Good Evening Mr. & Mrs. America, and All the Ships at Sea**.

ALL THE WORLD'S A STAGE

The really artificial (or artificially real) world of theater provides a wonderful backdrop for many types of fiction, from comedies of manners to mysteries to coming-of-age sagas and more.

A Company of Three by Varley O'Connor describes the loving but occasionally difficult relationship of three people—two men and a woman—whose friendship mostly sustains them through their attempts to carve out careers as actors in 1970s New York.

Also set in the 1970s is Reckless Eyeballing, a quintessential Ishmael Reed novel—bitingly satirical, fearless in its attack on all that is politically correct, and very very funny (even as you wince). It's the story of Ian Ball, a black playwright attacked and scorned by theater feminists, who hopes to redeem his career and reputation by writing a play in which the women get all the major roles.

Christopher Bram's delicious Lives of the Circus Animals takes place over the course of a week in the lives of six people, all of whom are involved with the New York theater scene: Henry Lewse, an aging British actor; his personal assistant, Jessie; her brother, playwright Caleb Doyle, who had one huge success on Broadway but whose second play was given a terrible review by the *New York Times'* second-string theater critic, Kenneth Prager, known as the "buzzard of Broadway"; Frank Earp, who is directing a play featuring Toby Vogler, the onetime boyfriend of Caleb Doyle and current gleam in the eye of Henry Lewse . . . along with assorted drivers and caterers as well as the gun-carrying, slightly agoraphobic mother of the Doyles.

In Janet Burroway's Opening Nights (one of the few theater novels set outside of Manhattan, in this case in a college town in Georgia), costume designer Shaara Soole becomes a reluctant ally of her ex-husband's new wife during rehearsals of the play he has come south from New York to direct.

Two British mystery novelists—Ngaio (pronounced Nyo, rhyming with "my toe") Marsh and Simon Brett—use a theater setting for many of their books. My favorite Marsh theater mystery is **Night at the Vulcan**, in which the main character, an aspiring actress who's just arrived in England from New Zealand, gets caught up in the general infighting and travails of a theater troupe. At the center of more than a dozen of Simon Brett's novels is Charles Paris, the bumbling and incompetent actor who is always able to detect his way to the ultimate solution of any crime he encounters. Two of Brett's best Charles Paris mysteries are **A Reconstructed Corpse** and **Dead Room Farce**.

"ALMOST HEAVEN, WEST VIRGINIA"

I don't know quite why I'm so taken with so many novels set in West Virginia, where I've never been but hope someday to visit. Maybe it's that I've always loved "Take Me Home, Country Roads," the John Denver song that gives this section its title; maybe it's the fact that I love native West Virginian Mary Lee Settle's writing so much. Whatever the reason, here are some awfully good works of fiction set in one of the smaller of the United States.

Mary Lee Settle's Beulah Quintet series covers three hundred years of American cultural and political history as lived by three fictional West Virginia families; the five novels are **Prisons, O Beulah Land, Know Nothing, The Scapegoat,** and **The Killing Ground.** (The two Settle novels that I most frequently settle down with are **Celebration,** the story of two emotionally wounded people—an American anthropologist and a Scottish doctor—who become the focal points of a star-crossed group of friends, and **Blood Tie**, about a group of American and British expats in Turkey, which won the 1977 National Book Award for Fiction. Although, neither book takes place in West Virginia.)

Dogs of God by Benedict Pinckney depicts the violence that ensues when two men become mixed up with DEA agents, illegal immigrants, and gunrunners in rural West Virginia.

Sisters Lenny and Alma become friends with Buddy, the abused son of the camp cook, in **Shelter** by Jayne Anne Phillips.

Katherine Mosby's **Private Altars**, set in the 1920s, and Keith Maillard's **Gloria**, which takes place in the 1950s, describe two women, each of whom tries to balance her own sense of who she is and what she wants from life against the expectations of family and fellow small-town citizens.

The coal miners at the heart of Denise Giardina's **Storming Heaven** and **The Unquiet Earth** struggle for their lives and livelihood against mine owners who are determined not to improve the working conditions or safety of the men and boys in the mines.

THE ALPHA, BETA, GAMMAS
OF GREECE

Without the Greeks, where would we be? In philosophy, art, literature, rhetoric, history, sports, and science, the Greeks were there—at least one step ahead of everyone else.

Much of what we know about Greek history we owe to two men: Herodotus and Thucydides. It is Herodotus, often referred to as the father of history, whose rousing **Histories** serve as our guide to understanding the epic battles between Greece and its archrival, Persia. But it's Thucydides who gave me one of the most meaningful reading experiences I had in college. I was assigned his **History** of the Peloponnesian War, the story of the twenty-seven-year war between two major Greek city-states, Athens and Sparta, which took place between 431 and 404 B.C. I read the translation by Thomas Hobbes, and was struck again and again by how events of the war echoed in World War II and the long Cold War that followed, and even its relevance to many of today's events.

Donald Kagan, Hillhouse Professor of Classics and History at Yale University and the foremost Thucydides scholar of this or probably any other day, wrote a four-volume history of the Peloponnesian War, but perhaps feeling that four books were a bit much to ask anyone except scholars in the field to read, he also published **The Peloponnesian War**, a wonderful one-volume condensation of his own work, which is intended for a general audience. Kagan's account supplements Thucydides, whose own account ends seven years before the war officially came to a conclusion, with added commentary from other Greek writers.

Other good books about ancient Greece include **The Battle of Salamis: The Naval Encounter That Saved Greece—and Western Civilization** by Barry Strauss, which recounts an epic sea battle between Persia and the Greeks, and Tony Perrottet's **The Naked Olympics: The True Story of the Ancient Games**. As Perrottet tells it, had those ancient games and related activities been filmed, they'd have gotten an R rating.

As for fiction, don't miss **The Last of the Wine** and **The Mask of Apollo** by Mary Renault, two novels set during Greece's classical period, and **The Sand-Reckoner**, Gillian Bradshaw's biographical novel of Archimedes, who is known for his boast "Give me a lever long enough, and a prop strong enough, and I can single-handedly move the world."

Two of the best-known novels of Nikos Kazantzakis, perhaps Greece's—or to be more specific, Crete's—most famous writer, are

Zorba the Greek and the more controversial The Last Temptation of Christ.

You definitely don't want to miss the four great Greek playwrights and these plays—Aeschylus's Oresteia trilogy, Sophocles's Oedipus Rex and Antigone, Euripides's Medea, and Aristophanes's Lysistrata.

Francine Segan's The Philosopher's Kitchen: Recipes from Ancient Greece and Rome for the Modern Cook is fascinating to anyone interested in ancient history and contemporary cooking, and my friends who cook assure me that the recipes work just fine.

For more about Greece, see the section "The Classical World" in Book Lust.

ALPHABET SOUP

I think my interest in books about the alphabet came from my childhood, when I read two of Rudyard Kipling's Just So Stories, "How the First Letter Was Written" and "How the Alphabet Was Made." Who'd have thought there would be such interesting books about those twenty-six little letters?

Language Visible: Unraveling the Mystery of the Alphabet from A to Z by David Sacks is a thoroughly delightful and delightfully thorough look at the history of the Roman alphabet, as well as a compendium of little-known facts about each individual letter. It includes essays on lexicographers, printing, and other lovely oddities sure to please language lovers. Despite the amount of research that Sacks obviously did for this book, he is refreshingly free of self-importance. His linguistic history is written in a conversational tone and is filled with puns that Sacks always apologizes for, admitting to a proclivity for these groaners.

In his breezy yet informative Quirky Qwerty: A Biography of the Typewriter and Its Many Characters, Torbjorn Lundmark offers readers not only the explanation for why the typewriter (and computer) keyboards are configured as they are (do you recognize the word qwerty?), he also gives the history and background of the alphabet and diacritical marks, along with other fascinating bits of information that are perfect for dropping into casual conversation at cocktail parties. Did you know that the Remington who became famous for the guns he produced also made the first typewriters? Did you know that you could type "typewriter" by using just the third row of letters on a keyboard? Did you know that consonants are much older than vowels? Wh nds vwls nyhw?

AND THE AWARD FOR BEST TITLE GOES TO . . .

I f you can't judge a book by its cover (see page 237), how do you pick a book out of the sea of titles out there? Why, you're drawn to a particular book by its title, of course. Some titles provoke a visceral reaction of pleasure that compels you to reach out and take the book off the shelf. Even if many of these turn out to be duds, a few are pure gold.

Leah Hager Cohen's Heart, You Bully, You Punk *(the title comes from a poem by Marie Ponsot called "One Is One")*

James Conrad's Making Love to the Minor Poets of Chicago

John Dufresne's Love Warps the Mind a Little

Dave Eggers's A Heartbreaking Work of Staggering Genius

Herbert Gold's She Took My Arm As If She Loved Me

Allan Gurganus's Oldest Living Confederate Widow Tells All

Alice Mattison's Men Giving Money, Women Yelling *and* The Wedding of the Two-Headed Woman *(in addition to being a superb novelist, she's hell on wheels at coming up with compelling titles)*

Sharyn McCrumb's If I'd Killed Him When I Met Him

Nicholas Mosley's Hopeful Monsters

W. M. Spackman's Armful of Warm Girl

ANIMAL LOVE

Now these are strange and wonderful novels, but they're sometimes a hard sell to readers. My advice is, give 'em a try, follow the fifty-page rule as promulgated in the introduction to this book, and see what you think. Personally, I adore them.

One of the funniest and tender novels I've ever read is **His Monkey Wife** by John Collier. Collier, who wrote many Hollywood screenplays including *The African Queen*, sets this novel in the 1920s in colonial Africa, where a chimp named Emily (one of the best creations in all fiction, and a real fan of the novels of Emily Brontë) falls in love with her owner, Alfred Fatigay, a British schoolteacher. When Mr. Fatigay goes home to England to marry his bluestocking wife, Emily goes along with him, contriving with great élan to prevent the wedding. From the first line of the introduction all the way to its oh-so-satisfying (and romantic) last sentence, this not-nearly-well-enough-known novel will warm the heart of even the most cynical reader.

Many a husband asserts that though his beloved wife may change, his love for her will remain constant, but Mr. Tebrick, the narrator of David Garnett's **Lady into Fox**, is challenged more severely than most when Mrs. Tebrick unaccountably—and suddenly—becomes a fox (that's a literal fox)—and leaves for an assignation with another fox, returning to the Tebrick family home some time later with her fox children in tow. Scholars can delve into the effect of the author's complex sexuality on the theme of the novel (he had a love affair with Vanessa Bell's lover, Duncan Grant, to whom this 1922 book is dedicated, and then, years later, married Grant and Bell's daughter), while the rest of us can simply enjoy this strangely affecting tale.

Of all the many odd novels I've read, Marian Engel's **Bear** ranks high on the list, not only because of how strange it is, but also because of its total believability. Winner of Canada's Governor-General's Literary Award in 1976, this novel tells of a young woman's love affair with—what else—a bear, on an ostensibly deserted island near Ontario, Canada. This gem of a novel has long been out of print, but it's well worth searching for.

Another out-of-print book about a close relationship between humans and animals is Peter Dickinson's superior mystery **The Poison Oracle**. British psycholinguist Wesley Morris comes to an unnamed Arab kingdom to study its language; when a murder occurs, the only witness is Dinah, a chimpanzee whom Morris has been teaching to communicate with humans. (A similar plot is at work in a terrific children's book called **The Highly Trained Dogs of Professor Petit** by Carol Ryrie Brink.)

BARSETSHIRE AND BEYOND

During my first *Book Lust* book tour, a gentleman in the audience at the Louisville Free Public Library in Kentucky stood up and asked in an aggrieved tone, "Where is Anthony Trollope?" Which gave me the chance to utter a sentence that I venture to say few others have had the opportunity to use: "In his grave, in Kensal Green cemetery, along with Wilkie Collins, William Makepeace Thackeray, and Charles Babbage," I said smartly. (Oh, the obscure facts one can pick up through a lifetime of reading!) More seriously, of course, the gentleman was reminding me that I'd forgotten to include one of my favorite writers, the indefatigable author of more than four dozen books, part of whose fame rests on the fact that he got up before dawn every day to write his self-imposed ration of pages, then went off to his job at the post office (where he invented the letter box).

My favorite Trollope novels are the whole Barsetshire series (in order): **The Warden, Barchester Towers, Doctor Thorne, Framley Parsonage, The Small House at Allington,** and The Last Chronicle of Barset, and the whole Palliser series (in order): **Can You Forgive Her?, Phineas Finn, The Eustace Diamonds, Phineas Redux, The Prime Minister,** and **The Duke's Children.**

Besides these, though, every Trollopian worth his or her salt will have an additional must-read list, and mine is headed by the amazingly prescient **The Way We Live Now.**

But what do you read when you finish all of Trollope? (You can, of course, as many of the most loyal Trollopians do, read them all again. And then again.) If not, though, you could go on to the novels of Angela Thirkell, who not only set her novels in the county of

Barsetshire, but also invented characters that are direct descendants of Trollope's. Thirkell wrote forty novels, beginning when she was forty-three. Her characters endure the home front of World War II with stoic fortitude, maintaining that particular sort of stability unique to the English, which was being threatened within and without. What's so hard about reading Thirkell—and this makes it really difficult to recommend her with all my heart—is that she allows her characters to say appallingly nasty things about blacks and Jews. Granted, this was the prevailing attitude of the English upper and middle classes (a good example of someone who thought this way was the English Nazi, Unity Mitford), and you find such sentiments in the novels of Agatha Christie and Dorothy Sayers as well, but I feel awfully uncomfortable every time I re-encounter a Thirkell novel.

Still, you can't beat Thirkell at writing about nostalgia and scenes of light romance amid domestic coziness and the minor vicissitudes of village life. Try **Pomfret Towers**, with its description of a party at a seventeenth-century English country house, and **What Did It Mean?**, set during Elizabeth II's coronation summer of 1953.

Other scenes of British village life can be found in the novels of Miss Read (**Thrush Green** and **Summer at Fairacre** are a good sampling) and in E. F. Benson's **Mapp and Lucia** and his other novels set in the small villages of Tilling and Riseholme.

If you're in the mood for good old-fashioned Trollopian storytelling, but want something set in the present-day United States, then **Morningside Heights** by Cheryl Mendelson (who is also the author of the nonfiction **Home Comforts: The Art and Science of Keeping House**) should go high on your list. Set on the Upper West Side of Manhattan, in the neighborhood around Columbia University, the richly detailed and complicated plot features a young couple living well beyond their means, a suspicious death, a missing will, a priest unhappy with his vocation, and an unscrupulous lawyer, as well as various friends and relations of all the characters. As in the novels of Anthony Trollope, to which this novel pays loving homage, the good are ultimately rewarded and the bad are suitably punished.

THE BEATS AND THEIR GENERATION

The phrase "Beat Generation" was first used by Jack Kerouac in an interview he did with his friend and fellow writer John Clellon Holmes, for an article (worth reading) called "This Is the Beat Generation" that appeared in the *New York Times Magazine* in November 1952. There were really very few "true" beats (Kerouac, Allen Ginsberg, Neal Cassady, Gregory Corso, Lawrence Ferlinghetti, and William S. Burroughs were among the earliest to identify themselves as such). But despite that fact, the Beats had a huge influence on succeeding generations of writers. Here are some of my favorite books by and about them and the period they defined.

First, take a look at Holmes's own chronicle of the times, **Go**, generally considered the first Beat novel (it was published five years before **On the Road**) and filled with lightly fictionalized portraits of his contemporaries.

Then move into the biographies. Ann Charters, who went on to be one of the acknowledged experts in the area of Beat literature and the men who wrote it, started it all with **Kerouac: A Biography**; a good companion read is Gerald Nicosia's **Memory Babe**, another view of the movement's best-known personage. (You'll also want to read Kerouac's autobiographical first novel, **The Town and the City**, which sets the stage for the man who goes **On the Road** a few years later.)

Steven Watson's **The Birth of the Beat Generation: Visionaries, Rebels, and Hipsters, 1944–1960** looks at the relationships among the major players. An added pleasure of this book is that it's cunningly designed to include many quotations, anecdotes, and relevant definitions in the margins.

The Beat Hotel: Ginsberg, Burroughs, and Corso in Paris, 1957–1963 by Barry Miles transports the Beats to the Left Bank and shifts the focus away from Kerouac to Allen Ginsberg, William Burroughs, and Gregory Corso, all of whom lived for a time in a cheap boardinghouse where they wrote (or finished) some of the best works of their careers, including Burroughs's **Naked Lunch** and Ginsberg's poem "Kaddish."

In Sam Kashner's **When I Was Cool: My Life at the Jack Kerouac School**, the author looks back on his experiences as the first student at the Jack Kerouac School of Disembodied Poetics, founded by Allen Ginsberg in 1976, long after the heyday of the Beat movement.

Joyce Johnson's claim to fame was her 1950s relationship with Jack Kerouac (whom she met on a blind date, arranged by none other than Allen Ginsberg) just months before **On the Road** made him the spokesman for the Beat Generation. Her book **Minor Characters: A Young Woman's Coming-of-Age in the Beat Orbit of Jack Kerouac** won the National Book Critics Circle Award and is one of the two best memoirs of the period. It includes solid portrayals of other luminaries of the time, including Gregory Corso and Peter Orlovsky.

The other great memoir about the Beats that came out of the 1950s and 1960s is **How I Became Hettie Jones**, in which the author writes of her transformation from Hettie Cohen, young daughter of Jewish parents in Queens, New York, into the wife of black poet and activist LeRoi Jones, only to find their marriage ended by forces (both personal and societal) that drove them apart in 1965.

THE BECKONING ROAD

Robert Louis Stevenson once wrote, "I travel not to go anywhere, but to go. I travel for travel's sake. The great affair is to move." Here are some wonderful nonfiction reads about traveling long distances, books that will make you want to buckle up your seat belt and take off—anywhere.

In 1964, when Peter Beagle was in his early twenties, he and a friend rode their Heinkel motor scooters from the East to the West Coast to meet up with Beagle's girlfriend, Enid, then living in Menlo Park, California. He describes their journey in **I See by My Outfit: Cross-Country by Scooter: An Adventure.**

Another two-wheeled trip is Robert Pirsig's classic, highly readable, and indispensable **Zen and the Art of Motorcycle Maintenance: An Inquiry into Values**, an account of a cross-country journey that he and his son took by motorcycle, which is only partially an account of the trip itself and mainly a philosophical musing on the importance of quality in a world that values quantity much more.

Among the many books by the prolific John McPhee, my favorites include the books he wrote about traveling up and down, back and forth, on Interstate 80 studying geologic history. **Annals of the Former World**, which won the Pulitzer Prize for nonfiction in 1998, is composed of four earlier books—**Assembling California; Rising from the Plains; In Suspect Terrain;** and **Basin and Range**—as well as an additional section, "Crossing the Craton."

After he finished his superb **Empire Express: Building the First Transcontinental Railroad**, historian David Haward Bain decided to take his wife and two children on a car journey from their home in Vermont out to California by way of old logging roads, superhighways, and railroad routes. The result is the equally readable **The Old Iron Road: An Epic of Rails, Roads, and the Urge to Go West.**

Other nonfiction travel accounts include John Steinbeck's **Travels with Charley: In Search of America,** in which the author, along with his poodle (the eponymous Charley), wandered by car the length and breadth of the United States in 1960; **Blue Highways: A Journey into America** by William Least Heat-Moon, the now-classic account of Heat-Moon's travels by car on all those back roads marked in blue on many maps; Michael Paterniti's **Driving Mr. Albert: A Trip Across America with Einstein's Brain,** which describes a car trip with a definite purpose: to deliver Einstein's brain (via Buick Skylark) to the great scientist's daughter in California; and Pete Davies's **American Road: The Story of an Epic Transcontinental Journey at the Dawn of the Motor Age,** in which a convoy of military vehicles wend their way across the country in the summer of 1919, averaging the mind-boggling speed of five miles per hour.

In 1988, ten years after Eric Hansen was rescued from a desert island in the Red Sea by a group of goat smugglers, he went back to collect the journals he had buried there before he left. He recounts his adventures (describing them as "madcap" would not be too far off the mark) in **Motoring with Mohammed: Journeys to Yemen and the Red Sea.** This intrepid traveler was also beckoned to Southeast Asia in **Stranger in the Forest: On Foot Across Borneo,** and recounts more travel adventures in **The Bird Man and the Lap Dancer: Close Encounters with Strangers.**

See also the "Road Novels" section of *Book Lust,* which covers fictional long-distance car trips.

BEST FOR BOYS AND GIRLS

To make your choosing easier (though far less politically correct), I've attached a symbol to each of these books indicating whether they'd appeal most to a boy or a girl or both. Many of these books will also appeal to young teens.

When both symbols appear, the one that appears first indicates that perhaps boys would enjoy the book a bit more than girls or vice versa.

♂♀ *Joan Aiken's* The Wolves of Willoughby Chase *and* Black Hearts in Battersea

♂♀ *Natalie Babbitt's* The Eyes of the Amaryllis

♂♀ *Blue Balliett's* Chasing Vermeer

♀ *Judy Blume's* Are You There God? It's Me, Margaret

♂♀ *Carol Ryrie Brink's* The Highly Trained Dogs of Professor Petit

♂♀ *Robert Burch's* Queenie Peavy

♀ *Betsy Byars's* The Pinballs

♂♀ *Andrew Clements's* Frindle *and* The Report Card

♂♀ *Sharon Creech's* Love That Dog

♂♀ *Helen Cresswell's* Ordinary Jack, Absolute Zero, *and all the other books in the Bagthorpe series*

♂♀ *Kate DiCamillo's* The Tale of Despereaux: Being the Story of a Mouse, a Princess, Some Soup, and a Spool of Thread

♀♂ *Elizabeth Enright's* The Saturdays, The Four-Story Mistake, Then There Were Five, *and* Spiderweb for Two

♀♂ *Eleanor Estes's* The Hundred Dresses, Ginger Pye, The Moffats, The Middle Moffat, *and* Rufus M.

♀♂ *Louise Fitzhugh's* Harriet the Spy *and* The Long Secret

♂♀ *Michael Hoeye's* Time Stops for No Mouse: A Hermux Tantamoq Adventure *(and sequels)*

♀♂ *Robert Lawson's* Rabbit Hill

♂♀ *Ursula Le Guin's* A Wizard of Earthsea *(and sequels)*

♀♂ *Patricia MacLachlan's* Sarah, Plain and Tall

♂ *John Masefield's* Jim Davis

♂♀ *Hugh Montgomery's* The Voyage of the Arctic Tern

♀ *Katherine Paterson's* Bridge to Terabithia

♂♀ *Philippa Pearce's* Minnow on the Say *and* Tom's Midnight Garden

♀♂ *Ellen Raskin's* The Westing Game

♂♀ *V. A. Richardson's* The House of Windjammer

♂♀ *Louis Sachar's* Holes

♀♂ *Zilpha Keatley Snyder's* The Headless Cupid *and* The Egypt Game

♀ *Cynthia Voigt's* Homecoming *and* Dicey's Song

BEST FOR TEENS

These are sure teen-pleasers, ranging from science fiction and fantasy to ultrarealistic and everything in between. Once again, I've attached a handy-dandy symbol to indicate whether a book may appeal more to girls or boys. But don't take these symbols as the final word—try them out on any teens in your life, or yourself.

♀ *Laurie Halse Anderson's* Speak

♂ *M. T. Anderson's* Thirsty *and* Feed

♂ *Lance Armstrong's* It's Not About the Bike: My Journey Back to Life

♂♀ *Amelia Atwater-Rhodes's* Hawksong

♂♀ *Joan Bauer's* Rules of the Road

♀ *Liz Berry's* The China Garden

♀ *Francesca Lia Block's* Weetzie Bat

♂ *Edward Bloor's* Tangerine

♀ *Ann Brashares's* The Sisterhood of the Traveling Pants *and its sequel,* The Second Summer of the Sisterhood

♀ *Libba Bray's* A Great and Terrible Beauty

♀ *Kate Cann's Love trilogy* Ready?; Sex; Go!

♂ *Stephen Chbosky's* The Perks of Being a Wallflower

♂ *Robert Cormier's* I Am the Cheese

♂ *Chris Crutcher's* Whale Talk

♀ *Sylvia Engdahl's* Enchantress from the Stars *and* The Far Side of Evil

♀♂ *Catherine Fisher's* The Oracle Betrayed

♂♀ *Alex Flinn's* Breathing Underwater

♂♀ *Neil Gaiman's* Neverwhere

♂ *Jack Gantos's* Hole in My Life

♀♂ *Nikki Grimes's* Bronx Masquerade

♂♀ *Ann Halam's* Dr. Franklin's Island

♀♂ *Susan Juby's* Alice, I Think

♀ *Annette Curtis Klause's* Blood and Chocolate

♀♂ *E. L. Konigsburg's* Silent to the Bone *and* The Outcasts of 19 Schuyler Place

♀ *Amy Goldman Koss's* The Girls

♂ *David Levithan's* Boy Meets Boy

♀ *Lois Lowry's* A Summer to Die

♀ *Melina Marchetta's* Looking for Alibrandi

♀ *John Marsden's* Tomorrow, When the War Began

♀ *Megan McCafferty's* Sloppy Firsts *and* Second Helpings

♀ *Robin McKinley's* Beauty: A Retelling of the Story of Beauty & the Beast

♂ *Walter Dean Myers's* Monster

BIG TEN COUNTRY: THE LITERARY MIDWEST

For those non–college football fans reading this, the Big Ten consists of eleven universities (don't ask me, ask the National Collegiate Athletic Association) in these states: Illinois, Indiana, Iowa, Michigan, Minnesota, Ohio, Pennsylvania, and Wisconsin. For me, growing up in Michigan, the Midwest was characterized by the Great Lakes, the steel mills, the automobile plants, the miserable winters, and also the great sports rivalries such as the University of Michigan vs. Ohio State University and the Green Bay Packers vs. the Detroit Lions. It wasn't until I started categorizing some of my favorite novels that I realized how many of them were set in Big Ten Country.

Michigan

Harriette Arnow's **The Dollmaker** is the story of a family who leaves their Kentucky home during World War II to find factory jobs in Detroit, where they struggle to make new lives for themselves.

A series of interesting Ann Arbor, Michigan, residents—from teenage lovers to a retired professor to Baxter's next-door neighbor and his two ex-wives—come to populate Charles Baxter's home in his inventive novel **The Feast of Love**. Each person relates his or her experiences of love—a force that variously sustains us, destroys us, and drives us crazy.

Beginning with 1990's **Whiskey River** and ending with 1999's **Thunder City** (in between are **Jitterbug**, **Stress**, **Edsel**, **King of the Corner**, and **Motown**), noted mystery writer Loren D. Estleman wrote seven "Detroit" novels, which taken together offer a sweeping (often gritty) history of the Motor City from the early twentieth century on.

But you sure can't talk about novels set in my home state, especially in Detroit, without mentioning the page-turning and highly entertaining novels of Elmore Leonard. By my count, he has so far written ten crime novels set in Michigan, and scores of others set elsewhere (don't miss **Get Shorty**). My particular Michigan favorites are **Pagan Babies** and **Freaky Deaky**, although **Mr. Paradise** is pretty wonderful too.

Iowa

The best-loved contemporary novel with an Iowa setting may well be W. P. Kinsella's **Shoeless Joe**, the story of Ray Kinsella, who builds a baseball field in back of his house after hearing a voice say, "If you build it, he will come."

We learn about events in fictional Grouse County, Iowa the setting for Tom Drury's **The End of Vandalism**, through the experiences of Sheriff Dan Norman; his wife, Louise; and Louise's ex-husband, Tiny, a thief and a plumber.

Jane Smiley's **A Thousand Acres** put this author on the literary map (although I still like one of her early novels, **Duplicate Keys**, and her story collection **The Age of Grief** even better). The plot—you'll recognize its relationship to Shakespeare's **King Lear**—revolves around a dysfunctional family comprised of an autocratic father and his three daughters. What with conflict over a disputed inheritance, deteriorating marriages, cancer, and groundwater pollution, these three-dimensional characters wrestle with a myriad of contemporary (and timeless) issues.

An Ocean in Iowa by Peter Hedges describes a year in the life of seven-year-old Scotty Ocean, a tumultuous year in which he must cope with the fact that his mother has deserted the family.

Minnesota

The earliest Minnesota novel is probably Sinclair Lewis's **Main Street** (originally published in 1920), the satirical story of librarian Carol Kennicott's attempts to bring culture to Gopher Prairie, Minnesota (clearly based on Lewis's own hometown, Sauk Center), and how everyone, from the townspeople to her physician husband, reacts to her plans. (Incidentally, Lewis was the first American to win the Nobel Prize in Literature.)

One of the best things about P. J. Tracy's novels **Monkeewrench** and **Live Bait** is that all the characters—major and minor—come vividly alive for the reader, whether they're homicide detectives (like Minneapolis cop Leo Magozzi or his cohorts) or software developers (the brilliant and traumatized Grace MacBride).

One of the authors I am most chagrined about having omitted from *Book Lust* (and about whose omission many readers wrote me) is Jon Hassler. My favorite books of his are the two set at Rookery State College and featuring Leland Edwards, first a faculty member (in **Rookery Blues**) and later dean of the college (in **The Dean's List**). Hassler's emphasis is on his characters, and what I so loved about **The Dean's List** is that he shows how it's never too late to start growing up.

One of my all-time favorite novels (which is also a terrific choice for book clubs) is **In the Lake of the Woods** by Tim O'Brien. It's the story of John Wade, whose race for political office is derailed by facts that are leaked to the press about his participation, years before, in a My Lai–type massacre during his Vietnam service. He and his wife, Kathy, retreat to a cabin at the Lake of the Woods to regroup—to come to terms not only with John's political future (and lack thereof) but also with what it means that he's kept secret from Kathy one of the most important events of his life.

Linda Hogan's **Solar Storms** tells about the return of seventeen-year-old Angel to the Minnesota village of her birth in order to get answers about the scars on her face and other events in her past.

Other Minnesota novels not to miss are the Jake Hines mysteries by Elizabeth Gunn (all with numbers in their titles—among them **Par Four** and **Six-Pound Walleye**); Leif Enger's novel about the bonds of family as seen through the eyes of an eleven-year-old boy, **Peace Like a River**; Karen Joy Fowler's lovely novel about a women's baseball team, **The Sweetheart Season**, based on her mother's life; and of course, both the fiction and nonfiction of Garrison Keillor, most of which is set in his beloved (and invented) Lake Wobegon, Minnesota. Among his best novels are **Love Me** and **Wobegon Boy**.

Ohio

Ruth McKenney's **Industrial Valley** (originally published to great controversy—at least in Akron—in 1939) is probably seen these days as outdated, irrelevant left-wing propaganda, and is therefore largely unread. This is a real shame, because McKenney's novel of strife in the rubber factories of Akron is a classic work of American labor history. (McKenney is far better known for **My Sister Eileen**, her lighthearted and immensely popular autobiographical collection of stories about two sisters who come to New York City's Greenwich Village to make their fortunes in the early 1930s. It became both a successful film and a Broadway play.)

In Mark Winegardner's novel **Crooked River Burning**, with its backdrop of Cleveland's sorry demise (from leading steel-producing city in the 1940s to a symbol of urban failure in the rust belt by the late 1960s), I most enjoyed the way he interwove the story of the on-again, off-again twenty-year relationship between an upper-class girl and her lower-class boyfriend who met as adolescents, with the chapters about major Cleveland movers and shakers, from disc jockey Alan Freed (who supposedly coined the phrase rock-and-roll) to the city's first black mayor, Carl Stokes. Reading Winegardner's novel reminded me, too, of how much I loved John Dos Passos's **USA** trilogy, which does the same sort of thing on a larger scale.

Toni Morrison, who was born in Lorain, Ohio, set some of her early novels there, including, most notably, the painful-to-read-but-oh-so-worth-it **The Bluest Eye**.

The Broom of the System was David Foster Wallace's first novel, published when he was just twenty-four, and a clear harbinger of the intelligence and inventiveness that would be manifested in his later books. It takes place in a recognizable but not quite realistic Cleveland, and its main characters include a cockatiel named Vlad the Impaler; his owner, Lenore Stonecipher Beadsman; and her boy-friend (and boss), Rick Vigorous.

Other Ohio novels include Conrad Richter's trilogy, which must be read in order, **The Trees, The Fields,** and **The Town;** Craig Holden's **The Jazz Bird;** Dawn Powell's **My Home Is Far Away;** the extremely violent mysteries of Jonathan Valin (**Final Notice, The Music Lovers,** and more); Les Roberts's detective series set in Cleveland starring private investigator Milan Jacovich, including **The Indian Sign;** and Robb Forman Dew's **Dale Loves Sophie to Death.**

Pennsylvania

Native Pennsylvanian John O'Hara fictionalized his childhood home of Pottsville in a series of novels, stories (incidentally, he published more stories in *The New Yorker* than any other writer), and novellas of unhappy love affairs, long drinking days, and the disappointments of even the best-lived lives. For a good sense of O'Hara's style, try his first novel, **Appointment in Samarra,** and then follow up with the three great novellas that make up **Sermons and Soda-Water:** "The Girl on the Baggage Truck," "Imagine Kissing Pete," and "We're Friends Again." (The book's title is from a Byron poem: "Let us have wine and women, mirth and laughter / Sermons and soda water the day after").

The Valley of Decision by Marcia Davenport is an oldie but goodie. Published in 1942, it follows the ups and downs of a steel mill—owning family in Pittsburgh from 1873 to Pearl Harbor.

Michael Chabon set his first two books in Pittsburgh— **The Mysteries of Pittsburgh,** a beautifully written coming-of-age novel, and the hilariously poignant story of a blocked writer, **Wonder Boys.**

The teenage hero of **Snow Angels** by Stewart O'Nan faces two tragedies: his parents' divorce and the murder of his favorite childhood babysitter.

Coal country is the setting for several gratifying Pennsylvania novels, including Lauren Wolk's **Those Who Favor Fire;** Tawni O'Dell's sad but ultimately redemptive **Coal Run;** and K. C. Constantine's gritty (but not noirish) long-running mystery series featuring policeman Mario Balzic. (Start with **The Rocksburg Railroad Murders,** which introduced Balzic way back in 1972.)

The subject of **A Good Doctor's Son,** a coming-of-age novel by Steven Schwartz set in suburban Philadelphia, is how one mistake can irrevocably change your life.

It's always a pleasure to read the latest in the Amanda Pepper series by Anthony Award–winning Gillian Roberts. Amanda is an English teacher (and amateur detective) at Philadelphia Prep who stumbles across mysterious deaths and suspicious behavior on a regular basis. Two good ones are **The Bluest Blood** and **How I Spent My Summer Vacation.**

Lisa Scottoline's series of mysteries featuring attorney Bennie Rosato and her law firm colleagues includes such doozies as **Everywhere That Mary Went** and **Final Appeal,** but her best is **Killer Smile,** in which attorney Mary DiNunzio takes on what appears to be a simple pro bono case concerning Amadeo Brandolini, who allegedly committed suicide while interned as an "enemy alien" during World War II, and whose family now wants to sue the government for reparations.

Wisconsin

Fond du Lac is the setting of one of the earliest (1942) and still most moving novels about young love written for young adults, **Seventeenth Summer.** According to the 1960 copy (thirty-eighth printing!) that my library owns, it won a prize from the Intercollegiate Literary Fellowship, whatever that was. This (just a tad dated, alas) novel was written when the author, Maureen Daly, was herself in college and relates the story of Jack and Angie, who fall in love during the summer after their high school graduation. (Why can't real life be like young adult novels, anyway? Or at least like young adult novels published before 1980?)

A. Manette Ansay brings small-town Wisconsin to life in her novels about religious faith and family ties. Take a look at **Sister** and **River Angel**, especially.

Stewart O'Nan's powerful and beautifully conceived historical novel **A Prayer for the Dying** is set just after the Civil War, when an epidemic is killing off the townspeople of Friendship at an alarming rate, confounding Jacob Hansen, who is both the sheriff and the undertaker.

I loved Mona Simpson's **Off Keck Road**, a slightly claustrophobic novella that is written with enormous grace and affection for the main character. Simpson explores what Thoreau referred to as a life "of quiet desperation" as that description applies to Bea Maxwell, who spends nearly her entire life in Green Bay, Wisconsin.

A Map of the World by Jane Hamilton explores how Howard and Alice Goodwin's family is turned upside down and inside out by two calamitous events: the death of a neighbor's two-year-old in the pond on their farm, and the accusation by one of Alice's students that she sexually molested him.

Other Wisconsin novels include **Orchard** by Larry Watson and **Crows over a Wheatfield**, a novel of domestic abuse by Paula Sharp, whose author, like her main character, is a criminal defense lawyer.

THE BOOK LUST OF OTHERS

I have spent many a happy hour poring over books that detail the book lusts of others. This has always been a great way for me to discover books I may have missed or overlooked, and it's so interesting to read the favorite books chosen by some of my favorite writers.

Linda Sternberg Katz and Bill Katz compiled **Writer's Choice: A Library of Rediscoveries**, which was published in 1983 with an introduction by Doris Grumbach. It offers annotated lists of about one thousand books, drawn from suggestions by various writers and divided into fiction and nonfiction sections. It's particularly heavy on books published in the 1950s and '60s, which are frequently hard to find, but it's still a valuable (and thoroughly enjoyable) resource. (I remember running across a library copy that had been [helpfully?] annotated by a previous reader, with check marks and comments of agreement or vociferous differences of opinion with the editors.) I first heard here about later faves of mine: Nigel Dennis's **Cards of Identity**; John Ashbery and James Schuyler's **A Nest of Ninnies**; George Kennan's **Tent Life in Siberia**; and Joanna Field's **On Not Being Able to Paint**.

The subtitle of **Lost Classics**, edited by Michael Ondaatje, Michael Redhill, Esta Spalding, and Linda Spalding, pretty much says it all: "Writers on Books Loved and Lost, Overlooked, Under-read, Unavailable, Stolen, Extinct, or Otherwise Out of Commission." This eccentric compendium includes essays by Philip Levine on the poetry of Alun Lewis, focusing on his collection called **Ha! Ha! Among the Trumpets**, and Russell Banks's introduction to Barbara Greene's memoir of her travels in Liberia, **Too Late to Turn Back**.

She accompanied her more famous cousin Graham, whose account of the same trip, Journey Without Maps, you will surely want to read as well.

Most importantly, Noel Perrin's A Reader's Delight confirmed my delight in Emily Eden's The Semi-Attached Couple and my great admiration for Diana Athill's wonderful (and painful to read) memoir Instead of a Letter, since he obviously agreed with me about the pleasures of both.

David Madden's Rediscoveries (originally published in 1971) and Rediscoveries II, with a publication date of 1988, are two other great resources for book-lusters. Major writers wrote one- or two-page essays on their favorite works of "neglected" fiction, whatever "neglected" meant to them. It's from reading Rediscoveries II that I discovered, in an essay by Elmore Leonard, author Richard Bissell's novel High Water (the cover of the first edition, from 1954, is a hoot; Bissell also wrote 7½ Cents, the novel that became the musical *Pajama Game*); Dawn Powell's three New York novels, The Locusts Have No King, The Wicked Pavilion, and The Golden Spur (thanks to Gore Vidal); John A. Williams's !Click Song (a novel that's far less read than his The Man Who Cried I Am), selected by Ishmael Reed; and William Kotzwinkle's comic novel of the Age of Aquarius, The Fan Man, which is a favorite of novelist Herbert Gold.

In A History of Reading and A Reading Diary: A Passionate Reader's Reflections on a Year of Books, Alberto Manguel displays in most readable prose his deep love of books and reading, and his wide-ranging knowledge of authors and their works.

BRONTËS FOREVER

Working in isolation in the village of Haworth, sur-
rounded by the bleak moors of Yorkshire, England,
the three Brontë sisters (Anne, Emily, and Charlotte)
wrote some of the best novels of their age (and, arguably, any other),
so it's not surprising that the sisters as well as their characters have
become talismans for other writers. Whether in reaction to a story
line, as a reimagined character, or with one of the authors herself
making an appearance, modern fiction is littered with all things
Brontëesque.

If you have not yet read Jane Eyre, rush out and do so now (really,
put this book down and go read it). If you haven't read **Wuthering
Heights** or **The Tenant of Wildfell Hall**, put them at the top of your
must-read list. All three are romantic novels of love and freedom set
against the strictures of society and class. **Jane Eyre** is the happiest
of the three, while **The Tenant of Wildfell Hall** is perhaps the most
powerful, and **Wuthering Heights** the most tragic. Here are some
Brontëesque books to read as well:

> *Jasper Fforde's* The Eyre Affair *(see page 6
> in* Book Lust*)*
>
> *Mardi McConnochie's* Coldwater *(an
> imaginative intertwining of fictionalized biog-
> raphy with literary fact)*
>
> *Jean Rhys's* Wide Sargasso Sea *(a prequel
> to* Jane Eyre *that describes Mrs. Rochester's
> childhood in the Caribbean)*
>
> *Sharon Shinn's* Jenna Starborn *(*Jane Eyre
> *in outer space—no kidding)*
>
> *Jane Urquhart's* Changing Heaven
> *(doomed lovers and the ghost of Emily
> Brontë)*

BILL BRYSON: TOO GOOD TO MISS

I once interviewed Bill Bryson for a radio program, and found him in person to be just like his authorial persona: one of the most affable and downright friendly people I've ever met in or out of the pages of a book. Whether he's recounting his excursions around Britain, in Australia, or on the Appalachian Trail, or talking about words and language and everything else in (and out of) the world, he is always entertaining, informative, and a pleasure to read. Here's a list of his books, alphabetical by title with the ones that you especially shouldn't miss marked with an asterisk.

Bill Bryson's African Diary

Bryson's Dictionary of Troublesome Words: A Writer's Guide to Getting It Right

I'm a Stranger Here Myself: Notes on Returning to America After Twenty Years Away

* In a Sunburned Country

The Lost Continent: Travels in Small-Town America

Made in America: An Informal History of the English Language in the United States

The Mother Tongue: English and How It Got That Way

Neither Here Nor There: Travels in Europe

Notes from a Big Country

* Notes from a Small Island: An Affectionate Portrait of Britain *(This is the single best book I know of to give someone who is depressed, or in the hospital recuperating [or not] from an illness or surgery.*

The only problem with giving it to friends who had stomach surgery is that they might split their stitches laughing.)

The Palace Under the Alps: And Over 200 Other Unusual, Unspoiled, and Infrequently Visited Spots in 16 European Countries *(This guidebook was published in 1985, so it's dated, but it's still fun to read.)*

* A Short History of Nearly Everything

* A Walk in the Woods: Rediscovering America on the Appalachian Trail

BUILDING BLOCKS

The stories surrounding the building of buildings—from the dreams of the architects, to the engineers who execute their plans, to the end users—can, in the right hands, make for fascinating reading.

In **City in the Sky: The Rise and Fall of the World Trade Center,** *New York Times* reporters James Glanz (who has an advanced degree in physics) and Eric Lipton (who writes for the Metropolitan section of the paper) describe the development of the World Trade Center, from its inception in 1939 (to recycle an unused building from the 1939 World's Fair), through the political infighting that preceded actual construction, to its shocking collapse on September 11, 2001. Along the way we are introduced to a large number of the women and (mainly) men involved, from steelworkers to Nelson Rockefeller, from the head of the Port Authority to the widow of one of 9/11's victims, from small-business owners who lost their shops to the architect of the project. This is one compulsive read, intensified because we know the story's ending; but it also explains, in terms accessible to the layperson, exactly how and why the building fell, and why there was such loss of life.

It's especially enlightening to read Glanz and Lipton's book along with **Great Fortune: The Epic of Rockefeller Center** by Daniel Okrent, since many of the same people appear in both. While Nelson Rockefeller was a relatively minor player in **City in the Sky**, he plays a major role in Okrent's social and cultural history of the building that bears the Rockefeller family's name, one of the most famous skyscrapers in the world. Well researched, well written, and an absorbing read, this is a good choice for people who love all things New York. (You will no doubt want to read Robert A. Caro's **The Power Broker: Robert Moses and the Fall of New York** as well, a magisterial study of the man who wielded enormous control over the development of New York for nearly half of the twentieth century. Winner of a Pulitzer Prize and the Parkman Prize for historical writing, Caro's is the classic book about urban politics and development.)

In **House**, his retelling of one family's house-building experiences in Amherst, Massachusetts, Tracy Kidder presents a literary blueprint of the entire process. You'll be caught up in the lives of the owners, the architect, and the builder as they work through the myriad complications that arise. By the time you turn the last page, you'll either be scared of even thinking about building a house (as I was) or psyched to go ahead and do it.

David Macaulay has written a number of wonderful books for children (which adults will find equally useful and entertaining) about how a particular type of edifice comes to be built. He's particularly good at explaining various technical terms in language that the layperson (no matter his or her age) can understand. **Pyramid, Cathedral, Mosque,** and **Mill** are all excellent, but my favorite is **Castle,** in which the author looks at the step-by-step process by which a thirteenth-century Welsh castle was created.

Slightly off the topic (but I couldn't resist) is a charming little book called **There Goes the Neighborhood: Ten Buildings People Loved to Hate** by Susan Goldman Rubin. Rubin offers brief histories of these ten buildings (and the reactions they engendered), which include such notables as the Pompidou Center in Paris, the Walker Community Library in downtown Minneapolis, modernist architect Philip Johnson's glass house, the Washington Monument, and the Eiffel Tower.

CENTRAL ASIA: CROSSROADS OF EMPIRES, CAULDRON OF WAR

For several years I've been deep in central Asia, or at least deep into books about central Asia. I think I read these books with such interest because I am at heart and at best simply an armchair traveler, and this is one place in the world in which I am almost certain I will never find myself.

Luckily for me, there are some great novels, biographies, and histories of people who lived, visited, or somehow found themselves caught up in the events of a region that includes Afghanistan and the newly independent countries that were once part of the former Soviet Union (Tajikistan, Kazakhstan, Turkmenistan, Uzbekistan, and the Kyrgyz Republic).

Fans of historical fiction will love Philip Hensher's **The Mulberry Empire**, which makes a wonderful companion read to Susanna Moore's **One Last Look** (see "India: A Reader's Itinerary"). Set in the 1830s, when Britain's cockiness about its empire-building was at its height, this is a story of the first Afghan War, when Lord Auckland sent fifty thousand British and Indian troops to unseat the amir, Dost Mohammed, the leader of the Afghans, and replace him with someone more acceptable to an important ally, the king of the Punjab.

In addition to its rousing tale of treachery, bravery, and foolhardy empire-building, **Beyond the Khyber Pass: The Road to British Disaster in the First Afghan War** by John H. Waller includes this ironic verse describing the deaths of ordinary soldiers, victims of British hubris: "When you're wounded and left on Afghanistan's plains / And the women come out to cut up what remains / Jest roll to your rifle and blow out your brains / An' go to your Gawd like a soldier."

People who don't read the subtitle of **Ghost Wars: The Secret History of the CIA, Afghanistan, and Bin Laden, from the Soviet Invasion to September 10, 2001** by Steve Coll may be forgiven if they think they're reading a spy thriller written by, say, John le Carré. Coll, a Pulitzer Prize–winning journalist for the *Washington Post*, describes (with meticulous attention to detail, buttressed by nonintrusive endnotes) the nature and history of U.S. policy in central Asia.

Jon Lee Anderson wrote about the Soviet invasion and the mujahideens' war against the communist-backed government in Kabul for *The New Yorker*. More than a decade later, he returned to write about life there following September 11, 2001. His essays are collected in **The Lion's Grave: Dispatches from Afghanistan.**

More about contemporary Afghanistan can be found in **The Bookseller of Kabul** by Asne Seierstad; **The Storyteller's Daughter: One Woman's Return to Her Lost Homeland**, a memoir by documentary filmmaker and native Afghani Saira Shah; and **The Sewing Circles of Herat: A Personal Voyage Through Afghanistan** by British journalist Christina Lamb, which chronicles her trip to the war-torn country following the World Trade Center attacks in 2001. For a wonderful novel set in nearly contemporary Afghanistan, don't miss Khaled Hosseini's **The Kite Runner.**

I greatly admire Karl E. Meyer's two eminently readable and fact-filled accounts of the region: **The Dust of Empire: The Race for Mastery in the Asian Heartland** and **Tournament of Shadows: The Great Game and the Race for Empire in Central Asia,** the latter written with Shireen Blair Brysac. It's helpful to have an atlas handy while you're reading these books, both of which have splendid suggestions for further reading.

In 1996 Tom Bissell was a Peace Corps volunteer in Uzbekistan, but his stint was cut short by personal issues. In **Chasing the Sea: Lost Among the Ghosts of Empire in Central Asia,** he returns in 2001 and, with the help of a trusty translator, takes a road trip through the now post-Soviet country, sharing with us his adventures and misadventures along the way.

LEE CHILD: TOO GOOD TO MISS

Even the most diligent reader has this happen: through some oversight or quirk of fate or willful neglect, you don't hook up with an author's books until late in his or her career. Then you feel compelled to make a mad dash through the complete works (which is often *not* the best way to read them, since you're bound to notice the repetitions) until you're caught up and are forced to sit and wait impatiently for the next book.

This happened to me most recently with the suspense novels of author Lee Child. Child's books have been getting great reviews ever since **Killing Floor** was published in 1997, but the reviews made them sound so violent that I avoided them. I even remember beginning one, not being able to get into it, and wondering, after I returned it to the library, what all the good press was about.

Then, a few months ago, in a moment of desperation that all reading addicts are familiar with ("Oh no, I have nothing good to read!"), I picked up **Persuader,** and from page 1, I was hooked by

Child's tight writing and terrific suspense-filled plots. So hooked, in fact, that when I was about a quarter of the way in, I pulled myself away from the book and placed all of his earlier books on reserve at the library. When I was three-quarters done, I started to get nervous that I wouldn't have another one on hand as soon as I finished this one, so I started making the rounds of the various bookstores in Seattle, both used and new, to buy all of his books that I could find.

And just as quickly, I read them. Now, having read all eight of Child's suspense novels, I'm still a bit breathless, but eagerly awaiting his ninth.

Child's main character is a former Army military policeman named Jack Reacher. Reacher is squarely in the mold of Travis McGee (hero of John D. MacDonald's well-known novels, all with a color in the title): a loner, incredibly tough yet with a heart of gold, who always stumbles onto or into trouble, mostly because he can't resist helping a lady (or, less often, a gentleman) in distress. Be forewarned: the books do indeed contain some intensely violent scenes (some I had to read with my eyes closed, really). I didn't feel that the violence was gratuitous, but I can certainly see how some readers might.

I recommend starting with **The Enemy**, then proceeding to **Killing Floor**, and finishing up with **Persuader**. If you're going to read the remaining five, the order in which you do so doesn't really matter.

> **The Enemy**
> **Killing Floor**
> **Die Trying**
> **Echo Burning**
> **Running Blind**
> **Tripwire**
> **Without Fail**
> **Persuader**

CHILD PRODIGIES

Everybody loves a talented child—with the exception, of course, of his or her siblings and peers. A gifted child provides a feel-good subject for most readers, and sensitive child prodigies battling unfair odds are somehow especially appealing. Think David, in his fight against Goliath. Or Frodo in his battle with Sauron. The abilities of the kids in the following novels run the gamut from chess to music to sports to a sort of overall intelligence.

Beth Harmon, the eight-year-old heroine of **The Queen's Gambit**, has one talent: chess. During her spectacular rise from her first game to the U.S. Open Championship, Beth struggles with all sorts of inner and outer challenges. The author is Walter Tevis, who is probably best known for his novel **The Hustler** (but who is also the author of **The Man Who Fell to Earth**, **The Color of Money**, and **Mockingbird**).

Helen DeWitt tells the story of Ludo, a young genius, in her first novel, **The Last Samurai**, vividly evoking the odd relationship between Ludo and his rather strange mother, Sibylla, as well as Ludo's urgent search for his real father.

In Myla Goldberg's **Bee Season**, nine-year-old Eliza Nauman, an indifferent student at best, surprises her family with her amazing skill at spelling—but her talent ultimately unravels the tenuous strands that are holding her family together and causes her father, a cantor, to question his faith in God.

In **My Name Is Asher Lev**, Chaim Potok traces the young and brilliant artist Asher Lev's struggle between his religious life in the cloistered Hasidic community in post–World War II Brooklyn and his compulsive need to paint what he sees in the world around him.

Children of the Atom by Wilmar Shiras is about a group of lonely teenagers with preternaturally high IQs, the result of a nuclear accident that claimed the lives of their parents and left them as infants destined to be geniuses. Watching these young people gather and form new relationships with each other and with the outside world is both heart-wrenching and heartwarming, particularly for anyone who ever felt out of place or "different" as a child.

Rose Tremain's **The Way I Found Her** describes the eventful thirteenth summer of Lewis Little, who becomes involved in the life of the oh-so-beautiful and mysterious Valentina Gavrilovich, the best-selling Russian émigré author whose book his mother has come to France to translate.

WINSTON CHURCHILL

There aren't many—if any—twentieth-century statesmen who have generated the sort of massive yet readable biographies that Winston Churchill has. Given the scope and intensity of his life, it probably would be hard to write an uninteresting biography about such a man. Among his many quotable lines are "Any man under thirty who is not a liberal has no heart, and any man over thirty who is not a conservative has no brains," "The best argument against democracy is a five-minute conversation with the average voter," "I have taken more good from alcohol than alcohol has taken from me," and "My most brilliant achievement was my ability to persuade my wife to marry me." He was also the first to use the phrase "iron curtain," in a speech after World War II ended.

Churchill's official biographer is Martin Gilbert, and his eight-volume work is more than all but the most dedicated Churchillians will want to tackle (or have the time to read). You might instead consider Gilbert's one-volume distillation (only the high points of his subject's life, which were many), **Churchill: A Life.**

Hands down, though, the most popular books on Churchill are William Manchester's **The Last Lion: Winston Spencer Churchill: Visions of Glory, 1874–1932** and **The Last Lion: Winston Spencer Churchill: Alone, 1932–40.** They are the first two of what was projected as a three-volume biography. Unfortunately, Manchester died before he finished the third book. This is a real shame, because these books are enormously enjoyable—sweeping and intimate, insightful and well written. They give us entrée into the mind of a complex and brilliant man whose vision and words shaped much of twentieth-century England and the world.

Churchill: A Biography by Roy Jenkins is also a must-read, partly because it was written by a man who held various governmental positions as a member of the Labor Party and was first elected to Parliament in 1948, when the Tory Churchill still commanded much respect and awe. Jenkins's one-volume biography shows his critical admiration of the man he calls "the greatest human being ever to occupy 10 Downing Street."

For a good picture of the young Churchill, don't miss Ted Morgan's **Churchill: Young Man in a Hurry, 1874–1915.**

In addition, Churchill himself wrote copiously; his output includes a series of wonderful memoirs, including seven volumes alone on World War II. But take heed: Reading Churchill himself or about him will likely tempt you down some fascinating highways and byways. Churchill's experiences in the Boer War sent me on a reading jag of many books—so my advice to readers of Churchilliana is to make notes on what you want to read next, but don't let yourself be detoured until you finish the biographies.

CIAO, ITALIA

You could probably spend more time reading these books about Italy than you'll ever have to vacation there. Now, I'm not necessarily recommending that you give up your trip, but there is certainly an awful lot of good reading that can be done before you depart.

First, here are three books you may want to pack along with your toothbrush. **Italy: A Traveler's Literary Companion**, edited by Lawrence Venuti (part of the Traveler's Literary Companion series), introduces you to twenty-three of the best twentieth-century Italian short stories. **Lives of the Painters, Sculptors and Architects** by Giorgio Vasari (who lived from 1511 to 1574 and seems to have invented the term "Renaissance" as applied to Italian art) presents a gossipy, opinionated look at many of the author's famous friends and contemporaries, including painters, sculptors, and architects such as Michelangelo, Leonardo da Vinci, Raphael, and Ghiberti. **Desiring Italy**, edited by Susan Cahill, is a collection of writings about the country by a stellar (and remarkably diverse) group of women, including Muriel Spark, Florence Nightingale, and Elizabeth Barrett Browning, to name just a few.

For a nice historical perspective, try Jeremy Black's **Italy and the Grand Tour**, an assemblage of excerpts from letters and diaries of travelers in the early eighteenth century, when it was considered *de rigueur* to study the ruins of Italy, and Rome in particular.

In **The Dark Heart of Italy: An Incisive Portrait of Europe's Most Beautiful, Most Disconcerting Country**, Tobias Jones, who left his native England to live in Italy in the 1990s, portrays a country that is far more complex than is usually seen in guidebooks or armchair travel accounts.

Italian American Barbara Grizzuti Harrison wrote **Italian Days** about traveling throughout Italy to acquaint herself with her ancestral homeland, and she gives us the benefit of her thoughts on art, architecture, and the Italian character (and characters) as she journeys from region to region.

Gary Paul Nabhan is an ethnobotanist who takes both a spiritual and scientific look at Italy in **Songbirds, Truffles, and Wolves: An American Naturalist in Italy,** as he travels from Florence to Assisi in the steps of St. Francis.

Poet and novelist Frances Mayes has made a name for herself writing about her love affair with Tuscany, where she bought and refurbished an abandoned villa in the village of Cortona. She tells the full story in **Under the Tuscan Sun: At Home in Italy; Bella Tuscany: The Sweet Life in Italy;** and **In Tuscany.**

Take a look at a map of Italy and you'll see that its shape resembles a boot. When I read Mark Rotella's **Stolen Figs and Other Adventures in Calabria,** I wanted to put the book down immediately and make reservations to visit the toe of that boot. And so will you, because of Rotella's cheerful and charming writing.

Two insightful and engaging books about the Italian character are Luigi Barzini's **The Italians** (published originally in 1964) and **That Fine Italian Hand** by Paul Hofmann, Rome bureau chief for the *New York Times.*

For a picture of Italy during World War II, try Eric Newby's **Love and War in the Apennines,** a memoir of the author's experiences as an escaped prisoner of war in Italy, and **Naples '44** by Norman Lewis, who came to Italy as an intelligence officer and grew to love the chaotic, challenging, contradictory country. (He writes, "Were I given the chance to be born again, Italy would be the country of my choice.")

If Venice is your destination, you won't want to go without at least dipping into historian John Julius Norwich's **A History of Venice** and immersing yourself in Jan Morris's less daunting **The World of Venice** and Marlene de Blasi's **A Thousand Days in Venice.** (Don't miss her **A Thousand Days in Tuscany: A Bittersweet Adventure**, either.) And you'll certainly want to take along some of the mysteries set there by Donna Leon, all featuring her Italian policeman sleuth, Commissario Brunetti, whose love of good food and despair about the political corruption in his native country play prominent roles in every book. **Uniform Justice** is a particularly good one, in which Brunetti is foiled at every turn by higher-ups in the government while seeking to discover the murderer of a student at a military academy. Others I've enjoyed a lot include **Acqua Alta**, **Death at La Fenice**, and **A Noble Radiance**. Michael Dibdin also sets his superior mysteries in Italy, and one of my favorites, **Dead Lagoon**, has Italian policeman Aurelio Zen traveling back to his native Venice from Rome to investigate the disappearance of a wealthy businessman. (Other good Aurelio Zen novels are **Medusa, Così fan Tutti**, and **A Long Finish**.)

R. W. B. Lewis, who wrote an award-winning biography of Edith Wharton, lived in Florence with his wife for many years, and **The City of Florence: Historical Vistas and Personal Sightings** is the result of his love affair with the city, its past and its present. Other good books about Florence—its art, architecture, and people—include Mary McCarthy's **The Stones of Florence** and Ross King's **Brunelleschi's Dome: How a Renaissance Genius Reinvented Architecture**.

I had to troll the used-book world to find a copy of **The Hand of Michelangelo** by Sidney Alexander, a novel that ranks right up there with the other great biographical novel about Michelangelo, Irving Stone's **The Agony and the Ecstasy**. (You'll want to read Ross King's nonfiction **Michelangelo and the Pope's Ceiling** along with these.)

Another good novel about Italy is Robert Harris's historical thriller **Pompeii**. Even though you know the outcome—Mount Vesuvius is definitely going to erupt and bury Pompeii and Herculaneum—you'll still find yourself turning the pages maniacally, eager to find out what happens to the characters.

Three other contemporary novels I thoroughly enjoyed were **Italian Fever** by Valerie Martin; **Any Four Women Could Rob the Bank of Italy** by Ann Cornelisen (who also wrote **Torregreca: Life, Death, and Miracles in a Southern Italian Village**, about her experiences setting up a nursery school in an impoverished section of the country); and Francesca Marciano's **Casa Rossa**.

A whole category could be devoted to good books on Italian cooking, but the one you must read (and drool over, while thinking ahead to great meals) is Marcella Hazan's **Essentials of Classic Italian Cooking**.

CIVIL RIGHTS AND WRONGS

Sometimes the best way to learn about a historical period is to read a memoir by someone who played a major role in it. This is certainly true of Melba Patillo Beals's **Warriors Don't Cry: A Searing Memoir of the Battle to Integrate Little Rock's Central High**, the story of her experiences as one of the first black students to try to enroll in Central High School in Little Rock, Arkansas, in 1957. It's impossible not to be moved by this group of teenagers whose bravery paved the way for the next generations of "reluctant warriors" in the struggle for civil rights. An accompanying emotion will certainly be outrage at the reception they were given by the local authorities and citizens.

Diane McWhorter's 2002 Pulitzer Prize–winning **Carry Me Home: Birmingham, Alabama: The Climactic Battle of the Civil Rights Revolution** is really two stories in one. The first is an extremely readable yet very detailed historical account of 1963, "the Birmingham year," when the Reverend Martin Luther King Jr. arrived in Birmingham and the civil rights movement came into its own. The second part of the book is equally interesting: it's the story of the author's family, prominent members of the white Birmingham community who were always on the segregationist side of the Civil Rights struggle. McWhorter devotes a good portion of the book to discussing how vigilante leaders (some of whom were her relatives) were willing to use any means, including violence, to keep blacks from achieving equality in education, jobs, and housing.

Compared to McWhorter's book, Paul Hemphill's **Leaving Birmingham: Notes of a Native Son** is more truly a memoir, describing Hemphill's relationship with his father, with whom he vehemently disagreed on political and social issues. It's an honest and painful look at what Hemphill feels to be the almost irredeemable shame of Birmingham's past.

Lamenting what he sees as a lost opportunity for true equality, Peter Irons, in **Jim Crow's Children: The Broken Promise of the Brown Decision**, takes readers behind the scenes of the historic *Brown v. Board of Education* decision in 1954.

Another excellent book—from a man who personally experienced the effects of the *Brown* decision—is Harvard law professor Charles J. Ogletree's **All Deliberate Speed: Reflections on the First Half-Century of Brown v. Board of Education,** in which he reflects on Supreme Court Justice Thurgood Marshall's career, the work of the Reverend Martin Luther King Jr., and the history of the civil rights movement.

CODES AND CIPHERS

The documented history of codes and code breaking is a long one, stretching back to the sixteenth century and the attempt by Mary, Queen of Scots, to oust her cousin,

Elizabeth, from the throne of England. But no doubt the biblical Joshua also used codes when he communicated with the agents he sent to spy throughout the land of Canaan.

Among the nonfiction available on this subject, you won't want to miss **The Code Book: The Science of Secrecy from Ancient Egypt to Quantum Cryptography** by Simon Singh, who offers his reasons for believing that the people who win wars tend to have the superior code breakers. (His **The Code Book: How to Make It, Break It, Hack It, Crack It** keeps all the really interesting parts of the adult book and omits anything that could possibly bore the most exacting teenage reader.)

For two behind-the-scenes peeks at what went on in this field during World War II, take a look at David Kahn's **The Codebreakers: The Comprehensive History of Secret Communication from Ancient Times to the Internet** and **Between Silk and Cyanide: A Codemaker's War, 1941–1945** by Leo Marks. The latter is the author's story of how his interest in codes began when he read Edgar Allan Poe's story "The Gold-Bug" as a child, and then continued through his wartime experiences in a top-secret British government project monitoring the security of codes being used. (Interestingly, Marks was turned down for British Intelligence's high-profile Bletchley Park code-breaking section.)

If you want to learn how to break codes and work on some examples yourself, the book you're looking for is Helen Fouché Gaines's **Cryptanalysis: A Study of Ciphers and Their Solution**, which includes more than 150 puzzles.

The Decipherment of Linear B by John Chadwick combines history and detection in a biography of the first person to decode the language of the Mycenaeans, who lived on the island of Crete, circa 1500 B.C. If you have ever been curious about how ancient languages are deciphered, this is the book for you.

For a fine novel about codes and code breaking, try Robert Harris's **Enigma**, about the Allies' attempts to break the Germans' codes during World War II. Somehow Harris keeps you reading, even though you know that (surprise!) the codes were broken, the Axis powers were defeated, and the Allies prevailed.

COMMONPLACE BOOKS

Commonplace books have existed at least since Aristotle's time, and I for one would not be surprised to learn that Noah kept his own collection of his favorite proverbs, *bon mots*, and quotations. Called *locus communis* in Latin and *topos koinos* in Greek, these collections (if they're in a language you know, like English) are frequently fun to read: it's a rather different way of getting to know the author. Commonplace books are not strictly diaries because the entries are triggered by something read or heard, not by something the author felt or did.

The title of Helen Bevington's **When Found, Make a Verse Of** comes from a Dickens character in **Dombey and Son**, Captain Cuttle, who, upon hearing something he deems important, takes out a notebook and writes it down while murmuring, "When found, make a note of." Bevington's commonplace book is an anthology of proverbs, oddities, excerpts from what she's reading, and descriptions of conversations with people she meets; most entries are complemented by Bevington's own comments, frequently in the form of a poem.

It's a little unfair of me to include E. M. Forster's **Commonplace Book** in this list. Although it's a record of his thinking about what he was reading from 1925 to 1968, and therefore invaluable to Forsterists and other scholars, it's a bit rough going for all but the most dedicated reader. There are, however, some priceless bits, as when he writes, "Long books, when read, are usually overpraised, because the reader wants to convince others and himself that he has not wasted his time." But to be honest, most of the best stuff here ended up in Forster's important and influential **Aspects of the Novel** (see page 236).

Poet W. H. Auden arranged **A Certain World: A Commonplace Book** in alphabetical order, from Accidie to Writing, with all steps in between. All fans of poetry, and Auden's in particular, will want to take a look at this.

Word lovers rejoice in the existence of Willard R. Espy's books on words at play. **The Word's Gotten Out**, one of his best, includes epigrams, verses, and quotations, along with a collection of ways in which to play with words—rebuses, palindromes, and the like. I never get tired of reading Espy's books.

THE COMPLEX NAPOLEON

I first became interested in Napoleon Bonaparte after I read a curious and charming little book called **Zarafa: A Giraffe's True Story** by Michael Allin. Although Napoleon plays only a bit more than a bit part in this nonfiction account of the first appearance of a giraffe in Western Europe, I was immediately taken with Allin's report that Napoleon read a book while leading his army in Egypt and tore out each page as he finished it, tossing it to the soldiers who rode behind him, so that each book he read eventually passed all the way down through the entire invading French army!

But it became clear to me almost immediately that it's impossible to have only a passing interest in Napoleon. Once one meets him, one is hooked, and there are dozens of good books to read about him. Historians either admire or revile Napoleon; nobody is halfhearted about him. The books below exhibit the full range of opinions.

Probably the most accessible book about Napoleon is Julia Blackburn's beautifully written **The Emperor's Last Island: A Journey to St. Helena**, the story of Napoleon's final years in exile at the seeming end of the world.

Emil Ludwig, author of a 1915 biography called simply **Napoleon**, has this to say about the general's love of reading: "He read so fast that a book lasted him scarcely one hour, and at Saint Helena, a servant was kept busy carrying away armfuls of finished books which only a day before had been brought from the shelves."

Three fascinating though dauntingly door-stopping biographies (but really, how could any normal-size book ever contain this man?) are Alan Schom's **Napoleon Bonaparte**; Steven Englund's **Napoleon: A Political Life**; and Frank McLynn's **Napoleon: A Biography**.

If you're looking for a shorter overview of the general's life, career, and influence, check out Paul Johnson's **Napoleon**, part of the Penguin Lives series; Alistair Horne's **The Age of Napoleon**; or Felix Markham's **Napoleon**.

And of course, once you start on the Napoleon track, you'll find yourself at some point heading straight for all those books about the Napoleonic Wars. A good place to begin is with Simon Forty's **Historical Maps of the Napoleonic Wars**. If you're looking for a gripping nonfiction account of a key episode in Napoleon's life, read Alan Schom's **One Hundred Days: Napoleon's Road to Waterloo**.

But don't forget that there's good fiction, too, in which Napoleon's campaigns and the man himself play an important role, including Leo Tolstoy's **War and Peace**, Brooks Hansen's **The Monsters of St. Helena** (based on a memoir by a woman who as a child knew Napoleon in exile on St. Helena), and two series of novels set during the Napoleonic Wars: the Hornblower novels, including **Captain Horatio Hornblower** by C. S. Forester; and Bernard Cornwell's series about Richard Sharpe, including **Sharpe's Honor** and **Waterloo**.

And certainly don't neglect the excellent biography of Napoleon's complicated wife, **The Rose of Martinique: A Life of Napoleon's Josephine** by Andrea Stuart.

For a fascinating little sidelight on the general's career, take a look at **Napoleon's Buttons: How 17 Molecules Changed History**, by Penny LeCouteur and Jay Burreson, in the "Science 101" section.

THE CONTRADICTORY CARIBBEAN: PARADISE AND PAIN

The literature of the Caribbean is filled with contradictions: the turbulence and violence of its history contrast with the great natural beauty of its setting. The tentacles of slavery and the area's subjugation to the great colonial powers have left their mark on the writers of the region and the stories they tell, whether they're focused on Cuba, Jamaica, Haiti, the Dominican Republic, or islands such as Antigua, Martinique, or Barbados.

Among the most interesting nonfiction books about Haiti are **The Serpent and the Rainbow** by Wade Davis (about an ethnobotanist's search for a powerful "zombie" drug), Amy Wilentz's **The Rainy Season: Haiti Since Duvalier**, and **The Best Nightmare on Earth: A Life in Haiti** (an impressionistic tour through the country by Herbert Gold, a man who loves it deeply). As for fiction, try Graham Greene's **The Comedians**; Madison Smartt Bell's three-volume novelistic history of the country, including **All Souls Rising, Master of the Crossroads**, and **The Stone That the Builder Refused**; and four books by Haitian-born novelist Edwidge Danticat: **Breath, Eyes, Memory** (about the lives of a Haitian mother and daughter in New York), **Krik? Krak!** (a National Book Award finalist about the brutality of life under Duvalier's dictatorship), **The Farming of**

Bones (a very political novel set in the Dominican Republic), and The Dew Breaker (the people's name for members of the Tonton Macoutes, the murderers who killed their fellow Haitians at their government's behest).

St. Lucia native Derek Walcott, the 1992 Nobel Laureate in Literature, is both a poet and a playwright. In Omeros (a retelling of Homer) and Collected Poems, 1948–1984, as well as in newer writing such as Tiepolo's Hound, he blends his love for his homeland and the sadness of exile with classical Western myths and history.

On the island of Martinique, a saucy, aging woman named Marie-Sophie Laborieux recounts her family's struggles from slavery to the founding of a shantytown called Texaco in the novel of the same name by Patrick Chamoiseau, who also wrote Chronicle of the Seven Sorrows, a vivid novel set in the marketplace of colonial Martinique.

Phyllis Ahand Allfrey's The Orchid House is the story of three sisters growing up on the island of Dominica, all of whom fall in love with the same man.

The Polished Hoe by Austin Clarke (which won Canada's prestigious Giller Prize and the Commonwealth Writers Prize Best Book Award, Caribbean and Canada region), set on a fictional island that is clearly Clarke's native Barbados, is told in the form of a monologue by Mary-Mathilda, who over the course of one day confesses to the murder of the manager of a sugar plantation, whose unwilling mistress she was for more than three decades.

Other good novels about the Caribbean include Roslyn Carrington's A Thirst for Rain, chronicling the loves and losses of three intertwined characters in a rural Trinidadian neighborhood, and Jamaica Kincaid's beautifully written coming-of-age novel Annie John, in which the title character quietly rebels against her loving parents on Antigua.

For more fiction and nonfiction about the Caribbean, see the "Cuba Sí!" section in Book Lust.

COZIES

Sometimes you just don't want to read about dysfunctional families, you don't want sadness, you don't want to wonder whodunit, and you don't, for heaven's sake, want to read about sex or violence. Instead, what you want is the literary equivalent of a warm (not hot) bubble bath. If that's the mood you're in, try these.

For years and years, Gladys Taber wrote a column called "Butternut Wisdom" in *Family Circle* magazine, in which she shared with readers recipes and stories of her life in an old farmhouse in Connecticut that was filled with dogs and cats. Portions of her columns were compiled into such nonfiction titles as **The Stillmeadow Road; Especially Dogs . . . Especially at Stillmeadow**; and (my favorite) the novel **Mrs. Daffodil**, an affectionate fictional self-portrait.

Sarah Orne Jewett's novel **The Country of the Pointed Firs** explores the life of a young woman writer who has come to live in the small town of Dunnet Landing. Originally published in 1896, Jewett's novel is the perfect choice when you're feeling overwhelmed with the weight of the contemporary world.

Sixpence House: Lost in a Town of Books is a loving memoir of the months Paul Collins, his wife, Jennifer, and young son, Morgan, spent living in Hay-on-Wye, Wales. Along with stories of the houses they tried to buy and Collins's part-time job in the town's biggest used bookstore are captivating accounts of books he discovered and ruminations on book titles, the vagaries of publishing, literary hoaxes, and the fate of the many unsung writers whose books never made the splash they deserved.

Daddy-Long-Legs, an epistolary novel written in 1912 by Jean Webster, is one of those books that's good for girls between the ages of, say, 12 and 112. An anonymous benefactor, Daddy-Long-Legs, agrees to send orphan Jerusha "Judy" Abbott to college on the condition that she write to him once a month to let him know about her progress. Does she ever meet her secret friend? I'll never tell—but keep in mind that Fred Astaire played opposite Leslie Caron in a 1955 movie adaptation.

Hilda Cole Espy's **Quiet, Yelled Mrs. Rabbit** is the perfect read for any mother, especially for fans of Jean Kerr. Espy left her job as press agent for bandleader Fred Waring when her twins were born, and discovered that the traits that made her a good employee—flexibility and a great sense of humor—also enabled her to raise four daughters and one son happily.

Other writers of gentle reads are Elizabeth Goudge (try her novels **Pilgrims Inn** and **Green Dolphin Street** or, for a special treat, **The Little White Horse**); D. E. Stevenson (I'd suggest **Anna and Her Daughters** and **The Young Clementina**, and the four "Mrs. Tim" books, beginning with **Mrs. Tim Christie**); and Elizabeth Cadell (start with **The Corner Shop**, **The Toy Sword**, or **Mrs. Westerby Changes Course**).

CRIME IS A GLOBETROTTER

Crime occurs everywhere, from Alaska to Zambia. That makes mysteries a good way to travel around the world, since one of the best things about this genre is the authors' skill in bringing to life the settings of their books.

Russia

No list of novels about crime fighters is complete without Martin Cruz Smith's **Gorky Park**, in which Arkady Renko tries to figure out who or what is behind three mutilated corpses discovered in Moscow's Gorky Park. In novels such as **The Winter Queen** and **Murder on the Leviathan,** both set in Czarist Russia, Boris Akunin assigns complicated cases to Erast Fandorin, a young detective in the Moscow police department.

Norway

Karin Fossum's psychological and atmospheric series features Inspector Konrad Sejer, who, in the first of this series to be translated into English, **Don't Look Back,** investigates the death of a teenage girl.

Sweden

Two good Swedish mysteries are **Blackwater** by Kerstin Ekman, a moody thriller about the death of two campers on the outskirts of a remote Swedish village, and **Firewall,** one of Henning Mankell's superior police procedurals, in which Kurt Wallander's squad confronts several disparate cases of murder and mayhem that, contrary to initial appearances, all seem to be part of one deadly plot.

Bosnia

Dan Fesperman's **Lie in the Dark** and **The Small Boat of Great Sorrows** are the only two mysteries I know of that are set in the former Yugoslavia; both concern cases investigated by homicide detective Vlado Petric.

Sicily

The **Terra-Cotta Dog** by Andrea Camilleri takes Inspector Salvo Montalbano into a secret mountain grotto, where he discovers two embracing lovers who have been dead for fifty years, as well as a life-size terra-cotta dog.

China

Xiaolong Qiu's **Death of a Red Heroine** has Inspector Cao Chen, the poetry-quoting intellectual of the Shanghai police force, investigating the death of a Chinese worker; in **A Loyal Character Dancer**, Chen puzzles out the fate of a missing woman; and in **When Red Is Black**, he and his associate, Guangming Yu, look into the murder of a woman writer.

Japan

Laura Joh Rowland's **The Concubine's Tattoo**, set in seventeenth-century Edo (Tokyo), is my favorite novel in the series about Sano Ichiro, the shogun's Most Honorable Investigator of Events, Situations, and People. In this case he is interrupted in the middle of his own wedding feast to investigate the death of a concubine in the Edo Castle's women's quarters.

Tibet

The best novel I've ever read about Tibet is the unforgettable **The Skull Mantra** by Eliot Pattison. The pleasures of watching Shan Tao Yun (formerly the inspector general of the Ministry of Economy in Beijing, now imprisoned in Tibet) unravel the mystery are equaled or exceeded by the opportunity to immerse yourself in Tibetan culture and religion.

Egypt

Michael Pearce has written a series of mysteries set in Egypt (nominally ruled by the Khedive, but really under the control of the British) in the first decade of the twentieth century. His detective is a Welshman named Gareth Owen who serves as chief of Cairo's secret police, the *mamur zapt*. This is a series that is probably best read in order, beginning with **The Mamur Zapt & the Return of the Carpet**.

Elizabeth Peters's delightful series of novels about amateur archaeologist (and amateur detective) Amelia Peabody takes place during the Victorian period. The series comprises more than a dozen mysteries, beginning with **Crocodile on the Sandbank**. This is definitely another series to read in chronological order.

Turkey

The multicultural aspects of contemporary Turkey are the subtext of Barbara Nadel's **Belshazzar's Daughter: A Novel of Istanbul**, in which Inspector Cetin Ikmen tries to uncover the motive and perpetrator in what appears to be a gruesome, racially motivated murder.

Israel

Batya Gur's police procedurals—which include **Murder on a Kibbutz: A Communal Case; The Saturday Morning Murder: A Psychoanalytic Case; Literary Murder: A Critical Case; Murder Duet: A Musical**

Case; and **Bethlehem Road Murder**—are marked by psychological insights, strong character development, and a gift for portraying the complexity of Israeli society in the guise of a mystery novel. It's best to read them in order, so that you can watch the characters, especially Michael Ohayon of the Jerusalem police department, develop throughout the books.

DEWEY DECONSTRUCTED

The heart of the new Rem Koolhaas–designed Seattle Public Library is a book spiral that gently winds from the sixth to the ninth levels, offering patrons a continuous run of the nonfiction collections in Dewey decimal order, from the government documents on level 6 (which have their own arcane classification system), up through the 900s and biographies on level 9. The book spiral makes for perfect browsing and the sort of reading serendipity that I thrive on.

Melvil Dewey (1851–1931) is known as the father of librarianship. When he was just twenty-one, he came up with the Dewey Decimal Classification system, which assigns all of human knowledge to ten broad groups known as "centuries." The DDC is used in most public libraries throughout the United States and Canada. Follow me, then, as we wend our way up through all of the Dewey centuries. (You'll find some fascinating government documents in the "Your Tax Dollars at Work" section.)

000s

The Dewey naughts encompass an interesting hodgepodge. There are books about books, such as my own *Book Lust*; Sara Nelson's **So Many Books, So Little Time: A Year of Passionate Reading**, a collection of essays by a devoted reader that links experiences in her life to books that she's read; Janice A. Radway's **A Feeling for Books: The Book-of-the-Month Club, Literary Taste, and Middle-Class Desire**, which looks at how the Book-of-the-Month Club both interpreted and guided Americans' desire for "culture"; and Noel Perrin's wonderful collection of essays on children's books, **A Child's Delight**, which includes essays on books that he feels ought to be more widely read by children.

But the 000s also include the encyclopedia collection (at 031, to be exact), and, if you're extremely lucky, you might run across the set that many people have long considered the best encyclopedia ever published, the eleventh edition—all twenty-nine volumes and more than 44 million words—of the **Encyclopedia Britannica**, published in 1911. Approximately 1,500 authors contributed to its forty thousand or so articles, many of which were written by the leading experts of the day, who did not hesitate to voice their opinions in their essays. (In **Another Part of the Wood: A Self Portrait**, Sir Kenneth Clark's memoir of his early, formative years, he wrote about his love for this edition: "[O]ne leaps from one subject to another, fascinated as much by the play of mind and the idiosyncrasies of their authors as by the facts and dates. It must be the last encyclopedia in the tradition of Diderot which assumes that information can be made memorable only when it is slightly coloured by prejudice. When T. S. Eliot wrote 'Soul curled up on the window seat reading the Encyclopedia' he was certainly thinking of the eleventh edition.")

100s

Within the 100s are books on philosophy and psychology, including lots of pop psychology and self-help tomes, astrology, demonology, logic, and ethics. The 100s include many books that I go back to frequently: for information, for sustenance, and for consolation.

The Cult of Personality: How Personality Tests Are Leading Us to Miseducate Our Children, Mismanage Our Companies, and Misunderstand Ourselves by Annie Murphy Paul offers a fascinating look at just what value (or lack thereof) very popular tests (including such hoary standards as the Rorschach and the Myers-Briggs Type Indicator tests) have in predicting behavior.

I think a regular rereading of David D. Burns's **Feeling Good: The New Mood Therapy** is a good tonic whenever one is hit with an attack of the blues. Burns's advice—counterattack those automatic (and usually debilitating) negative feelings that arise, and do it immediately—is a useful part of his technique of cognitive therapy.

Elisabeth Kübler-Ross's **On Death and Dying** grew out of a seminar in which she and others interviewed terminally ill patients. She describes the five stages of grief through which most dying people pass: denial and isolation, anger, bargaining, depression, and, at last, acceptance.

The Art of Dying: How to Leave This World with Dignity and Grace, at Peace with Yourself and Your Loved Ones by Patricia Weenolsen is a book everyone can benefit from reading. Both matter-of-fact and compassionate, ranging in subject matter from the spiritual to the practical, the author looks at the full range of issues surrounding death, including talking to the dying and living with a terminal disease.

Although Will Durant's **The Story of Philosophy** is old (it was first published in 1926), and philosophy has inevitably taken itself in new (though not necessarily better) directions, I've never found a more clear and precise introduction to the major Western thinkers, from Socrates to John Dewey.

Three other accessible philosophy books include Edward Craig's **Philosophy: A Very Short Introduction;** Colin McGinn's **The Making of a Philosopher: My Journey Through Twentieth-Century Philosophy;** and Bertrand Russell's **The Problems of Philosophy.**

David Abram's The Spell of the Sensuous: Perception and Language in a More-than-Human World looks at the relationship between our way of experiencing our surroundings and our description of them in words. He concludes that language comes between us and the natural world in many deleterious ways.

200s

Dewey devoted the 200s to books on religion. I am particularly fond of John Bowker's World Religions, because each chapter not only includes an overview of the history and belief system of a particular religion but also discusses its symbols, relationship to other religions, works of art, and more, all complemented by excellent illustrations, including a timeline.

When Huston Smith published his comprehensive book on the seven major religions of the world in 1958, it was perfectly okay to title it The Religions of Man. In subsequent editions, the title morphed to the more politically correct The World's Religions. And because we now live in a highly visual age, the middle 1990s saw The Illustrated World's Religions: A Guide to Our Wisdom Traditions, which added some spectacular art but took away a lot of Smith's valuable text. It's best to go back to the first edition, which has Smith's original thoughts and words.

God: A Biography by Jack Miles, winner of the 1996 Pulitzer Prize for biography, is scholarly, provocative, and thoroughly engaging. Miles, a former Jesuit priest, places God in the context of the Old Testament, where he is clearly the main character, and analyzes his relationships with Abraham, Moses, Joshua, and others.

Lesley Hazleton's Mary: A Flesh-and-Blood Biography of the Virgin Mother looks at a woman who is mentioned only briefly in the New Testament (which is essentially the biography of Jesus, her son). It's illuminating, fascinating, and wide-ranging.

I can't praise Karen Armstrong's books too highly: they are brilliant as well as brilliantly readable. In addition to the two books mentioned in *Book Lust*, one other is essential reading. **The Battle for God** is an incisive analysis of fundamentalist movements among the Israeli Jews, American Protestants, and Muslims from both Egypt and Iran. Here Armstrong contends that fundamentalism arose out of a reaction against and fear of modernity.

300s

The 300s seem to go on forever, including as they do all of the social sciences. (I could probably do a whole separate book of recommended readings on this Dewey century.) Although this is an information-heavy Dewey area, there is also some great reading to be found here. All the books I describe below are excellent choices for book discussion groups looking for meaty but eminently readable nonfiction.

Edward Tenner's **Why Things Bite Back: Technology and the Revenge of Unintended Consequences** somewhat scarily opines that even the snazziest new inventions or life-prolonging medical techniques often result in problems that were never anticipated by their creators.

I enjoyed—and learned so much from—Geraldine Brooks's **Nine Parts of Desire: The Hidden World of Islamic Women**, in which she describes her experiences traveling throughout the Islamic world, talking to women from all walks of life and every political persuasion, from fundamentalists to feminists.

David Fromkin's **A Peace to End All Peace: The Fall of the Ottoman Empire and the Creation of the Modern Middle East** focuses on the region as a whole (and as such is required reading for anyone interested in that topic) but is also immensely valuable in trying to understand contemporary Iran and Iraq. Fromkin places their history in the context of nineteenth- and twentieth-century European colonialism and World War I, and introduces a cast of characters who were instrumental in shaping the region into what it is today.

In his controversial **Killing Monsters: Why Children Need Fantasy, Super Heroes, and Make-Believe Violence**, Gerard Jones offers his theories on the benefits of violent cartoons and computer games for healthy child development, arguing that cartoons and games should be viewed from a child's point of view rather than from an adult's perspective.

Bruno Bettelheim, in a related (though much older) title, **The Uses of Enchantment: The Meaning and Importance of Fairy Tales**, argues that fairy tales are necessary to children's healthy psychological development.

Orchid Fever: A Horticultural Tale of Love, Lust, and Lunacy by Eric Hansen is a story of big business—in this case, the multibillion-dollar industry of orchid smuggling. Hansen encounters almost unbelievable characters in his journey through the underground world of these showy plants. (See *Book Lust* for a description of a similar account, Susan Orlean's **The Orchid Thief**. The two books are complementary rather than repetitive.)

The true-crime genre is one of the few book categories that I don't much enjoy, save one notable exception: **Shot in the Heart**, a memoir by Mikal Gilmore about his (in)famous brother, convicted killer Gary Gilmore, and their horrific shared upbringing.

Other books found in the 300s include Virginia Woolf's wonderful **A Room of One's Own**, which describes how British society denied women writers the advantages and privileges afforded to their male counterparts; Tracy Kidder's **Old Friends**, a respectful and loving look at elderly residents in a nursing home in Northampton, Massachusetts; and Nicholas Lemann's **The Big Test: The Secret History of the American Meritocracy**, which uses the history of the Educational Testing Service as a springboard for a discussion of elitism, civil rights, affirmative action, and education.

The arguments expressed in political philosopher Michael Walzer's **Just and Unjust Wars: A Moral Argument with Historical Illustrations** have become part of the national dialogue about war (the book itself is used as a text at West Point).

400s

The 400s are all about language—from dictionaries and grammars of Austronesian to Yiddish, to books about words and punctuation, and everything in between.

Simon Winchester is the sort of nonfiction writer who can't write an uninteresting book, no matter the topic (he's tackled everything from rivers to maps to murderers masquerading as lexicographers to volcanoes). In his best-seller **The Professor and the Madman: A Tale of Murder, Insanity, and the Making of the Oxford English Dictionary**, Winchester explored the life of one of the oddest of the many contributors to the making of the *OED*. In a sort of follow-up, Winchester's **The Meaning of Everything: The Story of the Oxford English Dictionary** focuses on *OED* editor James Murray, who devoted more than fifty years of his life to trying to bring this project to completion (he died before the book was finished). A good related book, by Murray's granddaughter K. M. Elisabeth Murray, is **Caught in the Web of Words: James Murray and the Oxford English Dictionary**, which is shelved in the biography section, following the 900s.

"Sticklers Unite" is the motto of author Lynne Truss in **Eats, Shoots & Leaves: A Zero Tolerance Guide to Punctuation**. She delves into such topics as the history of typefaces (did you know someone actually invented *italics*?) as well as discussing the use of apostrophes, commas (did you know that Peter Carey's Booker Prize–winning novel **True History of the Kelly Gang** has no commas at all?), colons, semicolons, hyphens, and dashes.

Christopher J. Moore's In Other Words: A Language Lover's Guide to the Most Intriguing Words Around the World includes a selection of foreign words that are clearly *le mot juste* but defy easy translation. One of my favorites is the Russian *razbliuto*, which means "the confusing bundle of emotions felt by Russian males for their ex-girlfriends." Assuming that the bundle of emotions crosses cultures and sexes, it's a very useful word.

Other entertaining 400s include The Superior Person's Book of Words by Peter Bowler, which supplies the reader with a myriad of hardly quotidian but perfectly wonderful words—just right to impress fellow workers, family, and friends; Samuel Johnson's Dictionary: Selections from the 1755 Work That Defined the English Language, edited by Jack Lynch; and Descriptionary: A Thematic Dictionary by Marc McCutcheon. Divided into more than twenty subject categories, including Environment, Art, Weapons, Food and Drink, and Music, then subdivided further (into such niches as Keyboard Instruments, Vocals and Songs, and so on), this is an extremely useful book when you know the idea you want to express (e.g., a deep and powerful singing voice) but not the exact word for it (basso profundo).

Take a look at the "Alphabet Soup" section for some of my other favorite books in the 400s.

500s

The 500s are another huge Dewey area. If you're looking for good reading (as opposed to strictly information) on the natural sciences and mathematics, try these selections.

Sharman Apt Russell's An Obsession with Butterflies: Our Long Love Affair with a Singular Insect is designed to introduce readers to the (brief) life and behavior of one of the most varied, fascinating, and graceful creatures in the world. No one who reads this lovely book will remain unawed by the simple existence of such an insect. This is a good companion read with Robert Michael Pyle's **Chasing Monarchs: Migrating with the Butterflies of Passage**, shelved close by.

Aldo Leopold was widely regarded as the father of wildlife conservation, and his **A Sand County Almanac** is a beautifully written classic of the field that is as important and relevant today as when it was published in 1949, the year after his death. Leopold is passionate in reminding us of not only the beauty of the natural world, but also the need to maintain it in the face of developers and other business interests. There's a transcendent section in which Leopold looks back on the events of the last two centuries as he saws, ring by ring, through a fallen oak tree on his property.

Thomas Pakenham's **Meetings with Remarkable Trees** and **Remarkable Trees of the World** draw our attention—in photographs, prose, and poetry—to these marvels of nature, which many of us would otherwise overlook.

It's in the 500s that you can find two of David Quammen's well-written and always fascinating natural history books. **Monster of God: The Man-Eating Predator in the Jungles of History and the Mind** takes Quammen to four different regions of the world to study these fearsome beasts, and his discussions of them touch on everything from art to mythology to film. In **The Song of the Dodo: Island Biogeography in an Age of Extinction**, he laments the increasing number of extinct species due to humans' unceasing need to expand civilization into "uninhabited" regions of the world.

It's not hard to see why Dava Sobel's unexpected best-seller **Longitude: The True Story of a Lone Genius Who Solved the Greatest Scientific Problem of His Time** was the inspiration for a whole new genre of "microhistories." Her lively writing about the unheralded (and almost uneducated) John Harrison, who invented the chronometer, is mesmerizing.

In the beautifully written **The Sea Around Us**, Rachel Carson not only presents the facts about oceans (tides and currents, how they came to be, how life began, and so on), but conveys the majesty and power of flowing water.

Stephen Jay Gould's **Wonderful Life: The Burgess Shale and the Nature of History** is just one of his many accessible and informative books about the natural world.

In **The Periodic Kingdom: A Journey into the Land of the Chemical Elements**, Peter Atkins asks readers to "accompany [him] on a journey of imagination through the austere navigation chart of chemistry." Along this journey he discusses the ways in which the periodic table assists us in making sense of the world around us, the origins of the elements, and the scientists who charted the building blocks of chemistry.

David Bodanis dissects what is arguably the most famous equation in history, in **$E=mc^2$: A Biography of the World's Most Famous Equation**, by offering historical and biographical information about each element in the equation.

In **The Joy of π**, David Blatner discusses the mathematical symbol that, as every good student knows, begins with 3.14 and then continues on, up to more than 8 billion digits, with no end in sight. Why is the ratio of the circumference of a circle to its diameter so fascinating? Fear not, Blatner explains all, in prose aimed at the interested non-mathematician, like me.

600s

The 600s are devoted to technology and applied sciences. This is where you can find, among many other topics, all you ever wanted to know about diseases (the 616s), cooking (641.5), and business (generally the 650s).

Jeff Taylor's **Tools of the Trade: The Art and Craft of Carpentry** is a collection of essays on twenty-five different tools, beautifully written by a man in love with his profession. It could be subtitled "The Zen of Carpentry."

Not content with his appearance in the 500s, David Bodanis can also be found here! His **The Secret Family: Twenty-four Hours Inside the Mysterious World of Our Minds and Bodies** elicits an uneasy combination of laughter, nausea (are there really 40,000-plus mites in the pillowcase on which I lay my head each night?), and amazement at just what goes on inside and around us every minute of every day.

Natalie Angier's **Woman: An Intimate Geography** takes readers on an excursion through all aspects of the anatomy and physiology of women, from breast milk to menstruation to exercise to hormones to childbirth, and does it all in totally accessible prose.

It's a fool's game to try to make even a semi-definitive list of great cookbooks, especially if you're basically a non-cook, as I am. But since I'm someone who rushes in where others fear to tread, here's a sampling of my favorite cookbooks. First, of course, is Irma S. Rombauer and Marion Rombauer Becker's **Joy of Cooking** (but not the most recent edition). Try the oatmeal cookie recipe with orange peel or the baked macaroni and cheese when you want comfort food to go along with a cozy book.

For me, the best part about baking bread is the upper-arm exercise involved with kneading the dough, and the times that you can curl up on the couch with a good book while the dough is rising. I've used Bernard Clayton's bread books since the first one was published in 1973, and have never found a bad recipe. The most recent incarnation is **Bernard Clayton's New Complete Book of Breads**. But my new favorite is, hands down, **The Book Lover's Cookbook: Recipes Inspired by Celebrated Works of Literature and the Passages That Feature Them** by Shaunda Kennedy Wenger and Janet Kay Jensen. What a great idea! Not only do you get introduced (and reintroduced) to works of fiction and nonfiction, but you get some awfully good-sounding recipes along the way. Where else can you find a pie crust recipe straight from a description by Eudora Welty in One Writer's Beginnings, and a recipe for orange-almond bisque from Billie Letts's novel Where the Heart Is? Not to mention recipes for empanadas (from Isabel Allende's Daughter of Fortune) and teacakes (based on a selection from F. Scott Fitzgerald's The Great Gatsby).

One of the books I treasure in my home library is the 1932 "complete new revised edition" of A Thousand Ways to Please a Husband with Bettina's Best Recipes by Louise Bennett Weaver and Helen Cowles LeCron. As they follow the first year in the married life of Bob and Bettina, the authors provide tips and tricks (and recipes) for keeping husbands happy. Chapters include "Home at Last," "Bettina's First Real Dinner" (the menu is pan-broiled steak, baking powder biscuits, new potatoes in cream butter, pea and celery salad, and strawberry shortcake with rhubarb sauce), "A Good-bye Luncheon for Bernadette," and "The Dixons Come to Dinner"— each with its own vignette, followed by the menu and recipes. It's a true nostalgia trip.

Laura Shapiro's two books on the social history of food, Perfection Salad: Women and Cooking at the Turn of the Century and Something from the Oven: Reinventing Dinner in 1950s America, are both entertaining and informative. From descriptions of early Pillsbury Bake-Offs to the frozen food industry's all-consuming interest in decorating home freezers for every kitchen decor, from the history of the Boston Cooking School to an appreciation of Fannie Farmer, these books will change the way you look at food and its preparation.

700s

In the 700s you can pore over photos of the art in great museums that you may never have a chance to visit; you can read a history of the film industry; and you can learn to juggle or play bridge, poker, or backgammon.

Since the Amon Carter Museum's holdings showcase less well-known work by very well-known artists, a browse through **An American Collection: Works from the Amon Carter Museum** offers not only the pleasure of seeing excellent reproductions of works by Thomas Eakins, John Singer Sargent, Winslow Homer, James McNeill Whistler, Mary Cassatt, and others, but also the sense that you're enlarging your understanding of these artists' work.

In **Vermeer in Bosnia: Cultural Comedies and Political Tragedies,** Lawrence Weschler offers readers the pleasure of his myriad interests, with penetrating and entertaining essays on subjects as diverse as Roman Polanski ("The Brat's Tale"), theater ("Henry V at Srebrenica"), family relationships ("My Grandfather's Last Tale"), and art ("True to Life: David Hockney's Photocollages").

More than fifty years ago, general manager Branch Rickey signed Jackie Robinson to play for the Brooklyn Dodgers, and that act, which broke the color barrier in professional baseball, changed the course of more than sports history. As Arnold Rampersad shows in **Jackie Robinson: A Biography,** Robinson was uniquely qualified to play the role he did, both on and off the field.

Only a writer as good as David Remnick and a subject as complex as Muhammad Ali could make boxing interesting to me; **King of the World** is definitely not for sports fans only.

Michael Lewis's **Moneyball: The Art of Winning an Unfair Game** looks at the Oakland Athletics, one of the least wealthy teams in Major League Baseball, and analyzes why they win year after year. (This book turned me into a big fan of the Oakland A's, which is not a good thing to be when you live in Seattle.)

In the more than twenty years since Suzanne Gordon published **Off Balance: The Real World of Ballet,** not a lot appears to have changed: the beauty of classical dance as you watch it unfold on stage seems to have no connection with the blood, sweat, tears, and hours of work of the dancers themselves.

800s

Ah, at last we get to the truly literary part of Dewey. Don't miss these gems!

Randall Jarrell once said that he had "an uneasy respect" for a poem I had written. I didn't realize what a compliment that was until I read **No Other Book: Selected Essays,** a treasure for anyone interested in literary issues. Precious few critics have ever equaled Jarrell's incisive intelligence, wit, and plain old common sense. And editor Brad Leithauser's introduction is, by itself, worth the price of the book. (A good companion read is **Remembering Randall: A Memoir of Poet, Critic, and Teacher Randall Jarrell** by his widow, Mary Jarrell.)

In **How to Read a Poem: And Fall in Love with Poetry,** Edward Hirsch demystifies the reading of poetry in a way that doesn't talk down to readers. Even longtime lovers of poetry will find much to contemplate here.

Stephen Greenblatt brings the foremost Elizabethan playwright to life in **Will in the World: How Shakespeare Became Shakespeare;** this is a biography that will inspire you to read (or reread) all the plays and sonnets.

The first essay in poet Patricia Hampl's **I Could Tell You Stories: Sojourns in the Land of Memory** is about memoir, which she defines so thoughtfully as "that landscape bordered by memory and imagination." Her other essays address such diverse subjects as her mother's response to a poem about herself in Hampl's first collection ("It is pointless to argue your First Amendment rights with your mother," she writes), Anne Frank, and the philosopher and saint Edith Stein.

Inside Out: A Memoir of the Blacklist is Walter Bernstein's account of his experiences during the 1950s as a victim of McCarthyism. He describes a Hollywood that was divided between those who cooperated with the FBI by naming names of colleagues, friends, and families, and those who chose to go to jail or lose their jobs rather than answer questions about their political beliefs from the House Un-American Activities Committee. Bernstein wrote the screenplay for the movie *The Front*, which deals with this very topic.

Award-winning University of Virginia professor Mark Edmundson passionately argues for the benefits of reading great literature—the major one being that it helps people change and develop their lives for the better—in the stimulating **Why Read?**

Take a look at the "Poetry Pleasers" section for more good 800s reading.

900s

The 900s cover history and geography and are full of good choices for readers.

The 1915 attack by a German submarine on the luxury liner *Lusitania* during a voyage from Liverpool to New York, and the resulting death of 1,200 of its civilian passengers (including more than 100 Americans), was key in bringing the United States into World War I. Diana Preston offers a fittingly moving account of the events surrounding the attack in **Lusitania: An Epic Tragedy.**

Tony Perrottet had a great idea—to retrace the travels of the ancient Romans as they ventured throughout their empire from Pompeii to Egypt and beyond. As he follows in their footsteps two thousand years later with his pregnant girlfriend—in **Pagan Holiday: On the Trail of Ancient Roman Tourists**—Perrottet compares the ancient cities and the modern ones, describing their inhabitants, their problems, and their entertainments, all the while interspersing delightfully prophetic quotes from ancient travelers. Classics majors will find this book heaven-sent, while travelers will delight in this guide with a twist.

Stuart Stevens's **Night Train to Turkistan: Modern Adventures along China's Ancient Silk Road** is the story of the author's travels through the wilds of China. Stevens went to China along with three friends (one of them Mark Salzman of **Iron & Silk** fame—see "Mark Salzman: Too Good to Miss") to replicate the famous 1936 journey of Peter Fleming and Ella K. Maillart, recounted by Fleming in **News from Tartary** and by Maillart in **Forbidden Journey: From Peking to Kashmir**. A sense of humor, a large tolerance for discomfort, and a willingness to appear foolish are prime requirements for a traveler, especially for someone who wants to write about his travels, and Stevens has those attributes in spades.

Christiane Bird writes about the people she met in 2002 while traveling through Kurdistan, "a country that exists on few maps, but in many hearts," in **A Thousand Sighs, A Thousand Revolts: Journeys in Kurdistan**.

On a related subject, try Stephen Kinzer's **All the Shah's Men: An American Coup and the Roots of Middle East Terror**. It reveals that there's nothing new about the United States stepping in to force regime change in the Persian Gulf: fifty years ago, Britain and the United States engineered a coup that toppled the government of Iran's popularly elected and very popular prime minister, Mohammed Mossadegh, and brought the shah back from exile in Paris. Kinzer's account is a fascinating, cautionary, and fluidly written look back at these events. He explores the effect of the overthrow on both the country itself and its political relationships with the United States and Britain afterward.

Although foreign correspondent Jon Lee Anderson reports regularly for *The New Yorker* from Afghanistan and Iraq, excerpts from **The Fall of Baghdad**, his new collection of stunning war reportage, have not appeared in the magazine.

Many young readers—including me, some years ago—were thrilled by books about the fabulous discoveries of the German amateur archaeologist Heinrich Schliemann, whose love of Homer's Iliad led him to dig up the ancient, long-lost city of Troy. Caroline Moorehead retells this story for adults in **The Lost and Found: The 9,000 Treasures of Troy: Heinrich Schliemann and the Gold That Got Away.**

Although the length of Jacques Barzun's **From Dawn to Decadence: 500 Years of Western Cultural Life, 1500 to the Present** might put you off at first, this is a most readable cultural history—almost like a conversation between you and the author, a longtime professor and historian.

The Day the World Came to Town: 9/11 in Gander, Newfoundland by Jim DeFede describes what happened when U.S.–bound planes were grounded in tiny Gander, Newfoundland, and the passengers found themselves welcomed, aided, and consoled by the residents.

In **My Kind of Place: Travel Stories from a Woman Who's Been Everywhere,** Susan Orlean brings together a varied collection of essays on an assortment of topics: fertility rites in Bhutan; climbing Mount Fuji; beauty pageants for little girls; and a taxidermy convention.

DICK LIT

Face it: If publishers had had the guts to call this subgenre what it really is—Dick Lit—rather than the wimpy-sounding Lad Lit, it might've had a chance to succeed. As it is, I have the distinct impression that Dick Lit has been written off, even as its distaff counterpart, Chick Lit, continues in all its glory, or at least in all its money-making potential.

Of course, the major problem with Dick Lit is that Nick Hornby, in **About a Boy** and **High Fidelity** (both of which I reread fairly regularly), set the bar very high (and it didn't hurt that both books were turned into very good and true-to-the-novel films).

Even though I am clearly not in the right demographic for these books—being neither male, nor twenty- or thirty-somethingish, nor Manhattan- or London-based—I heartily recommend the following two works of fiction.

If you can imagine A. S. Byatt writing a dick-lit novel, then you have a good idea of what **The Calligrapher** by Edward Docx is like. The hero—a twenty-something Brit—has two passions: women (Jasper's the sort of guy who cheats on the women he's cheating on other women with) and calligraphy, with his latest commission being to calligraph the songs and sonnets of John Donne (who was also a dedicated serial seducer). Jasper's two passions are joined when he falls truly, madly, and deeply in love with the beautiful Madeleine.

Although some might argue that David Schickler's **Kissing in Manhattan** doesn't belong in this category, these eleven linked stories do feature young, mostly upwardly mobile urban professionals (mostly men) who are all trying to connect with like-minded souls and are all looking for love in the same mysterious apartment building and in all the same Manhattan restaurants.

DIGGING UP THE PAST
THROUGH FICTION

The reason I didn't go ahead and earn a doctorate after getting my master's degree in history was that I didn't think any institution would accept a dissertation about novels that take readers back in time and make them believe that the world they're reading about is the way the world really was back then. Here are some of the books and authors I would have discussed.

When people talk about great writers of historical fiction, Dorothy Dunnett's name is most often at the top of their list. And no wonder—her attention to detail, adroit use of both real and imagined characters, and intricate plots distinguish her from the many other historical-novelist wannabes. Of her two series, the Lymond Chronicles (set during the seventeenth century around the reign of Mary, Queen of Scots)—which consists of **The Game of Kings, Queens' Play, The Disorderly Knights, Pawn in Frankincense, The Ringed Castle,** and **Checkmate**—is probably the most popular, but it would be a shame to miss out on her House of Niccolo series (set two centuries earlier, in what are now the Benelux countries of western Europe), composed of **Niccolo Rising, The Spring of the Ram, Race of Scorpions, Scales of Gold, The Unicorn Hunt, To Lie with Lions, Caprice and Rondo,** and **Gemini.**

A writer who shares Dunnett's enviable talent for exciting storytelling and accurate re-creations of history is Sharon Kay Penman. My favorites among her books are **When Christ and His Saints Slept** (about the struggle for control of England's throne between Queen Maud and her cousin Stephen of Blois) and **Time and Chance,** her story of the tumultuous marriage of Henry II and Eleanor of Aquitaine. (It would be hard to write a dull novel about this fascinating woman; one of the other good ones is a book for young people called **A Proud Taste for Scarlet and Miniver** by E. L. Konigsburg.) But my favorite Penman novel, and probably her greatest accomplishment, is **The Sunne in Splendour,** a novel about Richard III (who got a bad rap from Shakespeare, it appears, but was redeemed beautifully in Josephine Tey's marvelous historical mystery, **The Daughter of Time**).

Margaret George has written many superior historical novels— they're really fictionalized biographies—including **The Memoirs** of Cleopatra and a remarkable portrait of the Tudor period, The Autobiography of Henry VIII: With Notes by His Fool, Will Somers. (I've always wondered, though, how she imagined that Henry would ever have time to write an autobiography, given the numerous women he bedded, his many marriages, and all the subsequent beheadings and divorces.) George is a master at turning her subjects into living, breathing individuals.

After the War by Richard Marius introduces readers to Paul Alexander, a Greek veteran of World War I, who crosses the Atlantic after his horrific wartime experiences in Belgium and ends up in Bourbonville, Tennessee, trying to find peace from the battlefield memories that still consume him. In this painstakingly realistic novel, Marius asks readers to think about how much of our life is determined by the decisions we make and how much is simply fate, or bad luck, or just chance.

Barry Unsworth's The Rage of the Vulture takes place during the Ottoman Empire's collapse in the first decade of the twentieth century. It relates the story of Captain Robert Markham, an Englishman who comes to Constantinople as part of the British army but who considers his real job to be avenging the rape and murder of his Greek fiancée at the hands of the Turks a dozen years before. You will not want to miss Unsworth's Sacred Hunger either, an intensely moving novel of the eighteenth-century slave trade.

Also set during the dying days of the Ottoman Empire is the richly satisfying Birds Without Wings by Louis de Bernières. The novel is narrated in dozens of voices, including those of the men and women, the rich and the poor, the nobles and peasants, the Christians and Muslims, the Greeks and the Armenians who have lived peaceably together for generations in a small coastal town in Anatolia, far from the seats of influence and power. When war breaks out, they become simply pawns of history, subject to the decisions of their misguided, incompetent, and dangerously power-hungry rulers. Along with the story of the residents of this one small town, de Bernières tells of the rise of Kemal Ataturk, whose goal was to make Turkey a modern, secular country. These parallel tales play off one another brilliantly.

In **Unicorn's Blood, Firedrake's Eye**, and **Gloriana's Torch**, Patricia Finney vividly animates the complexities of late-sixteenth-century England, in which religious issues divided not only England but the known world; slavery continued to extend its tentacles ever further into the European continent; and Elizabeth, the Virgin Queen, was beset by threats to her rule from both within and outside England. Finney is remarkably talented at creating three-dimensional fictional characters.

Other good choices include Rose Tremain's **The Colour** (newly-weds try to adjust to a new life in gold-mining-mad New Zealand in the mid-nineteenth century); Sigrid Undset's three-volume **Kristin Lavransdatter** (set in fourteenth-century Norway and available in an accessible new translation by Tiina Nunnally); Diane Pearson's **Csardas** (a family saga set during the last years of the Austro-Hungarian Empire); Morgan Llywelyn's **1916** (about the struggle for Irish independence); Cecelia Holland's **Great Maria** (a strong woman in eleventh-century Italy) and **Until the Sun Falls** (a thirteenth-century Mongol general takes on the world); **The Clerkenwell Tales** (another of Peter Ackroyd's enticing novels, this one peopled with characters from Geoffrey Chaucer's **The Canterbury Tales**, set in a medieval England that Ackroyd evokes brilliantly); **A Place of Greater Safety** by Hilary Mantel (maybe the best novel I've ever read about the French Revolution); and Joanne Williamson's **Jacobin's Daughter** (the second best, which was written for young adults but makes fine reading for grown-ups as well).

For American historical fiction, there are James Fenimore Cooper's rousing tales of the early years of our country, including **The Deerslayer** and **The Last of the Mohicans**; the romances of Gwen Bristow, especially **Celia Garth**, set in Charleston, South Carolina, during the Revolutionary War; and the satisfying novels of Kenneth Roberts—particularly **Arundel**, which is set in Maine and Quebec and features Benedict Arnold in a starring role, and **Northwest Passage**, which tells the story of a young artist, Langdon Towne, working under the command of the legendary Major Robert Rogers during the French and Indian Wars.

For more historical fiction recommendations, see these sections in *Book Lust*: "Biographical Novels," "Civil War Fiction," "Historical Fiction Around the World," and "World War I Fiction."

FANTASY FOR YOUNG AND OLD

The children's fantasy novels of E. Nesbit, who was born in the middle of the nineteenth century and died in 1924, influenced not only the many fantasy writers who came after her, but also the course of children's literature as a whole. Her books were realistic (despite their fantasy elements) and filled with gentle humor. Two of her best (**The Phoenix and the Carpet** and **Five Children and It**) center on children who unexpectedly happen upon magic creatures or stumble into a magical situation.

Edward Eager—author of **Half Magic, Knight's Castle, Seven-Day Magic, The Time Garden, Magic or Not?, Magic by the Lake**, and **The Well-Wishers**—was greatly influenced by Nesbit. His books, like hers, are down-to-earth as well as fantastical: you can believe that events like these just might occur (maybe and if only . . .). The book of his that I most often reread is **Half Magic**, but a close second is **Seven-Day Magic**, perfect for those who know the enchantment to be found in books and libraries.

Alan Garner's first fantasy novel was **The Weirdstone of Brisingamen**, but his two best novels—written for young adults but enjoyed by fantasy-loving adult readers as well—are **The Owl Service**, which won both Britain's *Guardian* Award and the Carnegie Medal in 1968, and **Red Shift**. The Owl Service is about three contemporary teens who are tragically drawn into re-enacting an ancient Welsh myth, while **Red Shift** is a somewhat more difficult and scary novel that challenges the reader to make the connections among three characters living in different time periods in the same location.

Noel Streatfeild is probably best known for her "Shoes" books for children, including **Ballet Shoes, Skating Shoes**, and **Tennis Shoes**. But she deserves to be known as well for her wonderful fantasy **The Fearless Treasure**, in which a group of children are given the ability to go back in time to find their family's place in England's history. This is a wonderful way to learn British history and to contemplate how the past impinges upon and even defines the present.

Edward Ormondroyd's **David and the Phoenix** was originally published in 1957, which is when I first read it. It's the story of a young boy who meets a fabulous five-hundred-year-old bird (in their very funny first meeting, the phoenix is studying Spanish verbs); together they must foil a scientist who wants to capture the bird and study him. This is not so much high fantasy (like the J. K. Rowling books) as it is a charming adventure story that will entice readers from age eight on up.

In **Gregor the Overlander** by Suzanne Collins, eleven-year-old Gregor and his younger sister, Boots, fall through a grate in their apartment building's basement laundry room and find themselves in an Underland beneath New York City. All Gregor wants is to take his sister and go home, but when he learns that an ancient prophecy involving an ongoing war between humans and the giant rats who are menacing them seems to refer to him, he is forced to decide whom to trust—the enormous cockroaches, humans, bats, spiders, or rats. Page-turning adventure, a brave young hero, and a heart-warming ending—what more could fantasy fans ask for? A sequel, of course. So you won't want to miss **Gregor and the Prophecy of Bane**. Go Gregor!

One of the most haunting fantasies I've ever read is John Keir Cross's **The Other Side of Green Hills**. Five children spend a winter holiday at a remote house in the English countryside, where they learn to their shock that Green Hills has an Other Side, and that a mysterious couple—the Owl and the Pussycat—lives there. Long out of print (it was first published in 1947) and difficult to find, this is a must for fans of fantasy.

Other good fantasies include Patrick Carman's **The Dark Hills Divide**, which is the first book in the Land of Elyon series; **Earthfasts** by William Mayne; **Mr. Pudgins** by Ruth Carlsen (every child dreams of having a babysitter like Mr. Pudgins); Diana Wynne Jones's **Fire and Hemlock, Archer's Goon,** and **Howl's Moving Castle,** among her many others; P. B. Kerr's **The Akhenaten Adventure**, the first in the Children of the Lamp series; Dave Barry and Ridley Pearson's **Peter and the Starcatchers**, a prequel to J. M. Barrie's **Peter Pan**; and Cornelia Funke's **The Thief Lord** and **Inkheart**.

Three wonderful fantasies/romances just right for teenage girls (and like-minded adults) are **The Sherwood Ring** by Elizabeth Marie Pope, which takes place both in the present and during the Revolutionary War period, and two delightful fantasies by Patricia C. Wrede and Caroline Stevermer that will appeal to anyone who loves Regency romances and Jane Austen. The Wrede/Stevermer titles are two of the longest known to humankind: **Sorcery & Cecelia or The Enchanted Chocolate Pot: Being the Correspondence of Two Young Ladies of Quality Regarding Various Magical Scandals in London and the Country**, followed up by **The Grand Tour: Being a Revelation of Matters of High Confidentiality and Greatest Importance, Including**

Extracts from the Intimate Diary of a Noblewoman and the Sworn
Testimony of a Lady of Quality.

FATHERS, MOTHERS,
SISTERS, BROTHERS: THE FAMILY
OF THE CLERGY

I find reading about the clergy particularly interesting, perhaps
because these books give me insight into a world I'll never
know otherwise. I suppose that's why, as a teenager, I was so
entranced with Kathryn Hulme's **The Nun's Story** and Monica
Baldwin's memoir **I Leap over the Wall: A Return to the World
After Twenty-eight Years in a Convent.**

Novels about men and women of the clergy range from the
humorous to the serious, from mysteries to mainstream fiction.
Here are some I've particularly enjoyed.

Morte D'Urban, the National Book Award–winning first novel by
J. F. Powers, is the frequently comic and persistently ironic story of
a midwestern Roman Catholic priest who ministers to an unlikely
flock while hovering uneasily between the quotidian and true
faith.

If humor is what you're after, you'll find that many of the funniest
novels have as their protagonists lapsed (or lapsing) practitioners of
the faith (**Plain Heathen Mischief** by Martin Clark, about a lapsed
Baptist minister, is particularly entertaining). **Conclave** by Roberto
Pazzi is a subversively funny look at the College of Cardinals in the
process of selecting a new pope. And Herbert Tarr's **The Conversion
of Chaplain Cohen** is a delightful (and sometimes poignant) look at
a newly minted young rabbi trying to adjust to life in the army.

A man who leaves the seminary when he falls in love with a
visiting speaker is one of the main characters in Gail Godwin's
The Good Husband. Francis Lake has long been married to the

much-older Magda Danvers, a literary theorist who has always boasted that she stole her husband from God and who is now dying of ovarian cancer.

The unorthodox young priest Father Paul LeBlanc finds his life and faith in upheaval after he sees a dead girl come back to life, in John L'Heureux's **The Miracle**.

A graphic designer who has given up on men and a monk who has lost his faith in God meet and fall—most tentatively—in love in Tim Farrington's **The Monk Downstairs**.

The Starbridge series by Susan Howatch is a group of novels about the Church of England, in which she explores different aspects of religious life (for those within and without the Church) in the middle of the twentieth century. Minor characters in one novel take the starring role in others, which enriches the experience of reading them. In order, they are **Glittering Images, Glamorous Powers, Ultimate Prizes, Scandalous Risks, Mystical Paths, Absolute Truths,** and **The Wonder Worker**.

Although **The Name of the Rose** by Umberto Eco is nominally a mystery, it is much more than that: an entrée into the world of medieval Italy and its theological controversies, worldview, politics, and scientific and artistic endeavors. This novel is simply not to be missed.

Probably the best pure mysteries featuring a member of the clergy are those by Ellis Peters, set in twelfth-century England. The twenty superb novels about Brother Cadfael, a Benedictine monk (which should be read in order, beginning with **A Morbid Taste for Bones**), take place during the two decades of bloody battles between King Stephen and his cousin, the Empress Maud, who were fighting for supremacy over Britain. I've always found that reading Peters is also a pleasurable way to learn English history.

FICTION FOR FOODIES

When food plays a major role in a novel—because the main characters are chefs, bakers, or just heavy eaters—there's always a danger that you'll encounter a particularly tasty paragraph or luscious-sounding recipe, drop the book, and head directly for the kitchen to cook, bake, or simply eat. Woe to any diet you might be on! Luckily, these novels are all engrossing enough to keep you involved at least to the end of each chapter, when it's natural to take a food break.

Sunya, a pastry chef, the owner of a bakery/cafe, and the main character in Bharti Kirchner's **Pastries: A Novel of Desserts and Discoveries**, travels to Japan to try to recapture her love for her chosen profession. Kirchner is a cookbook writer turned novelist (try **The Bold Vegetarian: 150 Inspired International Recipes** if you're interested in expanding your culinary repertoire).

It Can't Always Be Caviar by Johannes Mario Simmel tells the story of Thomas Lieven, a German-born banker, gourmet cook, romantic, and involuntary spy for Germany, France, England, and the United States (none of whom know of his connections with any of the others). It's great fun to read, and complicated menus and recipes accompany each chapter.

Thomas Fox Averill's **Secrets of the Tsil Café** is a coming-of-age novel about young Wes Hingler, who must find his own way in the wider world as well as in the world of food—somewhere between his father's Mexican restaurant and his mother's Italian catering company.

A chef is the main character in Monique Truong's **The Book of Salt**, in which Gertrude Stein and Alice B. Toklas's personal chef looks back on his childhood in Vietnam under the French and his years cooking for the crème of bohemian Paris.

Catherine de Medici is the main character in both **The Stars Dispose** and **The Stars Compel** by Michaela Roessner, historical novels with a tinge of fantasy and lots of luscious-sounding recipes offered up by Catherine's cooks.

FLORIDA FICTION

Before Walt Disney World, Busch Gardens, spring training, and the draining of the Everglades, Florida meant miles of swamps, untamed wilderness, and unspoiled beaches. Whenever I think of that prelapsarian time, four writers inevitably come to mind: Marjorie Kinnan Rawlings, Zora Neale Hurston, John D. MacDonald, and Carl Hiaasen.

Rawlings is probably best known for **The Yearling**, about young Jody and Flag, the fawn that he loves, which was awarded the 1939 Pulitzer Prize (the only time the award went to a book that is essentially for children). But I like **Cross Creek** even better, in which Rawlings lovingly describes the fourteen years that she and her husband spent living on a farm in a citrus grove outside of Gainesville in the 1930s.

Hurston's not inconsiderable and well-deserved fame rests on her now-canonized novel **Their Eyes Were Watching God**, which tells (in a dialect that takes some getting used to) the story of spirited and strong Janie Crawford.

MacDonald wrote a series of hugely entertaining books (just a bit dated these days) that feature the archetypal tough-guy-with-a-heart-of-gold Travis McGee. McGee lives on his boat, the *Busted Flush*, in Fort Lauderdale when he isn't off helping men and women (mostly women) in distress. (You can go to Fort Lauderdale today and see the slip where the boat in the book was docked, if you're so inclined.) Though each novel in the series stands pretty much on its own, you may as well begin with the first, **The Deep Blue Goodbye**.

Hiaasen's novelistic romps through and rants about Florida (particularly South Florida) always leave me wanting more books from him—try **Stormy Weather** and **Tourist Season**. For other books by Hiaasen, see page 78 in *Book Lust*.

For some of the best contemporary fiction set in the Sunshine State, try these books.

Racism rears its ugly head in Beverly Coyle's **In Troubled Waters**, in which ninety-one-year-old Tom Glover hires two boys—one black and one white—to accompany his son-in-law (who's in the early stages of Alzheimer's) while fishing, and unwittingly sets in motion a series of devastating events.

In a novel filled to the brim with calamities (rape, accidents, marital woes, and amnesia—and that's just for starters), you'd think that Mary Hood's **Familiar Heat** would be depressing at best, but in fact, this beautifully written novel offers an equal measure of tenderness and testament to the enduring power of love, making it a book you won't want to miss. And best of all, it's all done without any cloying sentimentality whatsoever.

The plot of **Carter Clay** by Elizabeth Evans revolves around three people—Carter Clay, the teenaged Jersey Alitz, and Katherine, her mother—who are the victims of a car accident caused by Clay. It's an absorbing novel that offers neither a happy ending nor an easy answer to difficult questions of guilt and the possibility of forgiveness.

Larry Baker's **The Flamingo Rising** updates the Romeo and Juliet story, moving the action from Verona, Italy, to 1960s Jacksonville, and offering as hero and heroine the teenage children of an uptight funeral director and the ever-dreaming developer of the area's first drive-in theater.

FOUNDING FATHERS

Reading about the men who were instrumental in setting up the governing mechanisms that turned the former British colonies into a cohesive Union (cohesive, at least, for most of our 200-plus years of existence) is a great way to get a sense of both how far we've come and how far we have yet to go. Many of the issues the founders struggled with are still of concern today—among them voting rights, racial equality, and the need for a strong Bill of Rights.

Here are some particularly interesting and insightful biographies of these men, who have achieved iconic status but, as the books show, were as human as the rest of us.

Two excellent books about our first president are James Thomas Flexner's **Washington: The Indispensable Man**, the classic one-volume account of the first president of the United States, adapted from Flexner's five-volume history of Washington; and Joseph J. Ellis's **His Excellency: George Washington**.

Great biographies of Benjamin Franklin include H. W. Brands's sweeping **The First American: The Life and Times of Benjamin Franklin**, which demonstrates not only the range of interests and talents of the elder statesman of the founding generation, but also Brands's talent as a historian and writer; Walter Isaacson's **Benjamin Franklin: An American Life**; and historian Gordon S. Wood's **The Americanization of Benjamin Franklin**. But I would begin any reading about Franklin's life and times with **The Autobiography of Benjamin Franklin**, in which, in wonderfully readable prose (he wrote it as though it were a letter to his son William), Franklin reveals himself to be a man of wide interests and a sly sense of humor.

One of the most interesting and controversial figures among the founding fathers is Alexander Hamilton, unfortunately best known for the manner of his death (in a duel with Aaron Burr on July 11, 1804, in Weehawken, New Jersey). Ron Chernow's **Alexander Hamilton** is a fine biography of this complex man that also probes the world of late-eighteenth-century finance and banking, and the men and families who controlled it. Chernow has an almost uncanny ability to animate his characters and the period in which they lived (you might want to try his **The House of Morgan: An American Banking Dynasty and the Rise of Modern Finance; The Warburgs: The Twentieth-Century Odyssey of a Remarkable Jewish Family;** and **Titan: The Life of John D. Rockefeller, Sr.** as well).

See also the "Presidential Biographies" section in *Book Lust*, which includes some of the best books on Jefferson and John Adams.

THE FOURTH ESTATE

It's unclear whether it was the nineteenth-century political philosopher Edmund Burke or the writer Thomas Carlyle who first came up with the phrase "the fourth estate" to refer to newspaper reporters. Burke believed that journalists had both the power and the responsibility to protect democracy. How well do they do today? Read on.

Although David Halberstam's **The Powers That Be** was published in 1979, it remains necessary reading for anyone interested in how we got to where we are today. Halberstam deals with the development of twentieth-century media from the era of Franklin Roosevelt through the Watergate scandal, taking a close look at the major players in four important media organizations: CBS under William S. Paley; Henry Luce and *Time* magazine; the *Washington Post* under publishers Philip Graham and his wife, Katharine; and the *Los Angeles Times* and the Otis family of publishers. (For more about Halberstam, see "David Halberstam: Too Good to Miss.")

The Kingdom and the Power by Gay Talese should be read in tandem with Halberstam's book, since it's a history of the "Gray Lady," the paper that prints "all the news that's fit to print"—the *New York Times*.

Another good book about the *Times* is **The Trust: The Private and Powerful Family Behind the New York Times** by Susan E. Tifft and Alex S. Jones. It's an armful, but despite its weight it's an extraordinarily readable history and analysis of the people and policies behind "the paper of record."

City Room, Arthur Gelb's memoir of his career at the *Times* from copy boy to managing editor, makes for quite interesting reading, as does Max Frankel's companion work **The Times of My Life and My Life with the Times,** which follows him from his childhood as a refugee fleeing Hitler's Germany to his forty-five years at the *Times,* culminating in his appointment as executive editor.

But enough of the *New York Times.* Try these two wonderful reads about the *Washington Post*: **Personal History** by Katharine Graham, which won the 1998 Pulitzer Prize for biography, and **A Good Life: Newspapering and Other Adventures** by Ben Bradlee, who was executive editor of the paper from 1965 to 1991, a tenure that included, of course, the Pentagon Papers case and the Watergate investigation.

FRACTURED FAIRY TALES

There must be something awfully appealing about taking a well-known work of literature and putting your own stamp on it. Think of Tom Stoppard's appropriating two minor characters from William Shakespeare's **Hamlet** and making them the main characters in his own wonderful play **Rosencrantz** and Guildenstern Are Dead. Or Jean Rhys exploring the childhood of Mrs. Rochester from Charlotte Brontë's Jane Eyre in her own Wide Sargasso Sea. It's a tribute to the original author that he or she could create characters realistic enough to capture the imagination of another writer of a far different time, who then was moved to reconstruct them in an entirely different work.

Gregory Maguire has done this to perfection again and again—in Wicked: The Life and Times of the Wicked Witch of the West (based on Glinda the Good's nemesis in L. Frank Baum's The Wizard of Oz); Mirror, Mirror (the tale of Snow White transferred to sixteenth-century Italy); and Confessions of an Ugly Stepsister (from *Cinderella*).

Robin McKinley is another major contributor to this subgenre. Her books, many based on fairy tales by the Brothers Grimm, are great choices for teenage girls as well as their mothers.

> Beauty: A Retelling of the Story of Beauty and the Beast
>
> The Outlaws of Sherwood (Robin Hood *from Maid Marian's point of view*)
>
> Rose Daughter (*also a re-creation of* Beauty and the Beast*)*
>
> Spindle's End (*based on* Sleeping Beauty*)*

Other good choices for teenage girls are Donna Jo Napoli's reinterpretations of classic tales.

> Crazy Jack (*from* Jack and the Beanstalk*)*
>
> The Magic Circle (*based on* Hansel and Gretel*)*
>
> Spinners (*from* Rumpelstiltskin*)*
>
> Zel (*based on* Rapunzel*)*

FRIEND MAKERS

I know that when I stumble across someone who has not only read but loved one of these books as much as I have, I've probably made a friend for life. And gosh, they're great reading! So trust me—try them:

Cassandra at the Wedding *by Dorothy Baker*

The Home-Maker *by Dorothy Canfield*

The Man in the Window *by Jon Cohen*

Oh, Be Careful *by Lee Colgate*

The Last Good Kiss *by James Crumley*

Fool *by Frederick G. Dillen*

The Golden Youth of Lee Prince *by Aubrey Goodman*

The Eleven Million Mile High Dancer *by Carol De Chellis Hill*

The Cowboy and the Cossack *by Clair Huffaker*

The World in the Evening *by Christopher Isherwood*

Winners and Losers *by Martin Quigley*

Horace Afoot *by Frederick Reuss*

Halfway Down the Stairs *by Charles Thompson*

Brother of the More Famous Jack *by Barbara Trapido*

The Bright Young Things *by Amanda Vail*

A Matter of Time *by Jessamyn West*

GALLIVANTING IN THE GRAVEYARD

A graveyard might seem like a strange place to set a novel, but here are two that succeed splendidly.

A Fine and Private Place by Peter Beagle, a tale of a love that begins only after life ends, is as charming and romantic a fantasy (or is it?) novel as you'll ever read. It definitely proves wrong Andrew Marvell's assertion in "To His Coy Mistress" ("The grave's a fine and private place, / But none, I think do there embrace").

Bill Richardson is probably best known for his humorous novels **Bachelor Brothers' Bed & Breakfast** and **Bachelor Brothers' Bed & Breakfast Pillow Book**, both light-as-air concoctions about a (fictional, unfortunately) British Columbia bed-and-breakfast that would be a perfect vacation destination for any reader. But Richardson has also written the delightful **Waiting for Gertrude: A Graveyard Gothic**, which takes place in Père Lachaise cemetery in Paris, where the souls of the dead, including Alice B. Toklas (who is waiting for her great and good friend Gertrude Stein to join her in death), Edith Piaf, Jim Morrison, Marcel Proust, Maria Callas, and others, are now living in the bodies of felines who make the cemetery their home.

JANE GARDAM: TOO GOOD TO MISS

Gardam is equally talented at writing fiction for adults and for children, as evidenced by her winning Britain's Whitbread Prize twice, first for **The Hollow Land** (a collection of stories for children) and then for **The Queen of the Tambourine** (a hilarious and ultimately sad epistolary novel that explores a woman's delusions—or are they delusions? Just how reliable is this letter writer, anyway?). Her other novels for adults include **Faith Fox**, a comedy of manners about an unlikely cohort of people whose only connection to one another is a baby whose mother dies in childbirth, and **Crusoe's Daughter**, about another orphan, this one raised by two dotty aunts in a secluded house on a salt marsh in the north of England, who all of her life is obsessed with another castaway—Robinson Crusoe.

The experience of reading Gardam is often like eating a deliciously tart apple, and "The Tribute," which appears in what is probably her best collection of stories, **The Sidmouth Letters**, displays this and other aspects of her talent to perfection: she views her characters with wry compassion and conveys their complex nature in just a few perfect sentences. (Her **Black Faces, White Faces** won both the Winifred Holtby and David Higham prizes for fiction, though, so clearly somebody out there doesn't share my opinion that **The Sidmouth Letters** is her best collection.)

Because they are both coming-of-age novels, my favorite Gardam books are frequently mis-shelved and mis-cataloged as children's books. They're perfectly acceptable teen reading, but they're also wonderful for adults who want to look back, from a safe distance, at the ups and downs of adolescence. My absolute favorite is **Bilgewater**, but a close second is **A Long Way from Verona**.

GENDER BENDING

Needless to say, one's sexual orientation doesn't depend on (or even necessarily reflect) one's gender. These books (two novels and two memoirs) are required reading for anyone interested in the mysteries of love, gender, and self-identity.

In **Middlesex**, the Pulitzer Prize–winning multigenerational novel by Jeffrey Eugenides, the main character, Cal Stephanides, is a hermaphrodite whose attempts to come to an acceptance of the condition she/he was born with, and her/his final decision, are at the heart of this compelling novel.

Rose Tremain's **Sacred Country** tells the coming-of-age story of Mary Ward, whose journey to adulthood is made infinitely more complicated by the fact that, ever since she was six years old, she has known that she was supposed to be a boy.

I read **She's Not There: A Life in Two Genders** in one sitting, unable to pull myself away from this moving and funny memoir. Jennifer Finney Boylan (whose previous works include two novels, **The Planets** and **The Constellations**, and a collection of stories, all written as James Finney Boylan) relates the long life's journey that took her from male to female when she was in her early forties. Jenny knew from childhood that she was trapped in the wrong body, but, determined to overcome her desire to be a woman, she married, had two sons, and became a successful college professor and fiction writer. Her struggle to make peace with herself at long last is told with a light touch, which adds both poignancy and power to the memoir. An afterword by Boylan's best friend, fiction writer Richard Russo, provides a touching coda to the story.

Jan Morris's haunting 1974 memoir, **Conundrum**, is a necessary companion read to Boylan's book—because of the authors' many shared attitudes as well as their many differences. Writing almost three decades before Boylan's memoir, James Morris describes his determination to succeed as a boy rather than give in to his certain knowledge—almost from his first moments of conscious thought—that he was really a girl, mistakenly placed in the wrong body. (Pronouns are a difficulty in describing books like this.) James grew up to be a tireless traveler and adventurer (he climbed Mount Everest) and a writer of wide interests who penned several books before having the surgery necessary to make him at last, at age forty-six, a woman.

GIRL GUIDES, OR IT'S A DARK AND STORMY NIGHT, GOOD THING YOU HAVE A FLASHLIGHT

In the early 1950s Mary Stewart wrote wonderful novels filled with romance, mystery, honor, and courage. Her heroines were strong (but often didn't know it), smart (except when it came to themselves), and brave (which they discovered only when they were tested by life's vicissitudes). Stewart would later go on to explore the virtues of honor, courage, faith, and love in her novels about King Arthur, but she honed her skill by writing about women.

For all readers who delight in women of courage and valor, and love to read about women coming into their own, but don't care for the contemporary chick-lit novels, Mary Stewart is for you. Among my favorites (see page 205 in *Book Lust* for more) are **Nine Coaches Waiting**, **Wildfire at Midnight**, and **Madam, Will You Talk?** Thankfully, once you've read every Stewart novel two or three times, there are some other writers you can read who are nearly as good. Rest assured that most of these women were prolific writers, so you're probably set for a long time.

Mary Elgin's **A Man from the Mist**

Jane Aiken Hodge's **Maulever Hall**

Victoria Holt's **Mistress of Mellyn**

Barbara Michaels's **Shattered Silk**

Phyllis A. Whitney's **Window on the Square**

GONE FISHIN'

A friend once said of her own fishing experiences, "Often the catching has been slim, but the fishing has always been memorable!" I would add, "And so are the books about the sport." In fact, the best reason to take up fishing (in my view) is that you will have a perfect excuse to read all the great fishing literature, beginning with Izaak Walton's little masterpiece of pastoral life and the joys of fishing, **The Compleat Angler, or, The Contemplative Man's Recreation**. And even if you don't like fishing—baiting the hook, releasing the fish, or eating the catch—there's still a good chance you'll enjoy these books by people who love the whole process.

Norman Maclean begins **A River Runs Through It, and Other Stories** with the unforgettable sentence "In our family, there was no clear line between religion and fly fishing," and goes on to describe how the joy of fishing sometimes becomes the means by which everything that can't be said overtly is communicated from one family member to another.

A Different Angle: Fly Fishing Stories by Women, edited by Holly Morris, is filled with essays and stories by contributors including E. Annie Proulx, Lorian Hemingway, Pam Houston, and fly-fishing champion Joan Salvato Wulff. Morris also edited another collection of essays, fiction, and poetry about the satisfaction of fishing for women, **Uncommon Waters: Women Write about Fishing**.

Fishing's Best Short Stories, edited by Paul D. Staudohar, offers a rich collection ranging from classic tales by the Brothers Grimm and Guy de Maupassant to the more modern fireside yarns of contemporary fishing writers such as Thomas McGuane and Stephen King.

It's hard to choose the best book by the incomparable John Gierach, so you may as well just read and enjoy them all, but start with **Death, Taxes, and Leaky Waders: A John Gierach Fly-Fishing Treasury,** the best of his best essays from earlier collections. Once hooked, you'll want to read these as well: **At the Grave of the Unknown Fisherman; Another Lousy Day in Paradise;** and **Sex, Death, and Fly-Fishing.**

If you get a serious case of the fishin' bug, you'll probably want to own two copies of Dave Hughes's Trout Flies: The Tier's Reference— one to keep in your home library and one to use while you're tying flies. Beautiful color photographs show the artistry involved in making flies that will fool the trout into thinking they're real.

Robert Hughes is best known as an art critic. Who knew he was a fisherman as well? Not me, until I ran across his lovely collection of essays on the sport, **A Jerk on One End: Reflections of a Mediocre Fisherman.**

A beginner's growing love of the art and craft of fly-fishing, primarily in Northwest rivers, is joyfully described by Jessica Maxwell, former columnist for *Audubon* magazine, in **I Don't Know Why I Swallowed the Fly: My Fly-Fishing Rookie Season.**

Thomas McGuane, an author who is best known for his exquisitely tough and gritty fiction (try **Ninety-Two in the Shade** and **The Sporting Club**), won the coveted Roderick Haig-Brown Award for Literature from the Federation of Fly Fishers for **The Longest Silence: A Life in Fishing,** a collection of beautifully written essays on everything from practicing casting to the pleasures of releasing that just-caught fish.

David James Duncan's first novel, **The River Why,** describes the coming-of-age of Gus Orviston, in which his search for the elusive steelhead on Oregon's rivers mirrors his search for self-knowledge.

There's also a wonderfully funny section in Rose Macaulay's **The Towers of Trebizond** (which has nothing, really, to do with fishing otherwise) about Anglicans angling. Don't miss it.

GOOD THINGS COME IN SMALL PACKAGES

I'm a relatively late convert to the short story; for many years I would always choose a novel over any collection of stories because I much preferred the wider canvas on which the author could work. But in the last decade or so, I've grown to appreciate short-story collections. Here are some I've really liked, along with the particular story or stories in them that I most enjoyed.

Alice Adams's The Stories of Alice Adams: *"Verlie I Say Unto You" and "Roses, Rhododendron"*

Sherman Alexie's Ten Little Indians: *"What You Pawn I Will Redeem" and "The Life and Times of Estelle Walks Above"*

Andrea Barrett's Servants of the Map: Stories: *the title story (actually a novella) and "The Cure"*

Richard Bausch's The Stories of Richard Bausch: *"Aren't You Happy for Me" and "Someone to Watch over Me"*

David Bezmozgis's Natasha and Other Stories: *the title story and "Tapka"*

Stuart Dybek's The Coast of Chicago: *"Blight" and "Hot Ice"*

Joseph Epstein's Fabulous Small Jews: *"Artie Glick in a Family Way" and "The Executor" (the unusual title comes from a*

poem by Karl Shapiro called "Hospital":
"This is the Oxford of all sicknesses. /
Kings have lain here and fabulous small
Jews / And actresses whose legs were always
news.")

Nell Freudenberger's Lucky Girls: Stories:
"The Orphan" and "Outside the Eastern
Gate"

Laura Furman's Drinking with the Cook:
the title story and "Hagalund"

Adrianne Harun's The King of Limbo
and Other Stories: "Lukudi" and "The
Eighth Sleeper of Ephesus"

Jhumpa Lahiri's Interpreter of Maladies:
the title story and "A Temporary Matter"

Lorrie Moore's Birds of America: "People
Like That Are the Only People Here:
Canonical Babbling in Peed Onk" and
"Four Calling Birds, Three French Hens"

John Murray's A Few Short Notes on
Tropical Butterflies: Stories: "Watson and
the Shark" and the title story

Antonya Nelson's In the Land of Men: the
title story and "Goodbye, Midwest"

Ann Packer's Mendocino and Other
Stories: the title story and "Babies"

Tom Paine's Scar Vegas and Other
Stories: "General Markman's Last Stand"
and "The Spoon Children"

J. D. Salinger's Nine Stories: all of them
are classics, but perhaps the two best are
"A Perfect Day for Bananafish" and "For
Esmé—with Love and Squalor"

Daniel Stolar's The Middle of the Night:
"Marriage Lessons" and "Jack Landers Is
My Friend"

Hannah Tinti's Animal Crackers: "How to
Revitalize the Snake in Your Life"

David Foster Wallace's Oblivion: Stories:
*"The Suffering Channel" and "Mr.
Squishy"*

Mark Winegardner's That's True of
Everybody: *"Thirty-Year-Old Women Do
Not Always Come Home"*

GRAPHICA

At first glance, graphic novels and memoirs might appear
to be simply a collection of comic strips. Once you start
reading the text, though, you discover that they offer a
great deal more.

Daniel Quinn's **The Man Who Grew Young** (illustrated by Tim
Eldred) is set in a universe where time runs backward and everyone lives their lives in reverse. People don't die at the end of this
backward life, but instead finally disappear into the bodies of their
mothers. The only problem is, Adam Taylor doesn't seem to have
had a mother.

Joe Sacco's **The Fixer: A Story from Sarajevo** takes us to Sarajevo,
where the past is never far from the present, and introduces us to
an American war correspondent who leans heavily on a "fixer"—a
person who helps Western journalists develop their heart-wrenching
stories for public consumption. You might also want to look at his
Palestine, winner of an American Book Award in 1996 (presented
by the Before Columbus Foundation), a dark and unfortunately still
relevant picture of Israeli–Palestinian relations in the early 1990s, and
Safe Area Gorazde: The War in Eastern Bosnia 1992–1995, an account
of a prolonged attack by Serbian soldiers on a small Bosnian town
during the war in the Balkans in the 1990s.

Lewis Trondheim's funny and heartbreaking **Mister O** is a word-
less novel in pictures about the adventures of a little man trying to
find his way across a chasm.

Marjane Satrapi's outstanding **Persepolis: The Story of a Childhood** relates the author's experiences growing up as the daughter of Marxists in Iran, both before and after the revolution that toppled the shah and brought religious extremists into power. The sequel, **Persepolis 2: The Story of a Return**, describes the author's late adolescence at school in Austria and later when she returns home to Iran.

Craig Thompson's debut work was **Good-bye, Chunky Rice**, a touching parable about love and loss; the two main characters were Chunky Rice, a turtle, and his closest friend, a mouse named Dandel. Thompson's next book, **Blankets**, revisits some of the same themes, as he remembers his own childhood and describes what it was like to grow up in rural Wisconsin in a family of rigid fundamentalists.

Art Spiegelman's **In the Shadow of No Towers** is a visually arresting, angry, and moving account of his (and his family's, and the country's) experiences on the day of the attacks on the World Trade Center and in the days, weeks, months, and years that followed. (Perhaps the most striking image in the book is Spiegelman's portrayal of the glowing "bones" of the twin towers as they burned.) A "Comics Supplement" at the end of the book presents a brief history of the funnies that began appearing in the Sunday supplements of newspapers in the early years of the twentieth century, as well as some reproductions of vintage comics from those long-ago, more innocent days.

THE GREAT PLAINS

According to the Center for Great Plains Studies, the area stretches from Edmonton, in the Canadian province of Alberta, all the way down to Fort Worth, Texas. These primarily barren and windswept lands form the backdrop for a number of good novels. The cities seem not to have inspired novelists (yet), but the wilds . . . well, read for yourself.

The Dakotas

Susan Power's **The Grass Dancer** takes place on a Sioux Indian reservation in North Dakota, and reading it is like participating in an archeological dig, in that each successive chapter takes you further back into the past.

Most of Louise Erdrich's stories of American Indian life take place in North Dakota, including her three best: **Love Medicine, The Beet Queen**, and **Tracks**, all of which are character-driven novels about love, friendship, and complicated family relationships.

Larry Woiwode set two of his most engrossing novels—**Beyond the Bedroom Wall** and **Born Brothers**—in his native North Dakota. Each explores the intricate nature of family relationships.

From the Black Hills by Judy Troy is the coming-of-age tale of eighteen-year-old Mike Newlin, who finds his life in turmoil when his father commits murder and disappears from their small South Dakota town.

In **Leaving the Land**, set just after World War II, Douglas Unger explores what happens when the children of longtime farm families, who want nothing more than to be forever finished with farming, begin to make their way in the larger world.

Mystery novelist Harold Adams set his long-running (more than a dozen novels) Carl Wilcox series in small-town, Depression-era South Dakota. Wilcox, an ex-cop, a sign painter, and an amateur detective, frequently stumbles onto interesting conundrums that he can't resist trying to solve. Try **The Man Who Was Taller Than God** (which won the 1993 Shamus Award) or **Hatchet Job**.

Deadwood by Pete Dexter is a portrait of the last years of Wild Bill Hickok's life—the late 1870s—as seen through the eyes of his partner in crime, Charles Utter. This book is as well written as Dexter's other novels, but much funnier.

Kent Meyers's **The Work of Wolves** is the story of three misfits who find that their culture and destiny are often intertwined, sometimes in sorrow-filled ways.

But I have to confess that my all-time favorite books set in the Great Plains states (in and near the town of De Smet, South Dakota) are the last four of the original Laura Ingalls Wilder series of books about her life: **By the Shores of Silver Lake, The Long Winter, Little Town on the Prairie,** and **These Happy Golden Years.** Wilder's daughter, Rose Wilder Lane, also set some of her novels in the Dakotas, including **Let the Hurricane Roar** and **Young Pioneers.**

Nebraska

Willa Cather's remarkable **My Ántonia** is perhaps the classic Nebraska novel. In it Jim Burden looks back on the life of his childhood friend, the high-spirited Ántonia Shimerda, who lived with her immigrant parents on a hardscrabble farm on the plains in the late nineteenth century.

To me, the classic Nebraska short story is Carl Sandburg's wonderful tale "The Huckabuck Family and How They Raised Popcorn in Nebraska and Quit and Came Back," which first appeared in his **Rootabaga Stories.** Its major characters are Jonas Jonas Huckabuck, his wife Mama Mama Huckabuck, and their pony-faced daughter, the star of the story, Pony Pony Huckabuck. This is a great read-aloud for families, but don't forget to have the popcorn popped before you begin, because you'll be laughing too hard by the end to do much of anything.

Over the course of her long life, Bess Streeter Aldrich wrote what seems like a gazillion books, but it was her 1928 novel, **A Lantern in Her Hand,** that cemented her reputation as a chronicler of the pioneer experience. It relates the experiences of Abbie Deal as she accompanies her husband, Will, from Iowa to a homestead in Nebraska in the 1880s, and was followed by a sequel, **A White Bird Flying. A Lantern in Her Hand** is still on many high school reading lists, and it's a good choice for those of us (no matter our age) who loved the Laura Ingalls Wilder series.

Juvenile delinquent Randall Hunsucker ends up in a small town, where he tries—often unsuccessfully—to put his young life back together in Tom McNeal's **Goodnight, Nebraska.**

Plains Song, for Female Voices was Wright Morris's final novel in a writing career that spanned more than fifty years. It won the American Book Award in 1981, and was chosen that same year as an American Library Association Notable Book. The story is told mainly through the experiences of three women—matriarch Cora Atkins, her daughter, Madge, and her niece, Sharon. We read about their relationship to one another, to the men in their lives, and to their family farm on the Nebraska plains.

Jim Harrison's **Dalva** contains at least two unforgettable characters. There is, of course, the eponymous main character, who in her middle age begins a search for her son, whom she gave away at birth almost three decades before; but there's also a terrific portrayal—through his journals—of the life of her great-grandfather, who came to Nebraska as a missionary.

GROUP PORTRAITS

It's hard enough to write a biography of one person, so consider the complications (not to mention the huge amount of work) that goes into writing a biography of two or more famous people. To succeed, you obviously need a theme, or a thread that binds the subjects together, so that the book doesn't feel like separate chapters hitched uneasily together. I think the following writers overcame these problems and produced books that offer fascinating insights into their subjects.

Paul Elie's **The Life You Save May Be Your Own: An American Pilgrimage** looks at the lives of Thomas Merton, Dorothy Day, Flannery O'Connor, and Walker Percy through the prism of their Catholicism (they were known among their wide circle of interconnected friends as "The School of the Holy Ghost"). Elie manages to tell each of their stories fully, while at the same time showing the influences of one upon the other, as they individually and together struggled to understand what their religious convictions meant to them.

A work of great readability and historical importance, **First Great Triumph: How Five Americans Made Their Country a World Power** by Warren Zimmerman profiles five fascinating men (all close friends) whose vision and policies set the United States on an expansionist and imperialist course in the years between 1898 and 1903, during which time Cuba, Puerto Rico, the Philippines, Hawaii, and Guam came under our sway. The men who set this in motion and saw it through *con brio* included Theodore Roosevelt; Alfred T. Mahan, the great naval strategist; Republican senator Henry Cabot Lodge; Roosevelt's secretary of state, John Hay; and corporate lawyer Elihu Root, who ended up administering the whole imperial strategy.

When we think of wild women of the 1920s, Zelda Fitzgerald, Edna St. Vincent Millay, and Dorothy Parker immediately come to mind, women whose audacious and frequently outrageous behavior caught the imagination of their own generation as well as every one since. Marion Meade's **Bobbed Hair and Bathtub Gin: Writers Running Wild in the Twenties** takes a look at the lives of these three, along with that of Edna Ferber. These women were not only muses, lovers, and wives to the men in their lives, but all (save Zelda) made a living writing novels, plays, poems, and short stories. Yet their lives (except perhaps Ferber's) were anything but happy, and Meade perfectly catches their frantic and by and large futile attempts to stop drinking and carousing. Zelda was the saddest (Meade shows just how much Scott appropriated her life and writing in his hugely popular books); Dorothy was the wittiest ("Brevity is the soul of lingerie" is one of her *bon mots*); Edna St. Vincent Millay was the greatest sexual adventurer; and Edna Ferber was the most successful of this quartet of hard-living, hard-loving women. Two things struck me as I read: the amount of alcohol they consumed and just how brilliant Dorothy Parker was. Who else could have come up with a sentence, impromptu, using the word "horticulture"? ("You can lead a horticulture, but you can't make her think.")

David Laskin's **Partisans: Marriage, Politics, and Betrayal Among the New York Intellectuals** explores the connections and differences among writers who were associated with *Partisan Review* magazine in the 1940s and '50s, including Hannah Arendt, Philip Rahv, Mary McCarthy, and Delmore Schwartz.

GUILT-INDUCING BOOKS

Some books make you feel guilty—about what you (or our society) have done in the past, what we're doing right now, what we probably ought not do in the future, and how much more we should be doing with our lives. Read these books when you're ready to believe that not only can you change and improve, but society can (and should) as well.

> *Jason DeParle's* American Dream
>
> *Barbara Ehrenreich's* Nickel and Dimed: On (Not) Getting By in America

Jennifer Gonnerman's Life on the Outside: The Prison Odyssey of Elaine Bartlett

William Greider's The Soul of Capitalism: Opening Paths to a Moral Economy

Tracy Kidder's Mountains Beyond Mountains: The Quest of Dr. Paul Farmer, A Man Who Would Cure the World

Alex Kotlowitz's There Are No Children Here: The Story of Two Boys Growing Up in the Other America

William Lederer and Eugene Burdick's The Ugly American *(the only novel on this list)*

Susan Linn's Consuming Kids: The Hostile Takeover of Childhood *(in the spirit of full disclosure, this is written by my sister)*

Bill McKibben's The End of Nature *and* Enough: Staying Human in an Engineered Age

Eric Schlosser's Fast Food Nation: The Dark Side of the All-American Meal

Susan Sheehan's Is There No Place on Earth for Me?

David K. Shipler's The Working Poor: Invisible in America

Morgan Spurlock's Don't Eat This Book: Fast Food and the Supersizing of America

DAVID HALBERSTAM:
TOO GOOD TO MISS

I've never read a dull book by David Halberstam—he's certainly one of our best nonfiction storytellers. Even subjects that I'm not interested in make fascinating reading in Halberstam's capable hands. He's prolific, with large books seeming to alternate with shorter ones every few years, so you never have to wait too long for another "Halberstam" to arrive at a bookstore or library near you.

At the beginning of his career, Halberstam wrote two novels—**The Noblest Roman** (his first book) and **One Very Hot Day**—but then shifted exclusively to nonfiction. For much of the 1960s he was a foreign correspondent for the *New York Times,* and his experiences as a reporter in Vietnam led to two of his earliest books, **The Making of a Quagmire: America and Vietnam During the Kennedy Era** and **The Best and the Brightest** (for more about these two, see page 238 in *Book Lust*).

Following are some of his other books; I've put an asterisk by the ones that I particularly enjoyed.

> The Amateurs: The Story of Four Young Men and Their Quest for an Olympic Gold Medal
>
> * The Breaks of the Game
>
> * The Children
>
> * The Fifties
>
> Firehouse
>
> Ho
>
> The Next Century
>
> October 1964

Playing for Keeps: Michael Jordan and the World He Made

* The Powers That Be

The Reckoning

* Summer of '49

* The Teammates: A Portrait of a Friendship

The Unfinished Odyssey of Robert Kennedy

* War in a Time of Peace: Bush, Clinton, and the Generals

RUSSELL HOBAN:
TOO GOOD TO MISS

What other author do you know who has written a series of successful picture books, collections of poems for children, books for middle school boys and girls, and several (very different from one another) novels for adult readers? Only Russell Hoban. And you shouldn't miss reading him.

He's probably best known for his picture books about a very young badger named Frances, including **Bedtime for Frances, Bread and Jam for Frances**, and **A Baby Sister for Frances**. With perfect illustrations by Garth Williams (the one showing Frances's father in bed, opening one eye to look at Frances when she comes into the bedroom to tell her parents she can't sleep, still makes me smile when I think about it), the series shows Frances in many situations that will be familiar to parents of young children: Frances refusing to go to sleep, Frances refusing to eat anything but bread and jam, Frances facing the arrival of a younger sister. All the stories are told in language that will satisfy both the adult reader and the child who is listening.

Then there are his books for adults. **Turtle Diary** is a tender (but not soppy or sappy) love story about two lonely people who come together in an effort to free the turtles at the London Zoo (it was also made into a not-half-bad film).

Riddley Walker, set after a nuclear war has destroyed the world, is one of the best of the postapocalyptic genre of novels. I don't know of another novel that could arguably be called science fiction which was a finalist for the National Book Critics Circle Award as well as the Nebula Award (for best science fiction novel). If you have trouble deciphering the language of the novel (which Hoban invented), do as my mother did and read it aloud—you'll then find it reasonably easy (mostly) to figure out.

Her Name Was Lola is a wonderfully quirky novel about a writer (who bears more than a passing resemblance to Hoban) in the midst of a midlife crisis, who can't quite make up his mind between the woman he loves (Lola) and the other woman he sort of loves too (Lula Mae). An invisible dwarf named Apasmara ("forgetfulness" in Hindu mythology) advises him on his dilemma.

A HOLIDAY SHOPPING LIST

Friends and family (no matter what their age) know that when they get a gift from me, it's sure to be a book. Here's my recent holiday shopping list.

For Uncle Sol, who loves books with maps in them: Katharine Harmon's **You Are Here: Personal Geographies and Other Maps of the Imagination**

For Stephen, who reads The New Yorker *and loves cartoons:* **The Party, After You Left** by New Yorker *cartoonist Roz Chast*

For Donnie, who yearns for the simple life: **Better Off: Pulling the Switch on Technology** *by Eric Brende*

For Arnie, who loves to visit New York City:
Ross Wetzsteon's Republic of Dreams: Greenwich Village: The American Bohemia, 1910–1960, *and Russell Shorto's* The Island at the Center of the World: The Epic Story of Dutch Manhattan, the Forgotten Colony That Shaped America

For Louis, who is interested in both Buddhism and physics: Arthur Zajonc's The New Physics and Cosmology: Dialogues with the Dalai Lama

For Jen and Jan, who both love chick-lit novels: The Big Love *by Sarah Dunn and* The Other Side of the Story *by Marian Keyes*

For Marilyn, who loves to cook: Ian Kelly's Cooking for Kings: The Life of Antonin Carême, the First Celebrity Chef

For Tomese, who loves literary fiction: Philip Roth's The Plot Against America

For Clare, who's looking for her spiritual path: Sue Bender's Plain and Simple: A Woman's Journey to the Amish

For Neal, who loves funny British novels: Snobs *by Julian Fellowes*

For Sarah, age three: Tell Me a Mitzi *by Lore Segal*

For Maria, who loves poetry: Mary Oliver's A Poetry Handbook *and* New and Selected Poems

For cousin Brian, who loves historical novels: The Travels of Jaimie McPheeters *by Robert Lewis Taylor*

For Anand, who loves wine: The Accidental Connoisseur: An Irreverent Journey Through the Wine World *by Lawrence Osborne*

For Millie, who loves quirky novels: The Spirit Cabinet *by Paul Quarrington*

For Peter, who wants to laugh more: Dress Your Family in Corduroy and Denim *by David Sedaris*

For Craig, who loves baseball novels: Waiting for Teddy Williams *by Howard Frank Mosher and* The Celebrant *by Eric Rolfe Greenberg*

For Emily, age one: Roll Over!: A Counting Song *by Merle Peek*

For Andra, who loves tennis: Bruce Schoenfeld's The Match: Althea Gibson & Angela Buxton: How Two Outsiders— One Black, the Other Jewish—Forged a Friendship and Made Sports History

For Bill, who loves films: Spike, Mike, Slackers & Dykes: A Guided Tour Across a Decade of American Independent Cinema *by John Pierson*

For Andy, the architect: The Feud That Sparked the Renaissance: How Brunelleschi and Ghiberti Changed the Art World *by Robert Paul Walker*

For Joe, who likes to read about the stories behind the headlines: Endless Enemies: The Making of an Unfriendly World *by Jonathan Kwitny*

For Susan, who loves books about dysfunctional families: A Hole in the World: An American Boyhood *by Richard Rhodes*

For Charley and Beth, the birders: Brushed by Feathers: A Year of Birdwatching in the West *by Frances Wood*

For Beth, the textile designer: Victoria Finlay's Color: A Natural History of the Palette

For Alice, who is interested in exploring her Jewish roots: Eva Hoffman's Shtetl: The

Life and Death of a Small Town and the
World of the Polish Jews

*For David, who eats, sleeps, and dreams
golf: George Plimpton's* The Bogey Man:
A Month on the PGA Tour *and* The
Greatest Game Ever Played: Harry
Vardon, Frances Ouimet, and the Birth
of Modern Golf *by Mark Frost*

*For Jon, who wants to know everything
about everything:* The Experts' Guide to
100 Things Everyone Should Know
How to Do, *created by Samantha Ettus,
with sections on "How to Wash Your Hands,"
"How to Shovel Snow" (by the mayor of
Buffalo, New York), "How to Relax," "How
to Give and Receive a Compliment," and
ninety-six more gems of advice*

For cousin Lynda, the psychologist: Secrets,
Lies, Betrayals: The Body/Mind
Connection *by Maggie Scarf*

HONG KONG HOLIDAYS

I think that the main reason I've always loved reading about Hong
Kong is because years ago I was lucky enough to stumble across
the Yellowthread Street mysteries of William Marshall (who was
described on the cover as "living in a modest castle in Ireland," which
thoroughly delighted me). The first books in this series were published in the 1970s, and though Hong Kong has changed significantly
since then, especially since the 1997 transfer from British to Chinese
hands, some essential elements remain the same. Hong Kong's poly-
glot society comes across vividly in these often very funny police
procedurals starring Detective Chief Inspector Harry Feiffer and
his colleagues Spencer, Auden, and O'Yee. They're sometimes hard
to find, but worth looking for (especially if you enjoyed the television show *Barney Miller*) at libraries, in used bookstores, or over

the Internet. Start with the first, **Yellowthread Street**, but don't miss **Skulduggery** or **War Machine**.

One of the best novels to read if you want a strong sense of the history (from 1935 on) of contemporary Hong Kong is John Lanchester's **Fragrant Harbor**. (The title is the literal translation of the Chinese name of the former British crown colony.) This story is indeed worthy of the adjective "sweeping." It's a good choice for anyone who enjoyed Colleen McCullough's **The Thorn Birds** or other sagas of that ilk.

The Language of Threads, Gail Tsukiyama's sequel to her much-loved **Women of the Silk**, follows one of her earlier characters as she travels to Hong Kong and gets caught up in the terrible experience of the Japanese occupation during World War II.

It's easy to find good guidebooks to Hong Kong, as well as lots of history books, but it's harder to find compulsively readable armchair travel books about the country. Here are two, and it's no surprise that one is by that consummate traveler Jan Morris. Called simply **Hong Kong**, it's filled with facts as well as evocative writing. The other is **Travelers' Tales Guides: Hong Kong: True Stories of Life on the Road**, edited by James O'Reilly et al., part of a reliable series of well-written books about many different countries. In its more than fifty personal essays, written by authors as diverse as Paul Theroux, Simon Winchester, and Pico Iyer as well as lesser-known writers, you get a great introduction to everything Hong Kong—from food to language to sights and scenes of a search for the perfect pig.

HORROR FOR SISSIES

The trick to reading in the horror genre for those (like me) who tend to be squeamish is to stay safely within the boundaries of the spooky and not venture into the truly scary. Thus, creature books are usually safe bets, as most readers can convince themselves that either (a) they would never be in a position to be attacked by such a creature or (b) the creature could not really exist. Safely reassured that mayhem could not be wreaked on their world, readers can then gleefully read about others' doom. Both the Romantics and the Victorians were great at spooky writing, and the conventions of their day kept the gore at bay, so among them you'll find some fine choices.

Mary Wollstonecraft Shelley's **Frankenstein** is more an exploration of humanity than a story of a monster. The real question the novel asks is, who is the monster? And the answer is more upsetting than scary.

The short story "The Cask of Amontillado" by Edgar Allan Poe is psychological horror at its best, as Poe tells the story of a man who takes revenge in the most chilling of ways.

The Picture of Dorian Gray by Oscar Wilde is a true Victorian nightmare, in which Dorian sells his soul to keep his youth and hide his evil ways.

John Harwood's **The Ghost Writer** is the (just bearably) scary tale of a man obsessed with a century-old ghost story written by his great-grandmother, and with an email correspondent who refuses to let him meet her in person.

In a twist on just who or what defines horror, Robert Neville finds himself in a world overrun by vampires, where he must fight during the day and hide at night in order to survive, in **I Am Legend** by Richard Matheson, a contemporary classic.

Relic by Douglas Preston and Lincoln Child is the ultimate creature horror novel, set in the spooky halls of the American Museum of Natural History in New York.

I AM WOMAN—HEAR ME ROAR

Many people find this particular phrase—from a 1973 Grammy Award–winning song by Helen Reddy—rather corny, but you'll find that the books described in this section are anything but. The voice of women's liberation in the 1970s was distinct, loud, and clear. Such modern pioneers of the women's movement as Simone de Beauvoir (**The Second Sex**, published in 1952), Betty Friedan (**The Feminine Mystique,** which came out in 1963), and the authors of the now-classic **Our Bodies, Ourselves** (a seminal work that in 1969 urged women to take control of their own bodies) had a revolutionary impact on our society.

The political became personal with the release of a number of feminist novels by young women in the late 1960s and early 1970s, including **Diary of a Mad Housewife** by Sue Kaufman, the comic story of an unhappy woman married to an overbearing and priggish husband; Sheila Ballantyne's tale of a suburban carpooling mother of three who lives simultaneously in both real and imaginary worlds, **Norma Jean the Termite Queen; Up the Sandbox!**, Anne Roiphe's tale of Margaret Reynolds, another conflicted housewife balancing fantasy and reality; the sardonic **Memoirs of an Ex-Prom Queen** by Alix Kates Shulman, which tells the story of Sasha Davis, the ex–prom queen who questions her all-American-girl background; and Erica Jong's revolutionary **Fear of Flying**, which broke many barriers with its account of uninhibited heroine Isadora Wing's desire for freedom.

Other groundbreaking novels were Fay Weldon's **Female Friends;** Margaret Atwood's **Lady Oracle** (my favorite Atwood novel, about a woman trying to leave her old life behind); Marge Piercy's **Woman on the Edge of Time;** Lois Gould's **Such Good Friends** (in which a woman re-evaluates her life after her husband falls into a coma and she discovers that he's been chronically unfaithful to her); and the feminist science-fiction novel **The Kin of Ata Are Waiting for You** by Dorothy Bryant. Although I already wrote, in *Book Lust*, about Marilyn French's **The Women's Room** (which a friend of mine took to the hospital with her in 1978 when she was about to give birth to her first child), it too fits well in this section.

Other influential political books from the early 1970s were Germaine Greer's **The Female Eunuch**, Shulamith Firestone's **The Dialectic of Sex: The Case for Feminist Revolution**, and Kate Millett's **Sexual Politics**.

Even thoughts about motherhood underwent a sea change during this period. Both Adrienne Rich's **Of Woman Born: Motherhood as Experience and Institution** and Jane Lazarre's **The Mother Knot** were published in 1976.

Clearly, a lot of women were thinking a lot about their place in society and what it meant to be female. And even though it has been more than thirty years since many of these books were published, they remain as fresh and insightful as when they first came out.

IDAHO: AND NARY A POTATO TO BE SEEN

Pete Fromm is probably best known for his novels (**How All This Started** and **As Cool as I Am**—neither set in Idaho), but the intensity and honesty of **Indian Creek Chronicles: A Winter Alone in the Wilderness** are striking, as he describes the winter he spent working in the Selway-Bitterroot Wilderness, checking up on the state of salmon eggs for the Idaho Department of Fish and Game in 1990 after he had dropped out of college.

Native Idahoan Vardis Fisher wrote a series of sprawling auto-biographical novels (often compared to Thomas Wolfe's equally expansive **You Can't Go Home Again**) set during the early twentieth century in the mountains of Idaho; the series begins with **In Tragic Life** and continues with **Passions Spin the Plot, We Are Betrayed,** and **No Villain Need Be.**

Melanie Rae Thon's **Iona Moon** is the story of a young woman's attempt to escape from the poverty and sadness of White Falls, the small town where she's been stuck her whole life.

Thomas Savage usually set his novels in Montana, but **The Sheep Queen** (originally published with the much more evocative title **I Heard My Sister Speak My Name**) is about Emma Russell Sweringen, the matriarch of an Idaho sheep-ranching family, her daughter, and her grandchildren.

Tom Spanbauer's **The Man Who Fell in Love with the Moon** takes place in the late 1880s in Excellent, Idaho, where Shed, a bisexual half-Indian, leaves the Indian Head Hotel (populated by whores and their customers), where he grew up, in search of his true identity.

Two brothers who come to Snake Junction, Idaho, from their native Oklahoma find their bond challenged when one of them falls in love with an older woman, in **Finding Caruso** by Kim Barnes. Barnes also wrote **In the Wilderness: Coming of Age in Unknown Country,** a moving memoir of growing up in a fundamentalist Christian family in the Idaho logging camps. Here's one of my favorite quotations from the memoir, illustrating Barnes's difficult upbringing: "[My mother] professed to be the only one among her friends who knew how to raise children because she alone told children the truth. 'I have always loathed your father, Kim, and have no idea why I'm alive.' Later on, she explained, these truths would be the handles by which I would grasp reality.'"

I love the cover of **King of the Mild Frontier: An Ill-Advised Autobiography** by Chris Crutcher, which pictures the author as a buck- and gap-toothed kid grinning goofily at the camera. Crutcher tells the humorous and heartbreaking story of his formative years in Cascade, Idaho, with an overly demanding father and an alcoholic mother, and with the added burdens of a terrible temper and no athletic ability.

THE IMMIGRANT EXPERIENCE

Books about the immigrant experience have always been popular, whether they're written in the form of novels or memoirs, whether they're set in the United States or elsewhere. Here are some that I've especially enjoyed, ranging from tales of Scandinavian immigrants arriving on the Great Plains to illegal aliens trying to find safe harbor from their war-torn countries.

One of the earliest novels written about the immigrant experience is O. E. Rolvaag's 1927 classic **Giants in the Earth: A Saga of the Prairie.** The Norwegian-born Rolvaag, who became a professor of his native language at St. Olaf College in Northfield, Minnesota, himself emigrated to the United States in 1896. His novel follows the lives of a small group of Norwegians as they try, with varying degrees of success, to adjust both physically and psychologically to their new home in South Dakota.

I don't know that I've read any other novel about Maltese immigrants (in this case landing not in America but in Cardiff, Wales) besides Trezza Azzopardi's **The Hiding Place** (short-listed for Britain's prestigious Booker Prize). It's narrated by Dolores, whose tales of the emotional ups and downs (mostly the latter) of this tragic family read more like a memoir than a novel.

The first relationship that newly arrived Ilka, daughter of parents lost in Hitler's cauldron of death, finds in America is with Carter

Bayoux, a black intellectual, prodigious drinker, and teller of tales, in Lore Segal's **Her First American**.

In **Harbor**, a wrenching first novel by Lorraine Adams, Aziz, a Muslim from Algeria who arrives illegally in America in the 1990s, becomes caught up in America's domestic war on terror following 9/11.

At the age of six, Remi is sent from her grandparents' home in Lagos, Nigeria, to boarding school in England, where she is the only African student, in Simi Bedford's **Yoruba Girl Dancing**.

Rachel Calof's Story: Jewish Homesteader on the Northern Plains is the actual journal of Rachel Calof, who at eighteen left a shtetl in Russia for an arranged marriage in North Dakota. A good companion read for Calof's book is Willa Cather's **My Ántonia**.

Zadie Smith's first novel, **White Teeth**, begins with the unlikely friendship between Archibald Jones, who is British, and Samad Iqbal, a Muslim immigrant from Pakistan. It quickly adds their wives and children to the mix, along with a host of other colorful characters.

Lucy, the title character in a spare and elegant novel by Jamaica Kincaid, emigrates from Antigua to the United States to work as an au pair for a wealthy (and unhappy) couple in an unnamed northern city that resembles Manhattan.

America as defined by change—people changing their names and identities and the regions of the country where they live—is portrayed painfully but realistically in Bharati Mukherjee's **Jasmine**. A slightly less distressing read about Indians adjusting to the new world is Jhumpa Lahiri's **The Namesake**.

In Mary Gardner's **Boat People**, a diverse group of Vietnamese refugees try to make new lives for themselves far from all they've ever known in, of all places, Galveston, Texas.

INDIA: A READER'S ITINERARY

I've always been fascinated by India's history, culture, peoples, and cuisine; books can satisfy all but the last of these interests. Luckily, there are good Indian restaurants wherever I travel, my son-in-law Anand can often be persuaded to make a South Indian dinner, and as a last resort, I can salivate over the recipes in a winsome cookbook such as Madhur Jaffrey's **An Invitation to Indian Cooking.**

History

The place to start in any reading itinerary of India is with James Morris's histories of the subcontinent—**Heaven's Command: An Imperial Progress; Pax Britannica: The Climax of an Empire**; and **Farewell the Trumpets: An Imperial Retreat**—which together chart the rise and eventual decline of British empire-building. They are triumphs of historical analysis and accessible writing.

A good companion read to Morris is Margaret MacMillan's **Women of the Raj**, which covers the three and a half centuries of Britain-in-India, focusing on the mid-nineteenth century through 1947. **Women of the Raj** was not published until 1988, so MacMillan was able to interview some of the memsahibs who, having nothing to go home for after Indian independence, stayed behind. (This is also the subject of Paul Scott's Booker Prize—winning novel **Staying On.**)

Freedom at Midnight: The Epic Drama of India's Struggle for Independence by Larry Collins and Dominique Lapierre is required reading for those interested in understanding colonial and postcolonial India from a non-Indian point of view.

Karma Cola: Marketing the Mystic East by Gita Mehta is a vivid picture of the 1960s in India, where the hippie trail ended in (most often drug-induced) bliss for many nirvana-seekers.

Armchair Travel

Two of the best books for stay-at-home travelers are by William Dalrymple, whose City of Djinns: A Year in Delhi and The Age of Kali: Indian Travels and Encounters (which also includes sections on Sri Lanka, Pakistan, and other areas in the subcontinent) are well informed, amusing, and filled with interesting details.

Don Bloch and Iman Bijleveld's Seduced by the Beauty of the World: Travels in India includes stunning photos from all regions of India, celebrating its festivals, monuments, and culture.

Fiction

For many years all the novels about India published in English were written by Englishmen and -women, and their subject was the Raj, the period of British rule in India. Not until late in the twentieth century did American publishers take a chance on Indian novelists, a decade or two after British publishers saw the market for books by authors such as Arundhati Roy, Rohinton Mistry, and Salman Rushdie. With that in mind, here are some recommendations for books about India by non-Indians.

The Anglo-Indian John Masters wrote many romantic historical novels about his native land, several of which were made into not-so-great movies, including Bhowani Junction, in which an Anglo-Indian woman (played by Ava Gardner) searches for her place in what will be the newly independent India. Masters also wrote Nightrunners of Bengal, which deals with the great Indian mutiny of 1857, a seminal point in British-Indian relations (akin to our own Revolutionary War, perhaps). The mutiny is also the subject of J. G. Farrell's The Siege of Krishnapur, which won the Booker Prize in 1973.

M. M. Kaye was deeply in love with India, and that love is reflected in her romantic nineteenth-century sagas Shadow of the Moon and The Far Pavilions, both of which are on many people's lists of all-time favorite books.

Susanna Moore's One Last Look examines in fiction the real-life sisters Emily and Fanny Eden, who accompanied their brother, Lord Auckland, governor-general of India, to Afghanistan during what's known as the First Afghan War in the 1840s. Emily wrote about her love of India and her experiences there in Up the Country and Janet Dunbar edited Tigers, Durbars and Kings: Fanny Eden's Indian Journals, 1837–1838, both of which make good companion reading to Moore's novel.

For books by Indian writers (many of whom now live in England, Canada, or the United States), try these titles.

The Vintage Book of Modern Indian Literature, edited by Amit Chaudhuri, is a good place to start, as it includes writers from the mid-nineteenth century on, translated from many different Indian languages, including Hindi, Bengali, and Urdu. Many of the writers in the rest of this section are included in Chaudhuri's book.

Rabindranath Tagore's Gitanjali: A Collection of Indian Poems by the Nobel Laureate contains most of this South Indian's best poems.

Nirad C. Chaudhuri's two exceptionally informative memoirs, The Autobiography of an Unknown Indian and Thy Hand, Great Anarch!: India 1921–1952, explore Bengali society from the turn of the twentieth century until shortly after independence in 1947, from the point of view of someone educated by the British but able to plainly see both their weaknesses and the necessity for India's sovereignty.

Take a look at Amit Chaudhuri's **Freedom Song** and **A New World**; R. K. Narayan's **A Tiger for Malgudi** and **Malgudi Days**; Akhil Sharma's **An Obedient Father**; Rohinton Mistry's **Such a Long Journey**; Manil Suri's **The Death of Vishnu**; Anita Desai's **Fasting, Feasting** or the tragic **Baumgartner's Bombay**; Chitra Banerjee Divakaruni's **Sister of My Heart**; Anjana Appachana's **Listening Now**; Pankaj Mishra's **The Romantics**; Gita Mehta's **Raj**; Nayantara Sahgal's **Mistaken Identity, Rich Like Us**, and **Plans for Departure**; Arundhati Roy's **The God of Small Things**; and Meena Alexander's **Nampally Road**.

I can't leave India without mentioning Jon Godden's **Two Under the Indian Sun**, about the lives of Jon and her sister Rumer in India during World War I. Godden's memoir is tender, loving, and a splendid evocation of imperial India.

IT WAS A DARK AND STORMY NOVEL

In Elizabeth Strout's **Amy and Isabelle**, Isabelle feels at one point "that she might not read another book for a while, that life was difficult enough without bringing someone else's sorrows to crash down about your head."

But what can I say? Some of my best friends (and me, too) love dark novels. You know the sort, when you can read only a paragraph or two at a time because it's so depressing to be so close to someone else's low-down and endlessly tragic life. A friend once described slamming one of these books shut and shouting into the air at the author (who was in some other place entirely, of course), "Can't you find it in your heart to let one, just one, of your characters have something good happen to him?!"

If that's the kind of book you like, try these simply stunning novels.

Margaret Atwood's Oryx and Crake

Russell Banks's Continental Drift

Larry Brown's Dirty Work

Dan Chaon's You Remind Me of Me

Michael Cunningham's Flesh and Blood

Pete Dexter's Train

Joan Didion's Play It As It Lays

Andre Dubus III's House of Sand and Fog

Kent Haruf's Eventide

Tim O'Brien's In the Lake of the Woods

Michael Ondaatje's Anil's Ghost

E. Annie Proulx's Postcards

JERSEY GUYS AND GALS

Bruce Springsteen isn't the only one writing about New Jersey. Here are some terrific novels populated by the men and women of the state.

Richard Ford's **The Sportswriter** introduced alienated scribe Frank Bascombe. Its sequel **Independence Day**, about Bascombe's plans for a trip to the Basketball Hall of Fame with his troubled teenage son, won a well-deserved Pulitzer Prize for fiction.

Richard Price's novels are hard to classify: they're not exactly suspense novels, and to call them crime novels somehow confines them too narrowly. In **Freedomland, Clockers,** and **Samaritan** (all set in the slums of the fictional town of Dempsy), Price explores the lives of men who are caught up in situations beyond their control.

Frederick Reuss's **Henry of Atlantic City** is told through the eyes and voice of six-year-old Henry. After Henry is abandoned by his father, the former chief of security at Caesar's Palace in Atlantic City, his life is made both easier and more difficult by his photographic memory and his interest in the writings of the Gnostics.

Tom Perrotta's **The Wishbones** is the story of Dave Raymond, a thirty-one-year-old guitar player in a wedding band, whose unexpected proposal to his on-and-off girlfriend of the last fifteen years reminds him of just how ambivalent he is about marriage.

Among the other fine books set in New Jersey are James Kaplan's **Two Guys from Verona: A Novel of Suburbia** (where have the twenty-five years since high school gone?); Frederick Reiken's **The Lost Legends of New Jersey** (Anthony Rubin tries to rescue his next-door neighbor, Juliette, from an abusive boyfriend); Julie Schumacher's **The Body Is Water** (pregnant and unmarried Jane Haus returns to her father's house on the Jersey shore to figure out both the past and the future); and **Goodbye, Columbus**, the first collection of stories by New Jersey native Philip Roth, as well as his **Portnoy's Complaint, I Married a Communist**, and **The Plot Against America**.

JOURNALS AND LETTERS: WE ARE ALL VOYEURS AT HEART

Some of the books I've most enjoyed in my reading life are the journals and letters of interesting individuals. In part this may be because the art of letter writing seems to have died, and I am psychologically incapable of keeping a journal of my own. Luckily for me (and other readers), the following writers didn't have those problems.

I, along with hundreds of thousands of other people, remember reading **Gift from the Sea**, Anne Morrow Lindbergh's reflections on solitude and achieving a life of peace in a tumultuous, crowded world. When her journals began appearing in the 1970s, my friends and I, regardless of our negative feelings about Charles Lindbergh's behavior before and during World War II, would eagerly wait for each new book to appear. Some of us still reread them yearly to remind ourselves of what's important in this frantic world. They are, in order, **Bring Me a Unicorn; Hour of Gold, Hour of Lead; The Flower and the Nettle**; and **War Within and Without**.

I Will Bear Witness: A Diary of the Nazi Years 1933–1941 and I Will Bear Witness: A Diary of the Nazi Years 1942–1945 (also known as To the Bitter End) are the journals kept by philologist Victor Klemperer, who survived the Holocaust because his wife was Christian. He was one of the best observers whose records we have of those terrible, and ordinary, years inside Germany.

In **The Diaries of Dawn Powell, 1931–1965**, edited by Tim Page, you'll have the pleasure of meeting this intelligent, bitchy, witty, and desperate woman whose friendships spanned the literary world, from John Dos Passos to Edmund Wilson to Noël Coward (whom she describes as "a perfectly dazzling thoroughbred madman").

In **The Writer's Journal: 40 Contemporary Writers and Their Journals**, edited by Sheila Bender, a diverse collection of writers, including poets, novelists, and essayists—Ron Carlson, Linda Bierds, Reginald Gibbons, Craig Lesley, and Pam Houston among them—give examples of how they use their journals in their writing life.

One of those books that many readers remember with pleasure (and one that still maintains its charm even with annual rereadings) is **84, Charing Cross Road**, a compilation of the letters exchanged across the Atlantic during World War II between assertive New York book lover Helene Hanff, always looking for difficult-to-find titles, and Frank Doel, a London bookseller at Marks & Co. bookstore.

The Diaries of Kenneth Tynan (one of England's leading theater critics, and for two years also a regular drama reviewer for *The New Yorker*) reveal a man who was engaging, exceedingly witty (often at the expense of others' reputations), opinionated, and raunchy, and who wrote compulsively readable prose (exactly what you want in a diary, in fact). His **Letters**, edited by his wife, Kathleen, offers another chance to meet Tynan at his best.

JUST TOO GOOD TO MISS

You're just going to have to trust me on these—they're all wonderful reading, each in its own way. Some are light reading, some have unexpected (or expected) depth, some were written decades and decades ago, some were written yesterday or the day before. Most are fiction, but I've indicated (nf) which are nonfiction. Give them all a try!

Alessandro Baricco's Ocean Sea

William Boyd's Any Human Heart

Robert Cohen's Inspired Sleep

Dennis Covington's Salvation on Sand Mountain: Snake-Handling and Redemption in Southern Appalachia *(nf)*

Frederick Crews's The Pooh Perplex *and* Postmodern Pooh *(nf)*

Alain de Botton's How Proust Can Change Your Life: Not a Novel *(nf)*

Susan Dworkin's The Book of Candy

Jennifer Egan's Look at Me

Michelle Huneven's Jamesland

Naguib Mahfouz's Palace Walk, Palace of Desire, *and* Sugar Street

Brian Morton's Starting Out in the Evening

Stewart O'Nan's The Names of the Dead

Caroline Preston's Jackie by Josie

José Saramago's The History of the Siege of Lisbon *and* Blindness

Mary Webb's Precious Bane

John Welter's I Want to Buy a Vowel: A Novel of Illegal Alienation

Edmund White's Fanny: A Fiction

KRAKATAU

I know of only two books for the general reader about the 1883 eruption of this volcano on a small, uninhabited island in Indonesia located between Java and Sumatra. Both—the island and the volcano—are called Krakatau by the native people, but are usually referred to by their more familiar spelling, Krakatoa.

Many people will know about Krakatoa simply because they read anything and everything that best-selling author Simon Winchester writes, whether his subject is China, the *Oxford English Dictionary*, or, as in this case, a volcano, the eruption of which led to tsunamis that killed more than thirty-five thousand people and changed weather and climate patterns across the globe. Though **Krakatoa: The Day the World Exploded, August 27, 1883** is as interesting, well-written, and informative as Winchester's other books, it's not the final word on Krakatoa.

That would be **The Twenty-One Balloons** by William Pène du Bois, which won the Newbery Medal in 1948. (This award, named for eighteenth-century British bookseller John Newbery, is given annually "to the author of the most distinguished contribution to American literature for children" by the Association for Library Service to Children, a division of the American Library Association.) Du Bois's book is a glorious fantasy about a balloonist who lands on the island of Krakatoa and finds it populated with eccentric people, enormous wealth (he gets a fair share), and a society that takes turns cooking dinner. And they even have an escape plan, of sorts, for when their volcano erupts!

LEGAL EAGLES IN FICTION

A good suspense or mystery novel requires a protagonist who has a legitimate reason (and a frequent one, if it's a series) to come into contact with crimes and their alleged perpetrators. Who fits this definition better than a lawyer?

No list of this sort would be complete without Scott Turow's genre-defining novel **Presumed Innocent**, in which prosecuting attorney Rusty Sabich finds himself in deep waters when his lover is found raped and murdered and he's accused of the crime.

In Richard North Patterson's **Silent Witness**, attorney Tony Lord goes back to his hometown to help out an old friend who's accused of murder.

A World War II German prisoner-of-war camp is the setting for John Katzenbach's **Hart's War**, in which former law student Tommy Hart is given the assignment of defending an African American soldier accused of murdering a fellow G.I.

James Grippando's **Last to Die** has his series attorney, Jack Swyteck, needing to decide if his best friend's brother (who is in line to inherit $46 million if five other people die first) is a killer or an innocent victim of a vicious plot.

In **Death Row**, William Bernhardt's series lawyer/detective Ben Kincaid is trying to clear the name of an alleged murderer on death row. He runs into trouble when the witness who identified his client as the killer, but then recanted, is found dead herself.

Veritas is William Lashner's second novel starring Victor Carl (his first was **Hostile Witness**), a criminal defense lawyer in Philadelphia. When a young woman asks Carl to prove that her sister's death was murder, not suicide, he has no idea of the complications that will be heading his way.

LEGAL EAGLES IN NONFICTION

Even though I have never had the least desire to become an attorney myself (imagine reading nothing but legal briefs all day, every day!), I've always enjoyed reading about the inner workings of the legal profession, whether in a history of the Supreme Court or in accounts of major battles over misdeeds, law, and legislation.

Gideon's Trumpet by Anthony Lewis was first published in 1964 and remains an important book in the field of legal history. It is the fascinating account of James Earl Gideon's fight for the right to legal counsel—a landmark case decided in Gideon's favor by the U.S. Supreme Court under the leadership of Chief Justice Earl Warren. A must-read for anyone with even a passing interest in the law.

A Civil Action by Jonathan Harr tells the long, tangled, and enthralling story of a lawsuit filed by a group of citizens in Woburn, Massachusetts, against W. R. Grace and the Beatrice Corporation for dumping cancer-causing solvents into the city's water supply. Every player in the case—lawyers, plaintiffs, and defendants—is here, warts and all.

Simple Justice: The History of Brown v. Board of Education and Black America's Struggle for Equality by Richard Kluger is a massive (and massively readable), wide-ranging history of the historic 1964 Supreme Court decision that made segregated schools illegal. Kluger includes descriptions of all the people involved, their roles in the case, and their places in history.

If you're looking for readable histories of the Supreme Court, take a look at Peter Irons's **A People's History of the Supreme Court** and **The Brethren: Inside the Supreme Court** by Bob Woodward and Scott Armstrong. Irons, a professor of political science at the University of California, San Diego, and director of the Earl Warren Bill of Rights Project, describes the major cases, the plaintiffs, and the judges, from the court's earliest days to the last decade of the twentieth century. Irons's book focuses on Supreme Court cases involving individuals who believed their constitutional rights to free speech, freedom of religion, or other Bill of Rights protections had been denied.

Woodward and Armstrong's **The Brethren** (originally published in 1979) covers the years 1969 to 1975, the heyday of Warren Burger's years as chief justice. During these politically and socially volatile years, the court considered cases dealing with abortion, race relations, censorship, and definitions of pornography and obscenity. This is valuable reading for anyone trying to understand the state of the Union today, because in so many ways we are still grappling with similar issues. The authors also go behind the scenes to describe the personal relationships among the nine justices.

LEWIS AND CLARK: ADVENTURERS EXTRAORDINAIRE

The years 2004–2007 mark the bicentennial of Meriwether Lewis and William Clark's famous expedition to discover the Northwest Passage and to map the new territory just acquired from France. Their story never gets old—filled as it is with adventure, hardships, death, heartwarming friendships, good deeds, and, inevitably, heartbreak. In some ways, too, each succeeding generation has rethought the expedition in light of its own preoccupations and cultural beliefs, so that reading David Freeman Hawke's **Those Tremendous Mountains: The Story of the Lewis and Clark Expedition** (1980) is qualitatively different from reading, say, Stephen Ambrose's **Undaunted Courage** (1996). Neither is any less worthwhile to read; they just have different emphases and interpretations.

If you're going to read about these explorers, though, you need to begin with their own stories of the journey. Luckily, we don't all have to go to the immense trouble of deciphering that nineteenth-century handwriting. We can turn instead to a book such as Bernard DeVoto's **The Journals of Lewis and Clark**, which brings the journey to life in a way that even the best-written secondary accounts (and there are some great ones) cannot.

Two of the best secondary accounts, besides those mentioned above, are by two of our best contemporary historians: David Lavender's **The Way to the Western Sea: Lewis and Clark Across the Continent** and James P. Ronda's **Lewis and Clark Among the Indians.**

Castle McLaughlin's **Arts of Diplomacy: Lewis & Clark's Indian Collection** (with a general introduction by James Ronda) was written to commemorate the bicentennial. Page after page of fabulous reproductions demonstrate the breadth of the items (now at the Peabody Museum of Archaeology and Ethnology at Harvard University) that Lewis and Clark brought back from their travels.

Gardeners will especially enjoy **Common to This Country: Botanical Discoveries of Lewis and Clark** by Susan H. Munger, with illustrations by Charlotte Staub Thomas, which discusses the more than two hundred plants that Lewis and Clark brought back from their trek. (You can still see some of them at the Lewis and Clark Herbarium in Philadelphia.)

Three good novels about Lewis and Clark include Brian Hall's **I Should Be Extremely Happy in Your Company**, in which the story is told by multiple narrators; **From Sea to Shining Sea** by James Alexander Thom, which is much more about Clark's family than about the expedition; and **The True Account: A Novel of the Lewis & Clark & Kinneson Expeditions**, a laugh-aloud comic novel by Howard Frank Mosher, in which a Vermont ex-soldier named True Teague Kinneson and his nephew Ticonderoga race Lewis and Clark to the Pacific (and win).

LIBRARIES AND LIBRARIANS

Having spent the majority of my life inside a library, and most of my adult life as a librarian, I'm not surprised that I'm drawn to books in which libraries and librarians are featured prominently.

Eleanor Estes won the Newbery Medal for her novel **Ginger Pye**, but my favorite Estes novels are **The Moffats, The Middle Moffat**, and **Rufus M.**, whose characters all live in Cranbury, New Jersey, in the first decades of the twentieth century. In **Rufus M.** Estes has a rib-tickling, heartwarming chapter about young Rufus's arduous attempts to get his own library card. Such perseverance! If only all kids wanted to use the library as much as Rufus did.

Sydney Taylor's **All-of-a-Kind Family** tells the story of a Jewish family struggling with poverty on the Lower East Side of Manhattan in 1912, just before the outbreak of World War I. It includes a lovely chapter about what happens when Sarah, one of five young sisters, loses a library book and has to confess it to her beloved library lady.

The Grand Complication is Allen Kurzweil's clever and witty novel about a reference librarian's search for a watch that was supposedly made for Marie Antoinette. It's filled with wordplay amid very funny scenes set in a library (including a contest to see who can attach the correct Dewey catalog number to the most abstruse subjects).

Charity Blackstock wrote two great romantic suspense novels— **The Foggy, Foggy Dew** and **Dewey Death**. It's the latter, of course, that's set in a research library. It describes what happens when a young woman librarian falls deeply, desperately, and disastrously in love with the wrong man. He's clearly—à la Lord Byron—mad, bad, and dangerous to know. But is he a murderer as well? Romance fans should not miss this, and suspense readers should hunt it down as well.

Librarians play major roles in Elizabeth McCracken's **The Giant's House**, in which Cape Cod librarian Peggy Cort finds companionship and love in an unlikely relationship with James Sweatt, a teenager who has a growth disorder that eventually makes him the tallest man in the world; Larry Beinhart's forthrightly titled **The Librarian**, which has academic librarian David Goldberg called upon to foil a dastardly plot to steal a presidential election; Sinclair Lewis's **Main Street**, the tale of young newlywed Carol Kennicott's unhappiness in Gopher Prairie, Minnesota; Art Corriveau's **Housewrights**, the story of an unusual love triangle; and Jincy Willett's first novel, **Winner of the National Book Award: A Novel of Fame, Honor, and Really Bad Weather**, the tale of dissimilar twin sisters—librarian Dorcas and voluptuary Abigail—and the (loathsomely despicable) man who more or less falls in love with them both.

LINES THAT LINGER;
SENTENCES THAT STICK

When I finished *Book Lust*, the first omissions I noticed were the favorite first lines I'd somehow neglected to include—the lines that kept waking me up at night, pleading to be shared sometime, somewhere. And then readers began to send me their own examples of wonderful lines that opened into wonderful books. Finally, I can share them—a win-win situation all around.

First, here are the classic opening lines that simply slipped my mind:

> *"Happy families are all alike; every unhappy family is unhappy in its own way" opens Leo Tolstoy's* **Anna Karenina.**
>
> *"Call me Ishmael" begins Herman Melville's* **Moby-Dick.**
>
> *"Last night I dreamt I went to Manderley again" is the first line of Daphne du Maurier's haunting* Rebecca.
>
> *And, from Charles Dickens's* **David Copperfield:** *"Whether I shall turn out to be the hero of my own life, or whether that station will be held by anybody else, these pages must show."*

Here are some more of my favorite lines—first and otherwise:

The inimitable Rose Macaulay begins **Told by an Idiot** with this deliciously packed sentence: "One evening, shortly before Christmas, in the days when our forefathers, being young, possessed the earth, in brief, in the year 1879, Mrs. Garden came briskly into the drawing-room from Mr. Garden's study and said in her crisp, even voice to her six children, 'Well, my dears, I have to tell you something. Poor papa has lost his faith again.'"

Mary Roach's hilarious and informative **Stiff: The Curious Lives of Human Cadavers** begins with these arresting two lines: "The way I see it, being dead is not terribly far off from being on a cruise ship. Most of your time is spent lying on your back."

The Debut, Anita Brookner's first novel published in the United States, begins with a line that every compulsive middle-aged reader can identify with: "Dr. Weiss, at forty, knew that her life had been ruined by literature."

Hunter S. Thompson starts **Fear and Loathing in Las Vegas: A Savage Journey to the Heart of the American Dream** with ' We were somewhere around Barstow on the edge of the desert when the drugs began to take hold."

Middlesex by Jeffrey Eugenides begins this way: "I was born twice: first, as a baby girl, on a remarkably smogless Detroit day in January of 1960; and then again, as a teenage boy, in an emergency room near Petoskey, Michigan, in August of 1974."

In **Nervous Conditions,** Tsitsi Dangarembga begins provocatively: "I was not sorry when my brother died."

From Verlyn Klinkenborg's **The Last Fine Time:** "Snow begins as a rumor in Buffalo, New York."

"The past is a foreign country. They do things differently there," opens one of the great but relatively unknown novels of the twentieth century, **The Go-Between** by L. P. Hartley.

In **Parnassus on Wheels,** one of Christopher Morley's two novels celebrating the love of books (the other is **The Haunted Bookshop**), Helen McGill, who has spent years tending to her brother Andrew's needs on the family farm, impulsively buys a traveling bookstore from Professor Mifflin. In dismay and annoyance, Andrew chases after the couple and greets his sister with these memorable words:

"Upon my soul you ought to have better sense—and at your age and weight!"

The second chapter of Julia Blackburn's **The Emperor's Last Island: A Journey to St. Helena** begins, "St. Helena is further away from anywhere else than anywhere else in all the world."

The first paragraph of Michael Malone's detective novel **Uncivil Seasons** begins, "Two things don't happen very often in Hillston, North Carolina. We don't get much snow, and we hardly ever murder one another. Suicide is more our style. . . ."

You could almost believe that Gabriel García Márquez specialized in opening lines; **The Autumn of the Patriarch** begins, "Over the weekend the vultures got into the presidential palace by pecking through the screens on the balcony windows, and the flapping of their wings stirred up the stagnant time inside, and at dawn on Monday the city awoke out of its lethargy of centuries with the warm, soft breeze of a great man dead and rotting grandeur." **One Hundred Years of Solitude** opens with, "Many years later, as he faced the firing squad, Colonel Aureliano Buendía was to recall that distant afternoon when his father took him to discover ice." The first line of **Chronicle of a Death Foretold** is: "On the day they were going to kill him, Santiago Nasar got up at five-thirty in the morning to wait for the boat the bishop was coming in."

Lee Smith begins **Family Linen** with this line: "Sybill parks carefully at the curb in front of the hypnotist's house and stares at it for some time without getting out of the car, without even turning off the motor or the air conditioner."

And then there's "I am doomed to remember a boy with a wrecked voice—not because of his voice, or because he was the smallest person I ever knew, or even because he was the instrument of my mother's death, but because he is the reason I believe in God; I am a Christian because of Owen Meany," the opening of **A Prayer for Owen Meany** by John Irving.

Donna Tartt starts **The Little Friend** like this: "For the rest of her life, Charlotte Cleve would blame herself for her son's death because she had decided to have Mother's Day dinner at six in the evening instead of noon, after church, which is when the Cleves usually had it."

"Captain Ahab was neither my first husband nor my last," opens **Ahab's Wife, or, The Star-Gazer**, Sena Jeter Naslund's first novel.

In **Wonder Boys**, Michael Chabon describes one of his characters like this: "[His overcoat] emitted an odor of bus station so desolate that just standing next to him you could feel your luck changing for the worse."

"The last camel collapsed at noon" opens Ken Follett's best novel, **The Key to Rebecca**.

From Brady Udall's first novel, **The Miracle Life of Edgar Mint**, comes this great first line: "If I could tell you one thing about my life, it would be this: when I was seven years old the mailman ran over my head."

James Crumley's **The Last Good Kiss** begins, "When I finally caught up with Abraham Trahearne, he was drinking beer with an alcoholic bulldog named Fireball Roberts in a ramshackle joint just outside of Sonoma, California, drinking the heart right out of a fine spring afternoon."

"Short, fat, and of a quiet disposition, he appeared to spend a lot of money on really bad clothes, which hung about his squat frame like skin on a shrunken toad" is how John le Carré describes his hero, George Smiley, in **Call for the Dead**.

In **The Orchid Thief**, Susan Orlean portrays the main character this way: "John Laroche is a tall guy, skinny as a stick, pale-eyed, slouch-shouldered, and sharply handsome, in spite of the fact that he is missing all his front teeth. He has the posture of al dente spaghetti and the nervous intensity of someone who plays a lot of video games."

LITERARY LIVES:
THE AMERICANS

If you want to know more about a writer, either before or after reading his or her books, here are some top-notch literary biographies.

Ever since I first read R. W. B. Lewis's Pulitzer Prize–winning **Edith Wharton: A Biography** many years ago, I've thought that it set the gold standard for biographies: intensely readable, a page-turner, and a wonderful way to broaden and deepen one's appreciation of this marvelous writer. If you've never tried a Wharton novel or short story, then start with these: "Xingu," a little gem of a story about a women's book group, and her most famous novel, **The Age of Innocence**. Lewis also wrote a biography of Henry James and his family, **The Jameses: A Family Narrative**.

But to learn the most about Henry James, you can't do better than to read Leon Edel: either his magnificent five volumes about the author, or the one-volume abridgement, **Henry James: A Life**. The five are **Henry James: The Untried Years, 1843–1870; Henry James: The Conquest of London, 1870–1881; Henry James: The Middle Years, 1882–1895; Henry James: The Treacherous Years, 1895–1901;** and **Henry James: The Master, 1901–1916**. Edel won a Pulitzer Prize and a National Book Award for the second and third volumes of his massive biography. (Henry James is also the subject of Colm Tóibín's magnificent novel **The Master** and David Lodge's **Author, Author**.)

Most people think of Nathaniel Hawthorne only in terms of **The Scarlet Letter**, a book they were probably forced to read in high school. That's a shame, as Brenda Wineapple makes clear in her **Hawthorne: A Life**, because Hawthorne was a complicated and complex individual who struggled with many contradictory impulses in his life: writing vs. a more public life, living in the North while supporting the South in the Civil War, and much more. He showed himself fully to no one, and died leaving many unanswered questions.

Maybe **A Tragic Honesty: The Life and Work of Richard Yates** by Blake Bailey will revive interest in Yates's spare and crystalline prose, seen to perfection in the novels **The Easter Parade** and **Revolutionary Road**. The life of this sad, self-destructive writer can be read as a how-not-to manual for those aspiring to a career in fiction, but his legacy—he influenced the entire minimalist school of writers, including Richard Ford, Mary Robison, and Raymond Carver—is lasting.

Anyone who takes up the challenge of writing about a woman who changed lives and loves as fast and furiously as the writer Mary McCarthy did deserves a prize, so it's fitting that **Writing Dangerously: Mary McCarthy and Her World** by Carol Brightman won the National Book Critics Award. (There's more about McCarthy's novels on pages 3 and 53 in *Book Lust*.)

In **The Singular Mark Twain**, Fred Kaplan describes the life and development of a complex writer whose work includes some of the most popular (and controversial) books in the American canon, including, of course, **The Adventures of Tom Sawyer, The Adventures of Huckleberry Finn**, and **A Connecticut Yankee in King Arthur's Court**.

Arthur Mizener's **The Far Side of Paradise: A Biography of F. Scott Fitzgerald**, published in 1951, was the first, and remains the best, biography of F. Scott Fitzgerald, a self-destructive but extremely talented writer who died at a ridiculously young age while hard at work on what probably would have been his best novel, **The Last Tycoon**.

LITERARY LIVES: THE BRITS

Here are some gems of British literary biography, excellent reading whether or not you subscribe to the heresy that it's often more interesting to read about an author's life than to read what he or she wrote.

The romantic lives (and early deaths, each before the age of forty) of Charlotte, Emily, and Anne Brontë have certainly affected the way we think about their literary output. Two good antidotes to any of those misconceptions are Lucasta Miller's **The Brontë Myth** and Juliet Barker's **The Brontës**. Barker also edited **The Brontës: A Life in Letters**, which makes a good companion read to her biography.

According to one of his contemporaries, the nineteenth-century poet and literary critic Samuel Taylor Coleridge "did everything he shouldn't and nothing that he should." You can read all about him in Richard Holmes's excellent two-volume survey, **Coleridge: Early Visions, 1772–1804** and **Coleridge: Darker Reflections, 1804–1834**. Holmes also wrote about the wild life and beautiful writing of Percy Bysshe Shelley, in **Shelley: The Pursuit**.

One of the great "better than fiction" love stories of the nineteenth century is that of the poets Robert Browning and Elizabeth Barrett. Margaret Forster in **Elizabeth Barrett Browning** tells their whole romantic story—tyrannical father, lifelong illness, passionate love affair—with gusto and grace.

Lord Byron, who was described by his contemporary Lady Caroline Lamb as "mad, bad, and dangerous to know," had a life defined by his omnivorous sexuality. Needless to say, then, Benita Eisler's **Byron: Child of Passion, Fool of Fame** limns a life that far surpassed anything Byron could (legally) say in print.

The writing lives of a mother and daughter also make for fascinating reading. Mary Wollstonecraft, author of the influential feminist essay **A Vindication of the Rights of Woman**, was resolutely opposed to the institution of marriage, and made a career for herself as a journalist until she died shortly after giving birth to her daughter. Janet Todd reveals all in **Mary Wollstonecraft: A Revolutionary Life**. Her daughter, who would become the author of **Frankenstein**, lived an equally unconventional life, movingly told in Miranda Seymour's **Mary Shelley**.

A LITTLE LEFT OF CENTER

A lot has been written about the so-called rise and fall of the liberal establishment, but these two books led me to consider just what it means to be a liberal today, and how the meaning of that word has changed since the beginning of the twentieth century.

In **Blood of the Liberals**, George Packer looks at the evolution of the L word through the experiences of his maternal grandfather and his own father. Packer's grandfather, George Huddleston, was elected to Congress from Birmingham, Alabama, in 1914 as a Jeffersonian Democrat, and was finally defeated in 1936, having broken with FDR over the president's consolidation of power in the central government. Packer's father, Herb, believed that being a liberal meant that rational discourse and thought, rather than emotion, guided one's decisions. As an administrator at Stanford during the Vietnam War, Herb Packer was seen as the enemy by left-wing students, who wanted him to take immediate action against the war. Both Huddleston and Packer called themselves liberals, and both were destroyed by their beliefs. So what is liberalism? The third-generation Packer doesn't come to any real definition, but he raises some interesting and difficult questions about how we define ourselves in political terms.

The Guardians: Kingman Brewster, His Circle, and the Rise of the Liberal Establishment by Geoffrey Kabaservice uses the life of the president of Yale University during the turbulent decade from 1960 to 1970 to illuminate a circle of influential men (Republicans all) who came from privileged families, had inherited wealth, belonged to the toniest, most exclusive clubs, and yet worked to make important societal changes in civil rights, university admissions, and the problems of the inner cities. These liberal Republicans—Cyrus Vance, McGeorge Bundy, and Elliot Richardson among them—were the scourge of the conservative wing of the party, and were frequently scorned as well by those who felt they didn't go far enough in their reforms (just as George Packer's father was). Definitely not just for Yalies, this book is relevant to anyone interested in this era.

LIVING HIGH IN CASCADIA

Cascadia has been described as a state of mind as much as a geographic place. Geographically, it is the coastal Pacific Northwest region of North America, from northern California through southern British Columbia. The poet Denise Levertov (who lived there during the last years before her death) described Cascadia's mind-set this way:

> . . . I'll dig in,
> into my days, having come here to live, not to visit.
> Grey is the price
> of neighboring with eagles, of knowing
> a mountain's vast presence, seen or unseen.

Cascadia is fertile ground for both memoirs and fiction. The memoirs I describe here were written by transplants who dug in tenaciously and grew themselves deeply into the place, while still retaining an outsider's sense of awe. These books vividly portray people and wilderness with evocative clarity, with zest and passion. Read them when you want to summon sea fogs, cedar smoke, and salmon streams.

Living High: An Unconventional Autobiography by June Burn is a spirited account of a young couple's adventures homesteading in the San Juan Islands in the 1920s. The author's happy-go-lucky narrative of often-harrowing events is emblematic of the buoyant resilience that runs through all these memoirs. Floyd Schmoe, in A Year in Paradise, tells how he returned from World War I and landed a job as winter caretaker at Mount Rainier's Paradise Lodge. After moving the hotel's grand piano into their quarters for nightly recitals by his concert pianist bride, the couple settled in for a long snowbound winter, emerging in the spring to spend the rest of an idyllic year exploring the park and its surrounds.

For two views of Cascadia through the eyes of children read Opal Whiteley's The Diary of Opal Whiteley and Helene Glidden's The Light on the Island: Tales of a Lighthouse Keeper's Family in the San Juan Islands. Opal Whiteley's childhood diary, first published in The Atlantic Monthly in 1920, is now available in several different editions, including an online version from the University of Oregon. Written in the idiosyncratic prose of this six-year-old pioneer in an Oregon logging community, the diary chronicles the explorations of Opal and her extravagantly named animal friends, both wild and domestic. Helene Glidden's book tells of life on lonely Patos Island with her colorful lighthouse keeper father, mother, and twelve siblings. Smugglers and Indians, shipwrecks, and a visit from Colonel Teddy Roosevelt all make for plenty of family adventure.

For Love of Some Islands, another lovely book by Floyd Schmoe, recounts the author's summer sojourn on a houseboat with a difference. Wishing to study the marine ecosystem of the San Juan Islands, this biologist cut a picture window into the bottom of his boat in order to conduct research in the comfort of his own home.

A more adventurous boater was M. Wylie Blanchet, author of **The Curve of Time.** This intrepid Vancouver Island widow set off each summer with her five young children (and a dog) in a thirty-foot boat. Taking only their bathing suits and one change of clothes, they explored the chilly waters and sun-drenched shores of British Columbia's Inside Passage.

The Inside Passage is also the scene of Alexandra Morton's **Listening to Whales: What the Orcas Have Taught Us.** Like Jane Goodall, the woman she most admires, Morton earned her research credentials in the field and is a gifted storyteller. After breaking into cetacean research by getting hired to paint a mural in scientist John Lilly's house, her studies of captive orcas eventually led her to a new life among the whales of Johnstone Strait.

For a taste of Inside Passage life around the turn of the last century, read the remarkable **Klee Wyck** by Emily Carr. Traveling with only a small dog as companion, the maverick British Columbia artist braved dangerous seas and Victorian disapproval to forge strong friendships with First Nations villagers and sketch the vanishing monumental carvings on their remote islands. Klee Wyck, "The One Who Laughs," was the name the Indians gave to her.

Michael Modzelewski's **Inside Passage: Living with Killer Whales, Bald Eagles, and Kwakiutl Indians** tells of a solitary sojourn on one of these islands while learning the ancient alphabets of sky and wave, season and inner wisdom, challenged by a Kwakwaka'wakh visitor who observed, "You no survive here. . . . I be by neks time to pick up you bones."

Survival is also the theme of Totem Salmon: Life Lessons from Another Species by Freeman House, but here the bones in question are those of a watershed and its indicator species, one of the last genetically native chinook salmon runs in northern California. It's part legal thriller, part treatise on biology, and part hero's journey, but it all comes together as a gripping account of how human beings with little in common except the place they call home learn to work together to create a sustainable future for themselves and their non-human neighbors.

A Whale Hunt, Robert Sullivan's account of the Makah Nation's decision to reassert their tribal whaling rights, attempts to fathom the murky cultural and ecopolitical depths of the region from an outsider's point of view. Sullivan spent two years getting acquainted with participants in the hunt, and he sympathetically portrays the swirling currents surrounding them. But ultimately the cultural gulf dividing the multifarious stakeholders seems unbridgeable. Brenda Peterson's collection of essays, Singing to the Sound: Visions of Nature, Animals & Spirit, includes the author's thoughtful reports on the hunt as well as new revelations from her quarter-century apprenticeship to Puget Sound, first described in Living by Water: True Stories of Nature and Spirit.

In Having Everything Right: Essays of Place, Kim Stafford seeks to regain "the nourishing ways: listening, remembering, telling, weaving a rooted companionship with home ground." Jim Nollman also attempts to do just that in Why We Garden: Cultivating a Sense of Place. While ruminating on the etymology of the word "paradise," which originally referred to a walled garden, he discovers the futility of fencing out resident deer and learns to coexist by creating a permaculture garden. Jo Ann Ridley's San Juan Islands Journal chronicles life in the islands with economy and humor, portraying the marginal but deeply satisfying life of the independent and quirky San Juan Islanders, who cling as tenaciously to these rocky shores as do barnacles and lichens.

A final, more journalistic exploration of place is **The Good Rain: Across Time and Terrain in the Pacific Northwest** by Timothy Egan. Egan combines historical research, interviews, and his own experiences as a third-generation Westerner to seek "a common narrative in the land."

There's good historical fiction about Cascadia too.

Don Berry's trilogy of novels—**Trask, Moontrap**, and **To Build a Ship**—is set in the Oregon Territory in the mid-nineteenth century. Long out of print, the books have just been reissued and will give pleasure to a whole new generation of readers.

Molly Gloss's antiromantic western **The Jump-Off Creek** tells of Lydia Sanderson's experiences in the late nineteenth century as a single-woman homesteader in the high mountain region of Oregon.

Annie Dillard's **The Living** is an expansive novel about settling the area around Bellingham Bay in Washington, near the Canadian border, in the late nineteenth century. Well researched, well written, and filled with memorable characters and events, Dillard's novel is hard to put down.

Ken Kesey's classic **Sometimes a Great Notion** is on every list of top ten Northwest novels. Due to the stubbornness of the family patriarch, his two sons and daughter-in-law are caught up in a bitter conflict with striking fellow loggers—a Greek tragedy set in a coastal Oregon logging town.

Although Bernard Malamud's **A New Life** is set in the fictional town of Eastchester, in the fictional state of Cascadia, it was clear from the day it was published in 1961 that this novel about a New York writer who comes West to teach in the English department at a land grant college in the rainy Northwest was a thinly veiled autobiographical account of the twelve years Malamud and his family spent in Corvallis, Oregon, where he taught at Oregon State University.

Two novels use the high-flying dot-com world of 1990s Seattle as a backdrop: Michael Byers's **Long for This World** and Jonathan Raban's **Waxwings**. Byers's first novel is about a geneticist who has to decide whether the possibility of saving the life of a young patient is worth the likelihood of losing his license to practice medicine. Raban's novel is about an expatriate British writer going through a midlife crisis, and an illegal Chinese immigrant who comes into his life.

One of the best-known Pacific Northwest novels is David Guterson's **Snow Falling on Cedars**. Whether you're drawn to wonderful evocations of place, love a page-turning plot, or enjoy meeting a variety of well-drawn characters, you'll be engaged by this novel, set after World War II, about a returning Japanese internee who is arrested for murder.

Two other good novels set in Cascadia are Robin Cody's **Ricochet River**, set in the logging town of Calamus in the 1960s, about two high school seniors who are faced with difficult choices that will determine the rest of their lives; and **Educating Waverley** by Laura Kalpakian, which takes place at a progressive boarding school on an island in Puget Sound.

The mystery shelf is packed with tales set in Cascadia. M. K. Wren's series about bookseller/private investigator Conan Flagg includes **King of the Mountain** and **Wake Up, Darlin' Corey**. Kate Wilhelm's **The Hamlet Trap** is the first in a series of solid mysteries featuring Constance and Charlie Meiklejohn, a psychologist and former Manhattan policeman, that take place in Ashland, home of the Oregon Shakespeare Festival. (Wilhelm also has a series of mysteries about Oregon defense attorney Barbara Holloway, including **Clear and Convincing Proof** and **Defense for the Devil**.) Firefighter Earl Emerson has written a series featuring private investigator

Thomas Black (**Catfish Café** is a good one to begin with) as well as several novels with firefighter heroes, including **Vertical Burn** and **Pyro**. Aaron Elkins's **The Dark Place** has a main character who is a professor of anthropology. Lowen Clausen's **First Avenue, Second Watch**, and **Third & Forever** are police procedurals by a former Seattle cop. J. A. Jance's series starring Seattle homicide detective J. P. Beaumont includes **Failure to Appear** and **Lying in Wait**. Mary Daheim's **Silver Scream** is a cozy mystery set in a bed-and-breakfast in the heart of Seattle. G. M. Ford's novels about disgraced investigative journalist Frank Corso include **Fury** and **Black River**.

LIVING THROUGH WAR

Among the many accounts of wartime by men and women who were combatants are these excellent works: **Quartered Safe Out Here: A Recollection of the War in Burma** by George MacDonald Fraser, a candid account of the author's military service in the British army during World War II (for more about Fraser, see "George MacDonald Fraser: Too Good to Miss" in *Book Lust*); Robert Graves's **Good-bye to All That**, about his disillusioning experiences in World War I; and Siegfried Sassoon's **Memoirs of an Infantry Officer**. Sassoon's feelings about World War I are conveyed in his poetry as well, most strikingly in "Aftermath," written in 1919:

> *Have you forgotten yet?*
> For the world's events have rumbled on since those gagged days,
> Like traffic checked a while at the crossing of city ways:
> And the haunted gap in your mind has filled with thoughts that flow
> Like clouds in the lit heavens of life; and you're a man reprieved to go,
> Taking your peaceful share of Time, with joy to spare.

But the past is just the same,—and War's a bloody game. . . .

Have you forgotten yet? . . .

Look down, and swear by the slain of the War that you'll never forget.

Less readily available are memoirs by noncombatants who found themselves caught up in the most profound and life-changing events of their time. It's often through reading their stories that we come to understand the wider effects of war and wartime, and the bravery and courage it took for civilians to live through weeks, months, and even years of occupation or incarceration. These accounts of human suffering and terrible trials also attest to the power of the human spirit to overcome deprivation and despair.

In **Testament of Youth**, probably one of the finest accounts ever written of World War I, Vera Brittain describes her own and her friends' experiences during the war, including the deaths of those she loved most. Although Brittain served as a nurse—in London, Malta, and at the front in France—this memoir's strength is not so much her experiences in the thick of fighting but her depiction of a lost generation. She continued her memoirs in **Testament of Experience** (which covers the years 1925–1950) and **Testament of Friendship**.

Iris Origo's **War in Val d'Orcia: An Italian War Diary, 1943–1944** describes a momentous year late in the war, and concludes with a stirring description of her forced retreat across eight miles of heavily mined highway, shepherding sixty local and refugee children to what she hoped would be safety. (There's also a grand biography of Iris Origo by Caroline Moorehead called **Iris Origo: Marchesa of Val d'Orcia**.)

Emily Hahn, a longtime *New Yorker* writer (her first article appeared in the magazine in 1929, and she continued her contributions for sixty-seven years) and an indefatigable traveler, first went to China in 1935 and remained there through most of World War II. She wrote about her experiences in **China to Me**, an eccentric look at an expatriate's life during those difficult years. Particularly interesting is her description of the Japanese occupation of Shanghai, which changed everyone's lives dramatically and drastically, but especially her own: she was pregnant, and her lover was imprisoned by the invading army.

Three Came Home by Agnes Newton Keith is both an intensely moving story of her imprisonment, with her son, in a Japanese prison camp on Berhala Island on North Borneo during World War II, and a testament to her undying belief that it is war itself that is evil, not the men who are both its perpetrators and its victims. Despite the harsh treatment the British subjects received at the hands of their Japanese captors, Keith cannot find it in herself to hate them—only the circumstances that forced them to behave in inhumane ways. This is an invaluable record of what life was like in the prison camps. The movie version (which starred Claudette Colbert) isn't half bad, either.

We Die Alone: A WWII Epic of Escape and Endurance by David Howarth is a biography of Jan Baalsrud, a member of the Norwegian resistance whose escape from the Nazis is a tale of courage and adventure.

LIVING YOUR DREAM

I think poet Philip Larkin said it best in two of his poems. In "Toads," he writes, "Ah, were I courageous enough / To shout *Stuff your pension! /* But I know, all too well, that's the stuff / That dreams are made on." In "Poetry of Departures," he writes: "Sometimes you hear, fifth-hand, / As epitaph: / *He chucked up everything / And just cleared off. . . .*" Both poems describe the envy we feel when we hear about someone leaving their stodgy life and doing whatever it is they love best, be it building a medieval siege weapon, sailing around lush islands, or seeing more birds in one year than anyone else. Here are some good armchair dreaming books; perhaps they'll inspire each of us to live dreams, as these people did.

In **No Visible Horizon: Surviving the World's Most Dangerous Sport** by Joshua Cooper Ramo, the author meditates on the subject of extreme sports (with forays into Plato, the psychological theory of "flow," and his own sport, aerial acrobatics) and the men and women who risk their lives in pursuit of . . . what? Perhaps a certain purity of purpose, a loss of control in the midst of perfect control, the mind-altering sensations of approaching danger and paralyzing fear—the last two being feelings that most of us run from, screaming.

John Pollack, author of **Cork Boat,** describes quitting his job in Washington, D.C., and following his boyhood dream of building a boat made entirely from wine corks (his ended up using 165,321 corks, all held together by rubber bands) and sailing it in unfamiliar waters, in this case the Douro River, from Spain through Portugal to the Atlantic Ocean.

Sometimes it's enough to write about other people's obsessions, as Mark Obmascik did in **The Big Year: A Tale of Man, Nature, and Fowl Obsession.** He recounts the 1998 North American Big Year—in which devoted birders dashed around the United States and Canada trying to become the person who sighted the most birds—from the perspectives of the three top finishers.

In **Catapult: Harry and I Build a Siege Weapon,** Jim Paul describes what follows his realization that what he really wants to do in his life is build a catapult and shoot rocks into the Pacific Ocean. He enlists the help of his friend Harry, and the two begin the project. Ah, little does he realize all it will entail and where it will take him. . . .

Ann Vanderhoof and her husband left their high-powered, tension-filled jobs in Toronto and spent four years sailing to the Caribbean and back. She describes their trip—from the sublime to the ordinary, from sunsets to haircuts and recipes—in **An Embarrassment of**

Mangoes: A Caribbean Interlude, which nearly had me quitting my job, learning to sail, and leaving drizzly Seattle (but I settled instead for listening to Jimmy Buffett).

Lynne Cox writes about her almost mystical love of long-distance swimming, in **Swimming to Antarctica: Tales of a Long-Distance Swimmer**, in much the same way that Joshua Cooper Ramo describes his attachment to aerial acrobatics. We learn all about the training, the endurance (Cox swam across the Bering Strait, around the Cape of Good Hope, and through the Strait of Messina), and, most importantly, the joy she takes in doing it.

MAIDEN VOYAGES

I'm struck by the number of first novels that reside on my bookshelves. I suspect there are so many because, for me, the only thing more satisfying than reading a wonderful first novel is to discover a writer in midcareer, which means I'll not only have several books to go back to but I'll have many more to look forward to as well. Believe me, though I will give you no hint as to what these first novels are about, they're all wonderful books.

Monica Ali's **Brick Lane**

Diana Atkinson's **Highways and Dancehalls**

Ann Beattie's **Chilly Scenes of Winter**

Liam Callanan's **The Cloud Atlas**

Esi Edugyan's **The Second Life of Samuel Tyne**

Julia Glass's **Three Junes**

Andrew Sean Greer's **The Confessions of Max Tivoli**

Mark Haddon's **The Curious Incident of the Dog in the Night-Time**

Khaled Hosseini's The Kite Runner

Mick Jackson's The Underground Man

Seth Kantner's Ordinary Wolves

Hari Kunzru's The Impressionist

Adam Langer's Crossing California

Mary Lawson's Crow Lake

Ann-Marie MacDonald's Fall on Your Knees

Alistair MacLeod's No Great Mischief

David Maine's The Preservationist

Renée Manfredi's Above the Thunder

Bobbie Ann Mason's In Country

Larry McMurtry's Horseman, Pass By

Maile Meloy's Liars and Saints

Cheryl Mendelson's Morningside Heights

Anne Michaels's Fugitive Pieces

Audrey Niffenegger's The Time Traveler's Wife

Kate Phillips's White Rabbit

Jonathan Raymond's The Half-Life

Michael Redhill's Michael Sloane

Ben Rice's Pobby and Dingan

Suzanne Strempek Shea's Selling the Lite of Heaven

Aurelie Sheehan's The Anxiety of Everyday Objects

Ira Sher's Gentlemen of Space

Marisa Kantor Stark's Bring Us the Old People

Monique Truong's The Book of Salt

Debra Weinstein's Apprentice to the Flower Poet Z

Jincy Willett's **Winner of the National Book Award: A Novel of Fame, Honor, and Really Bad Weather**

Lolly Winston's **Good Grief**

MICHAEL MALONE: TOO GOOD TO MISS

One reads (and rereads) Michael Malone's novels for the pure joy of these often funny, sometimes tragic, and always well-written books. His wide range of subject matter makes him delightfully unpredictable, so that liking one novel doesn't always guarantee that you'll equally appreciate another. On the other hand, if one of his novels doesn't strike your fancy, there's a good chance another will.

For many years Malone was the head scriptwriter for the über–soap opera *One Life to Live*, and he's written the über–novelistic soap opera in **Dingley Falls**, which includes among its many charms a lovely map of the eponymous town, where a plethora of eccentric people are involved in everything from love affairs to murders.

In **Foolscap, or, The Stages of Love,** Theo Ryan's relatively staid and sober existence as a professor of theater studies comes to a rapid end when he agrees to write the biography of a hard-living, alcoholic, womanizing playwright.

Handling Sin finds Raleigh Whittier Hayes racing down the highway to find his elderly and outlandish father, who has escaped from the hospital in a yellow convertible (along with a young nurse). His search runs into many roadblocks, including a motorcycle gang, an escaped convict, the Ku Klux Klan, and a search for buried treasure.

Two more of Malone's best are **Uncivil Seasons** and **Time's Witness,** both mysteries set in a small town in North Carolina.

Uncivil Seasons introduces policemen Cuddy Mangum and Justin Savile; their crime solving is continued in Time's Witness.

MARRIAGE BLUES

It was **The Amateur Marriage**, the title of Anne Tyler's sad and wry novel about a spectacularly mismatched couple, that started me thinking that most, if not all, marriages (in fiction, at least) are amateur in nature: they are covenants between people who are inexperienced or unskilled in being part of a pair. This subject has been on Tyler's mind for years; **Earthly Possessions**, a much earlier novel, describes Charlotte Emory's decision to leave her husband after many years of marriage, and the complications that ensue as she attempts to do so.

Two of the best books about marriage are Evan S. Connell's **Mr. Bridge** and **Mrs. Bridge**, which together are devastating in their realism, their honesty, and their ability to convey the lives and emotions of an upper-middle-class couple in 1930s Kansas City. The Bridges are two people more to be pitied than envied.

Few writers are as talented as Alison Lurie at capturing the emotional—or maybe "mercurial" would be a more accurate term—ups and downs of marriage and relationships. Three of her novels, originally published in the 1960s and '70s (at the beginning of the sexual revolution), bring readers into the center of marriages that are on the verge of breaking up: **Love and Friendship**, **The Nowhere City**, and **The War Between the Tates** (probably her best known).

Tabitha King's **The Book of Reuben** is the story of a marriage gone bad and a man's search for redemption.

Other novels about marriage include **Light Years** by James Salter, one of the most painful to read and possibly the most realistic novel about the changes that married couples go through; Brian Moore's sensitive and compulsively readable **The Doctor's Wife**, in which a woman must choose between her husband and her lover; Cathie Pelletier's **A Marriage Made at Woodstock,** an often laugh-out-loud picture of the dissolution of a longtime marriage; and **Say When** by Elizabeth Berg, which looks at both halves of a separated couple and relates what happens when Ellen tells Griffin that she's in love with the teacher of her adult-ed class in basic auto mechanics and wants a divorce.

Alice Hoffman's novel **Illumination Night**, which takes place in Martha's Vineyard, Massachusetts, tells how lack of money and a teenager's obsession come to threaten a marriage.

After reading all these relatively realistic novels, you might want some pure fun reading about a couple who seem to have no problems whatsoever, even though they're involved in a dangerous search for a Nazi sympathizer. If so, I highly recommend Helen MacInnes's **Above Suspicion**, a novel I reread regularly.

ME, ME, ME: AUTOBIOGRAPHIES AND MEMOIRS

W. H. Auden once wrote that "great art is clear thinking about mixed feelings." If we substitute the word "memoir" for "art," and add something about painful honesty, we get a good definition of the best of this genre.

In **Rain or Shine: A Family Memoir,** Cyra McFadden looks at her parents' difficult marriage—they couldn't stand living together but couldn't bear to live apart—and her own relationship to each of them.

In **Early Morning: Remembering My Father, William Stafford,** Kim Stafford uses his own memories as well as excerpts from his father's poetry and prose to give readers a picture of a prolific writer and popular teacher whose personal life was shaped by his early and lifelong commitment to pacifism. (Kim, his father's literary executor, also edited a collection of his father's writings called **Every War Has Two Losers: William Stafford on Peace and War**, which includes much of Stafford's antiwar writings.) Reading the son's affectionate memoir should send you back to the library or bookstore shelves to acquaint (or reacquaint) yourself with Stafford's poetry (you might want to begin with **The Way It Is: New and Selected Poems**).

Sebastian Matthews wrote **In My Father's Footsteps** as an attempt to understand his father, the poet William Matthews, who died suddenly at age fifty-five in 1997, and also to understand his father's legacy to him: how much is he his father's son, he asks. "A lush and a lech," Matthews says one of his female students called his father, "without a trace of malice." Drinker, womanizer, successful poet, and tenured professor at Cornell University, Williams was a thrice-divorced, difficult, often absent father who still played an enormous role in the lives of his sons. Read **Search Party: Collected Poems** to appreciate the depth and range of William Matthews's talent.

Patrimony: A True Story, Philip Roth's National Book Critics Circle Award–winning memoir of his father, relates Herman Roth's life and hard-fought death with sensitivity and great love, a quality of Roth-the-son and Roth-the-writer that we don't often see.

Call me a romantic, but even though Diana Athill went on to write several interesting books about her career in the publishing industry (including **Stet: An Editor's Life**), my favorite has always been her first memoir, **Instead of a Letter**, in which she describes the great lost love of her life.

Another heartbreaking and romantic memoir is Irish poet P. J. Kavanagh's **The Perfect Stranger**, the story of his unexpected meeting with (and marriage to) Sally, "the perfect stranger." The heartbreak comes at the end, and it is almost as difficult for the reader to bear as it was for the young man who lived through it.

American Childhood, Annie Dillard's memoir about growing up in Pittsburgh, Pennsylvania, in the 1950s, is suffused with her discovery of the beauty beneath the everydayness of her life.

In Sidetracks: Explorations of a Romantic Biographer, Richard Holmes describes the highways and byways he traveled in the course of writing the lives of Samuel Coleridge and Percy Bysshe Shelley, and tells the tales he couldn't quite fit into the published biographies.

Nine Hills to Nambonkaha: Two Years in the Heart of an African Village by Sarah Erdman is an insightful and thought-provoking memoir about the author's experiences as a health care worker in a small West African village. She introduces American readers to a place, a people, and a way of life that most of us will never experience—an Africa that is both devoutly Muslim and devotedly animistic.

Marie Arana's American Chica: Two Worlds, One Childhood, nominated for the National Book Award, is a beautifully written memoir about the difficulties and pleasures she experienced in moving between the cultures of her Peruvian father and her American mother.

London Times journalist Peter Godwin describes growing up in Rhodesia in the 1960s in Mukiwa: A White Boy in Africa, a powerful and moving testament and tribute to a land and people he loves.

Love in the Driest Season: A Family Memoir is the story of reporter Neely Tucker (a white man from Mississippi) and his African American wife Vita's attempts to adopt an abandoned baby in 1997 in AIDS-ravaged Zimbabwe, where their good intentions were thwarted at every turn by cultural biases and bureaucratic nightmares.

For more than thirty years, M. E. Kerr has been writing great novels for teens (I still think the best is Dinky Hocker Shoots Smack!). Her memoir of her own teen years, Me, Me, Me, Me, Me: Not a

Novel, not only recounts that period but also suggests how she used her own experiences to inform her novels.

Two wonderful memoirs set in the Persian Gulf are **Reading Lolita in Tehran: A Memoir in Books** by Azar Nafisi, which tells of the author's experiences in Iran with a group of women students using literature to explore their own lives and the political realities of their country during the rule of Islamic fundamentalists; and Roya Hakakian's **Journey from the Land of No: A Girlhood Caught in Revolutionary Iran**, which offers a moving portrait of growing up Jewish after the fall of the shah—the parallels to Nazi Germany are chilling.

Jay Neugeboren's **Imagining Robert: My Brother, Madness, and Survival: A Memoir** is a loving book about the author's brother, who was diagnosed with schizophrenia as a teenager. Paul Fussell's intense and angry memoir **Doing Battle: The Making of a Skeptic** is about how being an infantryman in World War II turned him into the man he is today—someone disinclined to take orders from anyone. In **Blue Blood**, Edward Conlon tells of graduating from Harvard and returning home to join the New York Police Department as a housing-authority cop. Katy Lederer's **Poker Face: A Girlhood Among Gamblers** is a fascinating memoir of life in a highly dysfunctional, poker-playing family. In **Turbulent Souls: A Catholic Son's Return to His Jewish Family**, Stephen J. Dubner writes about his strongly Catholic upbringing as the youngest of eight children and his decision as an adult to convert to Judaism, the religion that his parents had given up years before. **Cider with Rosie** is an affectionate memoir by Laurie Lee of growing up in the Cotswolds in the years following World War I. And Margot Adler's **Heretic Heart: A Journey Through Spirit and Revolution** includes this wonderful tribute to the author's mother: "[S]he was at home with physical affection and a wide range of emotions and was so absolutely and totally unconditional in her love that it sometimes still takes my breath away."

MEN CHANNELING WOMEN

Even though I know that the best writers can and usually do create characters who are very different from themselves, I am still shocked (or at least surprised) when a male author can get inside a woman's head and write so persuasively, so authentically, that I find myself frequently turning to the back cover to see if it is, indeed, a man who wrote the book. Of course, the classic novels in this category (as in the "Wayward Wives" section) are **Madame Bovary** by Gustave Flaubert and **Anna Karenina** by Leo Tolstoy, but here are some others.

The Darling *by Russell Banks*

Hannah Coulter *by Wendell Berry*

Mrs. Bridge *by Evan S. Connell*

A Yellow Raft in Blue Water *by Michael Dorris*

Middlesex *by Jeffrey Eugenides*

Memoirs of a Geisha *by Arthur Golden*

The Saskiad *by Brian Hall*

Dalva *by Jim Harrison*

Kate Vaiden *by Reynolds Price*

Mating *by Norman Rush*

I Heard My Sister Speak My Name *by Thomas Savage*

The Easter Parade *by Richard Yates*

MIDCENTURY: FROM WORLD WAR II TO VIETNAM

Even though, at well over eight hundred pages, this is a hefty book by anyone's standards, The Wise Men: Six Friends and the World They Made: George Kennan, Dean Acheson, Charles Bohlen, Robert Lovett, Averell Harriman, John McCloy by Walter Isaacson and Evan Thomas makes for fascinating and informative reading. Exploring the lives (minimally) and contributions (maximally) of the men who (arguably) had the most impact on both foreign and domestic policy from the 1930s onward, Thomas and Isaacson (both writers for *Time* magazine) illuminate much of the inside-the-Beltway (indeed, inside the State Department) thinking that led us through the Cold War and into the quagmire in Vietnam. This is required reading for anyone interested in American politics and policy of the mid- to late twentieth century.

You will find all six of these men cropping up in most books about U.S. foreign policy, and their own accounts of their lives in government service are also well worth reading. George F. Kennan's two-volume set of memoirs covers the years 1925 to 1963, but the best place to begin an encounter with Kennan's wit and sharp intelligence is in Sketches from a Life, which starts at his first diplomatic posting in 1927 and continues through the 1980s. The others' accounts include Dean Acheson's Present at the Creation: My Years in the State Department; Clark Clifford's Counsel to the President; Charles E. Bohlen's Witness to History, 1929–1969; and W. Averell Harriman's America and Russia in a Changing World: A Half Century of Personal Observation.

The president under whom these men served is given a lengthy but highly readable profile by David McCullough in Truman, which deservedly won the 1993 Pulitzer Prize for biography.

Another excellent group biography that focuses on the leaders of this era is **In the Time of the Americans: FDR, Truman, Eisenhower, Marshall, MacArthur—The Generation That Changed America's Role in the World** by David Fromkin. Like all of Fromkin's books, this is chock-full of facts, interpretations, and thought-provoking ideas.

WALTER MOSLEY: TOO GOOD TO MISS

Walter Mosley hit the ground running with his first published Ezekiel "Easy" Rawlins novel, **Devil in a Blue Dress** in 1990, and hasn't stopped since. Mosley's series of mysteries featuring Rawlins—almost all with a color in the title—are much more than simple whodunits. The novels take place in the black ghetto of East Los Angeles during the middle decades of the last century, against the background of the great black migration north in the 1940s to the riots in Watts in the 1960s. Rawlins, divorced, father to two unofficially adopted kids, is always (though usually reluctantly) drawn into solving crimes within the black community. Mosley offers readers a unique "everyman" view of the black experience as experienced from Rawlins's perspective. In Mosley's tight, lucid descriptions, realistic dialogue, and uncanny ability to immediately draw readers into the world he's created, his writing is not unlike that of Raymond Chandler's novels about Philip Marlowe.

In addition to the fine quality of Mosley's writing, what I most admire about his books is that he's impossible to pigeonhole as this or that kind of writer: in the last decade and a half he's written mysteries, literary fiction, and science fiction (**Blue Light**).

Here are the Easy Rawlins books, in the order in which you should read them:

Devil in a Blue Dress

A Red Death

White Butterfly

Black Betty

A Little Yellow Dog

Gone Fishin' *(the prequel to the series)*

Bad Boy Brawly Brown

Six Easy Pieces: Easy Rawlins Stories

Little Scarlet

Mosley has another series too, about a black bookstore owner in 1950s Los Angeles who is writing about the exploits of his best friend, Fearless Jones:

Fearless Jones

Fear Itself

Then there are his stand-alone collections of stories and novels:

Always Outnumbered, Always Outgunned

Blue Light

The Man in My Basement

R L's Dream *(which received the 1996 Literary Award for Fiction from the Black Caucus of the American Library Association)*

MS. MYSTERY

When mystery fans talk about their favorite female detectives, they always mention Kinsey Millhone, Sue Grafton's sleuth; V. I. Warshawski, the main character in Sara Paretsky's series; and Sharon McCone, Marcia Muller's heroine. (We probably shouldn't forget Nancy Drew and Judy Bolton, either, since they were the heroines of the first mysteries many of us ever read.) But female protagonists star in a wide range of good mystery novels—both stand-alones and books that are part of an ongoing series. Try a few of these while you're waiting for the next Grafton, Paretsky, or Muller.

Writer and scholar (as well as one-time murder suspect) Harriet Vane, the main character in four of Dorothy L. Sayers's classic mysteries (**Strong Poison, Have His Carcase, Gaudy Night,** and **Busman's Honeymoon**), is both a product of her time (the early 1920s) and far ahead of it (in her attitude toward love and marriage). Plot is probably the least of Sayers's concerns—she was far more interested in the lives of her characters.

Another novel set during the 1920s is Jacqueline Winspear's **Maisie Dobbs**. Maisie's first position was as a housemaid; she elevates herself to a career as a private investigator. Winspear, like Sayers, does an outstanding job of conveying post–World War I English society.

The mysteries by Gillian Linscott that star Nell Bray (among the best are **An Easy Day for a Lady** and **The Perfect Daughter**) take place in pre–World War I England. Many of the subplots of the novels deal with Nell and her friends fighting for women's rights in an inhospitable time and place.

I love the Laurie R. King novels that feature Mary Russell and Sherlock Holmes, who meet in **The Beekeeper's Apprentice**, where Mary becomes Holmes's student in detection. In subsequent books (**A Monstrous Regiment of Women**, for example) she becomes his partner, and finally (in **The Moor** and **The Game**) his wife.

Mma Precious Ramotswe, the proprietor of **The No. 1 Ladies' Detective Agency** in the novel by Alexander McCall Smith, is less a detective than a folk hero. This delightfully intuitive sleuth in rural Botswana helps friends, neighbors, and relatives with twenty-two cases, each of which reveals another facet of both Africa and Precious Ramotswe herself. It's followed up with **Tears of the Giraffe,**

Morality for Beautiful Girls, The Kalahari Typing School for Men, and The Full Cupboard of Life.

You can't exactly label as mysteries the hilarious series by Janet Evanovich about the beautiful, raunchy former discount lingerie buyer turned bounty hunter Stephanie Plum (from Trenton, New Jersey), although that's where you'll find them shelved in bookstores and libraries. They're better described, I think, as irresistible romps through the world of lowlifes. Begin with **One for the Money** and continue, laughing all the way, through **Two for the Dough, Three to Get Deadly, Four to Score, High Five, Hot Six, Seven Up, Hard Eight, To the Nines,** and **Ten Big Ones.**

Other contemporary series featuring female sleuths include Barbara Wilson's Cassandra Reilly series (including **The Death of a Much-Travelled Woman** and **Gaudí Afternoon**); Lia Matera's novels about lawyer/detective Willa Jansson (especially **Prior Convictions**); S. J. Rozan's series about Lydia Chin and her occasional partner, Bill Smith (**Mandarin Plaid** and **Reflecting the Sky** are two good ones); Eleanor Taylor Bland's series about Chicago-based African American detective Marti MacAlister (including **Whispers in the Dark** and **Windy City Dying**); Sujata Massey's series featuring Japanese American antiques dealer Rei Shimura (my favorite is **The Pearl Diver**); J. S. Borthwick's cozy series featuring teacher and sleuth Sarah Deane, including **Murder in the Rough** and **The Bridled Groom**; Laura Lippman's grand (and multi-award-winning) series about Baltimore newspaperwoman turned P.I. Tess Monaghan (including **Butchers Hill** and **By a Spider's Thread**); and Diane Mott Davidson's series featuring caterer Goldy Bear Schulz, which begins with **Catering to Nobody** (in which Goldy meets her future husband while investigating the death of her former father-in-law).

NAGGING MOTHERS,
CRYING CHILDREN

Some of the earliest accounts of the perils (many) and pleasures (somewhat fewer) of modern motherhood are still entertaining today. Jean Kerr's **Please Don't Eat the Daisies** (1957) and Erma Bombeck's **Just Wait Till You Have Children of Your Own!** (1971), **Motherhood: The Second Oldest Profession** (1983), and **Family: The Ties That Bind—and Gag!** (1987) all made a fine art of maternal kvetching.

More recent authors have continued to bang the pots and pans of family life. Joyce Maynard's **Domestic Affairs: Enduring the Pleasures of Motherhood and Family Life**, filled as it is with descriptions of family strife and just plain exhaustion, probably convinced many readers that they'd be better off childless.

It's hard to imagine that the true account of two Harvard academicians parenting a Down syndrome child can offer any humor, let alone be hysterically funny, but **Expecting Adam: A True Story of Birth, Rebirth, and Everyday Magic** by Martha Beck is a unique mixture of sophisticated humor, satire, self-deprecation, and spirituality.

Lori Borgman, a nationally syndicated columnist, presents a collection of her columns in **I Was a Better Mother Before I Had Kids**, offering advice on everything from driving with your teenager to protecting against household hazards to keeping it all together.

"Geezers with children" is columnist Judith Newman's description of her husband and herself as they cope with their infant twin sons in **You Make Me Feel Like an Unnatural Woman: Diary of a New (Older) Mother**. This humorous look at late-in-life pregnancy and motherhood considers such profound questions as whether parenthood is worth $70,000 and eight months of throwing up.

Operating Instructions: A Journal of My Son's First Year by Anne Lamott depicts with unusual candor the frequent hilarity and exhaustion of single parenthood.

Callie's Tally: An Accounting of Baby's First Year (Or What My Daughter Owes Me!) is another irreverent look at parenthood, this one in the form of a daily diary in which Betsy Howie itemizes the cost of her new daughter.

Rachel Cusk's A Life's Work: On Becoming a Mother looks at her new experience of being a mother from the perspective of the psychological and emotional changes it brings, puncturing a few accepted truths (that new motherhood is an unalloyed joy, for instance) along the way.

NATURE WRITING

When a friend lent me her copy of Ann Zwinger's Downcanyon: A Naturalist Explores the Colorado River through the Grand Canyon, she apologized that it was in such bad shape—so warped and water-stained. It turned out that she'd taken it with her while rafting down the Colorado River and used it both as a guide and as pleasure reading. Even if you're not actually going down the rapids on the Colorado, this book will make you feel as if you are.

The Last Wild Edge: One Woman's Journey from the Arctic Circle to the Olympic Rain Forest by Susan Zwinger, Ann's daughter, includes descriptions of her travels "over twelve years and eighteen degrees latitude," inviting readers to share her delight in the world around her.

Kathleen Dean Moore is a philosopher, and her two award-winning collections of nature writing, **Riverwalking: Reflections on Moving Water** and **Holdfast: At Home in the Natural World**, connect readers with a world of beauty and grace.

Green Treasury: A Journey through the World's Great Nature Writing, edited by Edwin Way Teale, includes selections from writers from the mid-nineteenth to mid-twentieth centuries. Teale's own love of nature is seen in a quartet of books about the journeys he and his wife took across the country: **North with the Spring; Autumn Across America; Journey into Summer;** and **Wandering Through Winter**. On their car trips, Teale noted not only the natural world about them but also the people they met and the experiences they had en route. Since these books were written more than fifty years ago, much has changed—there are interstates, for example, and "nature" is far less readily found—but these books beckon us to emulate Teale's own travels, and they paint an enchanting portrait of a world that is, sadly, nearly lost to us.

David James Duncan's subtitle for **My Story As Told by Water** says a lot: **Confessions, Druidic Rants, Reflections, Bird-Watchings, Fish-Stalkings, Visions, Songs and Prayers Refracting Light, from Living Rivers, in the Age of the Industrial Dark**. But even this seemingly comprehensive phrase does not fully convey the beauty of the writing and Duncan's crusading spirit about the absolute necessity of keeping the wild, wild.

When you're looking for good books about the natural world, you're bound to run into a worthy bird book or two or three, such as Candace Savage's **Bird Brains: The Intelligence of Crows, Ravens, Magpies, and Jays;** Robert Winkler's **Going Wild: Adventures with Birds in the Suburban Wilderness;** and Alan Tennant's **On the Wing: To the Edge of the Earth with the Peregrine Falcon**. *Book Lust* also has a section on birds and birding, called "Bird Brains."

NEAR NOVELS:
LINKED SHORT STORIES

What's the appeal of a collection of linked short stories? Short-story aficionados will appreciate the fact that they get to spend more time with an especially loved character. And lovers of novels will feel that these stories have nearly the depth and expansiveness of a full-length fictional work. Here are some particularly good examples of the genre.

Sherwood Anderson's **Winesburg, Ohio,** published in 1919, is a chronicle of small-town life in Ohio. This collection of loosely con-nected short stories reveals the inner lives of a number of the town's residents, and gives readers a sense of the range of secrets—from silly to profound—that we all keep hidden from even those closest to us.

In 1930s Homewood, the black community of Pittsburgh, three generations are united by the music of Albert Wilkes in John Edgar Wideman's collection of linked short stories, **Sent for You Yesterday.**

Life on both sides of the racial divide in a small Ohio town is the subject of Lynn Lauber's collection of linked stories, **White Girls.** She continued chronicling the lives of many of the same characters in **21 Sugar Street.**

Justin Cronin's **Mary and O'Neil** is a little less about the title characters, two people who eventually marry each other, than about the people surrounding them, especially O'Neil's family. The sto-ries focus on decisive moments in the lives of the characters: the unmarried Mary's decision to have an abortion; the moment that O'Neil's sister learns from her son that her husband is having an affair; a visit by O'Neil's parents to meet his first serious girlfriend; Mary and O'Neil's wedding day. The first story, especially, is heart-breaking and true.

No Bones by Anna Burns is an edgy and surreal collection about Amelia, whom we meet as a young schoolgirl during Ireland's "Troubles" and follow through her own internal troubles as well.

"Quirky" is the best word to describe the life and adventures of the central character in **Disappearing Ingenue: The Misadventures of Eleanor Stoddard** by Melissa Pritchard. It's also a good word to describe the book itself, as we discover that locations change, names are switched, marital status is uncertain, and careers are fuzzy. Throughout Eleanor's life people deceive her—husbands, friends, students, parents—just as Eleanor's life deceives the reader, who is always trying to figure out what is real.

The stories in **Island: The Complete Stories** by Alistair MacLeod all take place on Cape Breton Island, Nova Scotia, and are marked by their observant and honest portrayals of human behavior, set against the pace and texture of rural life.

The central character of **The Elizabeth Stories** by Isabel Huggan doesn't fit into her family, her body, or her narrow-minded small town in 1950s Canada.

The Family Markowitz by Allegra Goodman links the lives of a Jewish-American family, from grandmother Rose, who's dealing with old age, loneliness, and widowhood by downing Percodan pills, to granddaughter Miriam, who shocks her secular parents with her desire to become an Orthodox Jew.

Buddy comes of age in small-town New Jersey in Tom Perrotta's heartfelt yet unsentimental **Bad Haircut: Stories of the Seventies.**

Few fictional characters are as memorable as Rhoda Manning, a recurring character in Ellen Gilchrist's writings (and, as we learn in the introduction to **Rhoda: A Life in Stories,** based at least some of the time on Gilchrist's own life). She is Gilchrist's most captivating, complex, and, as a child, precocious character—someone you can't forget.

Other notable near novels include Julie Hecht's **Do the Windows Open?** and Bliss Broyard's **My Father, Dancing.**

NEW ENGLAND NOVELS

Nnew England is known for its long, harsh winters, its storied history, and the variety of its geography—from ocean to mountains, from small mill towns to vibrant big cities. All of which makes it a worthy setting for a lot of good fiction, including a hefty stack of mysteries. Try these:

National politics in New Hampshire is the backdrop for Mark Costello's **Big If,** a terrific character-driven novel, postmodernly big in scope but intimate in its depictions of a group of people whose lives converge during a primary presidential election campaign.

New England mysteries include Robert B. Parker's tough and atmospheric Spenser series (my two favorites are **The Godwulf Manuscript** and **The Judas Goat**). Linda Barnes's series of mysteries features private investigator Carlotta Carlyle, who operates out of Boston and environs; two recent chronicles of her exploits, **The Big Dig** and **Flashpoint,** are especially entertaining. Philip R. Craig (**The Woman Who Walked into the Sea; Vineyard Blues**) sets all his mysteries on Martha's Vineyard. George V. Higgins, best known for his great use of dialogue to propel his plots forward, has been writing about Boston for more than a quarter of a century; his first novel, **The Friends of Eddie Coyle,** is often cited as one of the seminal works of crime fiction. Margaret Lawrence's **Hearts and Bones** is the first of a fine historical mystery series set in the post–Revolutionary War period, all featuring midwife Hannah Trevor.

Although Elizabeth Gilbert is probably better known for her well-reviewed (and very interesting) biography **The Last American**

Man, I took more pleasure from her entertaining character-driven first novel, **Stern Men**. Set in the 1970s, it's the story of the long-time rivalry between families of lobstermen living on two fictitious islands off the Maine coast, and the young woman who somehow brings them together. This is a good choice for readers who like quirky characters and interesting settings.

Other good novels set in New England include John Gardner's **October Light**, Richard Russo's **Empire Falls**, Bret Lott's **The Man Who Owned Vermont**, Howard Frank Mosher's **A Stranger in the Kingdom** and other novels, Donna Tartt's **The Secret History**, Lynn Stegner's novella, **Pipers at the Gates of Dawn**, Douglas Hobbie's **This Time Last Year**, Alix Wilber's **The Wives' Tale**, Don Metz's **King of the Mountain**, and Sinclair Lewis's **It Can't Happen Here**. And don't miss **Judevine**, David Budbill's collection of narrative poems that capture the hardscrabble life in Vermont.

THE 1960S IN FACT AND FICTION

I'm a product of the 1960s; I think that's why I'm drawn to the books in this section.

Three novels about the lives of political radicals of the 1960s (à la the Weather Underground) make for good reading indeed. **Vida**, the eponymous main character of Marge Piercy's best novel, went underground during the late 1960s and is still living in fear of being captured by the government a decade later. Her claustrophobic and panicky life is both vividly drawn and unforgettable. **Vida** was published in 1979, so it is more contemporaneous with the events it's describing than is Susan Choi's **American Woman** or Neil Gordon's **The Company You Keep**, which were published almost a quarter of a century later. Taken together, these three novels convey the essence of 1960s radicalism (and its consequences).

Reading David Hajdu's group biography **Positively 4th Street: The Lives and Times of Joan Baez, Bob Dylan, Mimi Baez Fariña, and Richard Fariña** brought back all the hours and hours of music that gave me such pleasure throughout the 1960s. (Richard Fariña was himself the author of a novel set during the late 1950s, **Been Down So Long It Looks Like Up to Me.**)

Mark Kurlansky looks at a crucial year in **1968: The Year That Rocked the World.** He covers not just the United States (where the murders of Robert Kennedy and Martin Luther King Jr. and the violent demonstrations at the Democratic National Convention in Chicago occurred) but also events in France, Vietnam, and Prague, to name just a few places. Like all of Kurlansky's books, this is compulsively interesting reading. Clark Clifford, a quintessential Washington, D.C., political animal, called 1968 "the year that everything went wrong," and when you read this book you'll understand the truth of that statement. (For lots more about Mark Kurlansky's books, see "Mark Kurlansky: Too Good to Miss" in *Book Lust.*)

A copy of Kirkpatrick Sale's **SDS: Ten Years Toward a Revolution** is expensive these days, but it's worth every dollar if you have any interest in the 1960s. This is the still-unsurpassed history of Students for a Democratic Society, from the organization's formation in 1960 to its split into two separate groups competing for the soul of the American New Left in 1972. Another, complementary perspective on SDS is offered by James Miller, in **Democracy Is in the Streets: From Port Huron to the Siege of Chicago**, while Todd Gitlin's **The Sixties: Years of Hope, Days of Rage** is written from an insider's perspective: Gitlin was elected president of SDS in 1963.

No discussion of books about the 1960s would be complete without a mention of the books written about a 1964 cross-country trip that the Merry Pranksters, a group led by Ken Kesey, took in

Kesey's psychedelically painted 1939 International Harvester school bus called Further. Read Tom Wolfe's **The Electric Kool-Aid Acid Test**, Paul Perry's **On the Bus**, and Ken Kesey's own **The Further Inquiry**.

OH, BROTHER!

Cain and Abel, Romulus and Remus, Seth and Osiris, Eteocles and Polyneices, and Jacob and Esau—brothers have loved and hated one another (sometimes at the same time) throughout history. And they provide a fertile subject for writers, as seen below:

Russell Banks's Affliction

James Carlos Blake's In the Rogue Blood

Ethan Canin's Blue River

Dan Chaon's You Remind Me of Me

Pete Dexter's The Paperboy

Ivan Doig's Bucking the Sun

Tim Gautreaux's The Clearing

Sherwood Kiraly's Big Babies *(the only even marginally humorous book in this list)*

Wally Lamb's I Know This Much Is True

J. Robert Lennon's On the Night Plain

Martin Quigley's Winners and Losers

Thomas Savage's The Power of the Dog

John Steinbeck's East of Eden

Guy Vanderhaeghe's The Last Crossing

Larry Watson's Montana 1948

OTHER PEOPLE'S SHOES

There are some books—both fiction and nonfiction—that succeed in putting you inside the main character's head in such a way that you experience the world as they do. And when their experiences are colored by psychological or physical disorders, we are privileged to know exactly what it must be like to live differently in the world. I found each of these books both eye-opening and deeply moving.

The Curious Incident of the Dog in the Night-Time by Mark Haddon is a terrific novel about fifteen-year-old Christopher, who has Asperger's syndrome (a form of autism), and his decision to find out who murdered the dog next door. A memoir about the experience of Asperger's is Dawn Prince-Hughes's **Songs of the Gorilla Nation: My Journey Through Autism,** in which the author describes how her autism went undiagnosed throughout her childhood; not until she was a young woman working with gorillas at the zoo did she begin to be able to connect to the world beyond herself.

Two good books about stuttering are **Dead Languages,** an autobiographical novel by David Shields, and Marty Jezer's memoir **Stuttering: A Life Bound Up in Words.**

The Diving Bell and the Butterfly: A Memoir of Life in Death by Jean-Dominique Bauby shows just how strong the human spirit can be in overcoming seemingly insurmountable injuries. Bauby, who was the editor of *Elle France,* suffered a stroke that left him unable to communicate except by moving his left eyelid; painstakingly, blink by blink, he wrote this moving memoir (and died two days after the book was published in France).

Reading about the people whom Oliver Sacks describes so compassionately in **The Man Who Mistook His Wife for a Hat and Other Clinical Tales** makes us painfully aware of the mysteries of the mind and the nervous system, and how quickly our lives can be turned upside down by chance or bad luck or perhaps a rogue gene.

When you finish Sacks, read Floyd Skloot's collection of essays, **In the Shadow of Memory**, a moving account of his life after he contracted a virus in 1988 that caused profound neurological damage to his brain, but also a thought-provoking discussion of how the brain operates (or doesn't) in people suffering from Alzheimer's or other brain injuries.

Other good nonfiction written from the inside out includes **As I Live and Breathe: Notes of a Patient-Doctor** by Jamie Weisman, a physician suffering from a congenital autoimmune deficiency disorder; **Breathing for a Living** by Laura Rothenberg, the story of a young woman with cystic fibrosis (be sure to read this during a happy period in your life, and not during the oppressive darkness of winter); and **Autobiography of a Face** by Lucy Grealy, about growing up with a deformed face (due to cancer of the jaw at the age of nine) in a society that seems to value physical beauty above all else. (And when you're done with that, read Ann Patchett's moving memoir of her relationship with Lucy, **Truth & Beauty: A Friendship**.)

Two compelling books about life in a wheelchair are Nancy Mairs's **Waist-High in the World: A Life Among the Nondisabled** and John Hockenberry's **Moving Violations: War Zones, Wheelchairs, and Declarations of Independence**.

Two novels about the experience of being deaf are Canadian author Frances Itani's **Deafening** and Joanne Greenberg's **In This Sign**.

PARROTS

I think the first parrot I ever met in fiction was Polynesia, the good Doctor Dolittle's right-hand man—er, bird—in Hugh Lofting's **The Voyages of Dr. Dolittle**. Then I discovered Kiki, who accompanies the children in Enid Blyton's Adventure series (e.g., **The Island of Adventure**) on their various adventures. So, fond as I am of Iris Murdoch, I was pleased to discover a parrot in **The Book and the Brotherhood** and then to find other tales in which parrots play a significant role.

Those include **The Loop** by Joe Coomer; Michael Chabon's **The Final Solution: A Story of Detection**; Julian Barnes's **Flaubert's Parrot** (although one of them is stuffed); Jim Paul's **Elsewhere in the Land of Parrots**; "Birdland," one of the stories in Michael Knight's **Goodnight, Nobody**, about pet parrots let loose in Rhode Island who spend their winters in Elbow, Alabama; and Bill Richardson's **Bachelor Brothers' Bed and Breakfast Pillow Book**, throughout which the delightful parrot Mrs. Rochester mutters darkly.

PLOTS FOR PLOTZING

Some novels' plots are so bizarre, so off-the-wall, so quirky, that they almost beggar description. Whenever I encounter one of these books, I cannot fathom how someone came up with the idea, let alone carried it through with such panache. Try these, and you'll see what I mean.

Gilligan's Wake by Tom Carson is a postmodern romp through the last half of the twentieth century, narrated in turn by the seven characters who were marooned, with Gilligan, on the television show

Gilligan's Island. The Professor, Ginger, Mrs. Howell, and all the rest interact with the likes of Robert Oppenheimer, John Kennedy, Alger Hiss, Sammy Davis Jr., and fictional entities such as Daisy Buchanan. At least read the chapter narrated by the Professor—which all by itself is worth the price of the book.

In **Gentlemen of Space**, George Finch looks back, from the perspective of adulthood, on the central event of his childhood: in 1976 his father, science teacher Jerry Finch, won a contest to be the first civilian to go to the moon with Buzz Aldrin and Neil Armstrong. (It was Apollo 19, in case you don't remember.) Unlike the two "professional" astronauts, Jerry Finch decides to remain there, high above earth, regularly updating his son with phone calls from the moon. The real subjects of Ira Sher's tender and imaginative novel are the trickiness and slippery nature of memory and all our protective self-deceptions.

Okay, take a libido-driven liberal president dying under suspicious (but clearly sexual) circumstances in the apartment of a beautiful young woman from Texas, throw in a cokehead vice president, a grieving but realistic widow, a recently fired newspaperman, a homeless poet who spiraled into mental illness after a bad review many years back by book critic Jonathan Yardley of the *Washington Post*, a certifiably stupid Mafia bagman on the run from both the Secret Service and the Mafia with $656,000 and the president's head in an attaché case, a gay football player, an aging Mafia don, his impressionable grandson, and several White House staffers (some crooked and conniving, others just conniving), and you have all the ingredients that make Tim Sandlin's **Honey Don't** so much fun to read.

The engaging and frequently chuckle-inducing **The Underground Man** by Mick Jackson was a finalist for the 1997 Booker Prize (losing out to Jim Crace's **Quarantine**) and is loosely drawn from the life of one of the most outlandish members of the Victorian-era peerage. It's written in the form of a journal so that we watch, firsthand, as the fictional duke is—as he fears—losing his mind. (Mystery writer Ross MacDonald wrote a mystery with the same title, so don't pick up the wrong one; MacDonald's is also great, but different.)

Clearly, Mark Dunn's imagination knows no bounds—consider both **Ella Minnow Pea: A Progressively Lipogrammatic Epistolary Fable** and **Ibid: A Life**. The former, whose subtitle is "A Novel in Letters," is laugh-out-loud funny (but also thought provoking). In order to find the solution to a nightmarish situation, the citizens of Nollup must construct a sentence of thirty-two letters or less that includes every letter in the alphabet. The latter is, as its title might imply, a novel written entirely in footnotes.

If you're looking for an adrenaline rush of a read, pick up Richard K. Morgan's **Altered Carbon**, a stylish mixture of hardboiled mystery and high-tech science fiction. It's set in a very realistic twenty-fifth-century world (in Morgan's capable hands, that's no oxymoron) in which hotels pack lethal weapons, the essence of humans is the digital pack that contains all of their memories and personality (and that can be downloaded into new body after new body), and life is dirt cheap. There's plenty of graphic violence, several scenes of drug-enhanced sex, and enough going on to entice even the most jaded reader. The second in the series, **Broken Angels**, is no less imaginative but a whole lot darker.

Some of the most interesting stories are those in which the author begins with real events and takes off from them, as Elwood Reid does in **D.B.**, a reimagining of the mysterious case of D. B. Cooper, who in 1971 hijacked an eastbound Northwest Airlines 727 from Portland, Oregon, and threatened to blow it up unless he received $200,000 in cash and two parachutes. What we know is that after his demands were met, he jumped from the plane somewhere in the Pacific Northwest and was never seen or heard from again. Reid's prose is uncluttered, his characters are three-dimensional, and the plot is resolved brilliantly, all adding up to one great read.

If you can imagine Stephen King writing satirical fiction, then **Kings of Infinite Space** by James Hynes is just the book for you. A devilishly vindictive cat named Charlotte, zombies, a human cog in a bureaucratic machine, and an attractive mailwoman who wants to better her life all come together to force Paul Trilby (first met in Hynes's **Publish and Perish: Three Tales of Tenure and Terror**) into a decision worthy of Faust.

Max Barry's satirical writing is both very funny and extremely scary. In **Jennifer Government**, a fast-moving, cautionary tale of the near future, the world is run by competing corporations, the NRA and the police force are publicly traded companies, crimes get investigated only if the victim can afford to pay the bill, and everyone's last name indicates their employer. Hack Nike is hired by two shadowy figures way up on the corporate ladder to commit murder in order to increase the popularity—that is, to develop the street cred—of the company's new line of $2,500 (per pair) sneakers. Enter Jennifer Government (who has a barcode tattooed under her eye), determined to bring the wrongdoers to their knees and avenge herself on John Nike, one of the men who hired Hack. It's chill-inducing, pointed, and a picture of an oh-so-possible future.

Susanna Clarke's **Jonathan Strange & Mr. Norrell** is a winsome example of an "alternative history" that falls in the fantasy and science fiction genre. (This means that fans of historical fiction will find it in the sci-fi/fantasy section of bookstores and libraries.) Set in the early 1800s in a perfectly plausible though imagined England, Clarke's novel tells the story of two warring magicians who come up against the sinister and even more powerful magical machinations of the Raven King, who has ruled his kingdom for more than three hundred years. Clarke uses period language, tone, and even spellings to successfully persuade the reader that what she's conjured up is absolutely true. She's even included footnotes to "refresh" the memories of readers who might have forgotten some of the more arcane events of the magical past. The Napoleonic Wars are raging, people can be brought back from the dead (though at a price), and magic is alive in the world—what could be more real than that?

POETRY PLEASERS

When I read through *Book Lust* months after it was published, I realized that it included very little poetry. Because poetry is one of my most enjoyable reading experiences and I participate in a weekly poetry discussion group, I found this surprising. So I determined that *More Book Lust* would have a lot more poetry.

Each week I am confirmed in my belief that reading aloud and discussing a work of poetry—considering the two halves of a poem, as Laurence Perrine suggested in **Sound and Sense: An Introduction to Poetry**—deepens most people's appreciation for the work itself. It certainly deepens mine. Of course, in reading, discussing, or thinking about a poem, you don't want to get into the sort of situation that Billy Collins describes in his wonderfully sly poem "Introduction to Poetry":

> I want them to waterski
> across the surface of a poem
> waving at the author's name on shore.
>
> But all they want to do
> is tie the poem to a chair with rope
> and torture a confession out of it.

Here are some poems that not only make for wonderful reading but also have the potential to generate great discussions. Most can be found in the poets' collected works, or you can ask your friendly librarian to help you track them down. (There are many, many more poems—and poets—that I'd have liked to include, but space constraints prevented it.)

W. H. Auden—"Musée des Beaux Arts" and "As I Walked Out One Evening"

Raymond Carver—"What the Doctor Said"

Almost everything by Billy Collins, including "Forgetfulness" and "Workshop"

Countee Cullen—"Yet Do I Marvel" and "Incident"

ee cummings—"anyone lived in a pretty how town"

Carl Dennis—"Prophet"

Stephen Dunn—"A Secret Life"

Cornelius Eady—"Why Do So Few Blacks Study Creative Writing?"

T. S. Eliot—"The Love Song of J. Alfred Prufrock"

Almost all of Robert Frost, especially "Provide, Provide" and "The Oven Bird"

Louise Glück—"Celestial Music"

Edward Hirsch—"The Welcoming" and "Colette"

Jane Hirshfield—"Rebus"

Gerard Manley Hopkins—"Spring and Fall: To a Young Child"

Ted Hughes—"Wind"

Randall Jarrell—"The Death of the Ball Turret Gunner" (there is so much feeling and meaning compressed into this five-line poem)

Jane Kenyon—"Happiness"

All of David Kirby's poems, especially "The Search for Baby Combover," "The Elephant of the Sea," and "The Ha-Ha, Part L: I Cry My Heart, Antonio"

Philip Larkin—"I Remember, I Remember" or "Church Going" or, really, anything he wrote

Philip Levine—"The Mercy" and "Clouds Above the Sea"

Heather McHugh—"What He Thought"

Sharon Olds—"I Go Back to May 1937"

Mary Oliver—"Wild Geese"

Wilfred Owen—"Dulce et Decorum Est"

Carl Phillips—"Luncheon on the Grass"

Katha Pollitt—"The Wisdom of the Desert Fathers"

Marie Ponsot—"Winter"

William Stafford—"The Discovery of Daily Experience"

Wallace Stevens—"Table Talk"

Michael Swift's mysterious "At Marlborough House"

Wislawa Szymborska—"Funeral (II)" and "The End and the Beginning"

James Tate—"The Blind Heron"

Dylan Thomas—"In My Craft or Sullen Art"

William Carlos Williams—"Tract"

Terence Winch—"The Bells Are Ringing for Me and Chagall"

QUEEN VICTORIA
AND HER TIMES

Queen Victoria ascended to the throne of England in 1837, when she was only eighteen, and ruled Britannia (which ruled the waves) until her death in 1901. We tend to think of Victorian England as being a time of repression (in dress, libido, and social mores), but it seems to have been quite the opposite, seething with emotions and outré behaviors. Here are some good choices among the many available histories, biographies, and memoirs of this incredibly rich period—a time that encompassed the Industrial Revolution and produced such luminaries as Charles Dickens, Charles Darwin, Karl Marx, Rudyard Kipling, Benjamin Disraeli, Thomas Hardy, and Robert and Elizabeth Barrett Browning.

Gwen Raverat, the granddaughter of Charles Darwin, writes enchantingly about growing up in Cambridge, England, in the late nineteenth and early twentieth centuries, in her memoir **Period Piece: A Victorian Childhood**. It's filled with genuine characters— Cambridge dons, her American mother, her many cousins, her various aunts and uncles—and much affection for that time and place. There's a smile to be had on every page, and it's an indispensable read for anyone interested in that time period.

A. N. Wilson's **The Victorians** surveys the age and is replete with mini-biographies of the leading figures and their accomplishments, while **Inventing the Victorians** by Matthew Sweet debunks all the received truths about the Victorian age. (You just know, reading Sweet, how much he enjoyed writing this book.)

Lytton Strachey, one of the leading Bloomsberries (that group of writers and artists whose best-known member is Virginia Woolf), disliked the whole Victorian aesthetic. In Eminent Victorians, he had a lot of fun debunking the myths surrounding the period's most well-known figures: Florence Nightingale, Cardinal Manning, Dr. Arnold (the headmaster of Rugby School), and Charles George Gordon, who died at Khartoum.

Strachey also wrote Queen Victoria, and even though he was not her biggest fan, he produced what is arguably one of the better biographies of her. Other biographies not to be missed by Anglophiles are Christopher Hibbert's Queen Victoria: A Personal History and Elizabeth Longford's compact Queen Victoria, which is perfect for those who want to decide whether they're interested in reading deeper into the topic.

There's also a whole group of novels that fall under the heading of "Faux Victoriana." They're the work of contemporary writers who re-create the Victorian era: novels in which you can hear the horses' hooves striking the cobblestones and the hiss of gas lamps being lit, and feel immersed in the chill of the London fogs. So when you've done Dickens to death, try these novels.

Rose by Martin Cruz Smith is quite a departure from his best-known novel, Gorky Park. Jonathan Blair, an adventurer down on his luck who was kicked out of Africa for misbehavior, and who is suffering from both malaria and an overdependence on gin, arrives in a mining town in England, where's he's been hired by a bishop to locate his daughter Charlotte's missing fiancé, a young cleric.

Maurice Edelman's two biographical novels about the great prime minister Benjamin Disraeli, Disraeli in Love and Disraeli Rising, illuminate the politics of the nineteenth century and the Jewish Disraeli's particularly anomalous position in society.

Anne Perry has been producing solidly enjoyable and true-to-the-times mysteries for more than a quarter of a century. She writes two different series, both set in Victorian England. One features Inspector Thomas Pitt and his wife, Charlotte; my favorites are **Resurrection Road** and **Bedford Square**, but you can't go wrong with any of them. The other series is about private "enquiry agent" (i.e., investigator) William Monk; try **The Shifting Tide** and **Death of a Stranger**. Neither series must absolutely be read in order, but you may enjoy them a bit more if you begin at the beginning with Pitt's first adventure, **The Cater Street Hangman**, and Monk's first, **The Face of a Stranger**.

READY, SET, LIFTOFF:
BOOKS TO IGNITE DISCUSSION

I think the best books for groups to discuss are those in which the ending is deliberately ambiguous, so that every reader will have a different answer to the question "Well, what really did happen?" Or books in which the main character is faced with a difficult choice that resonates with readers no matter their age or race or ethnicity. Here are some that I've found work extremely well in generating heated discussion among book group participants.

Deborah Schupack's **The Boy on the Bus** begins with every parent's worst nightmare—the disappearance of your child. Only in this case, a boy who looks a lot like Meg's eight-year-old son, Charlie, gets off the school bus at the end of the day. The problem is, he seems to be very different from the real Charlie in some definable ways (he doesn't have asthma and Charlie did) and in some indefinable ways (Meg just knows it's not her son). Many readers will no doubt wonder why the family doesn't just do a DNA test to find out, but the questions the novel raises about identity are fascinating.

First-time novelist Ann Packer's **The Dive from Clausen's Pier** asks readers to consider the following question: what do we owe those we love, and what do we owe ourselves? Or, in plainer language, how much sacrifice is too much? When Carrie's fiancé, with whom she's just about fallen out of love, dives off the pier on Memorial Day into water that is much too shallow, he breaks his neck and will be paralyzed for the rest of his life. What should Carrie do? Readers everywhere react to twenty-something Carrie's choice differently—some with frustration (I know someone who actually threw the book across the room in disgust when she read what Carrie decided to do), with applause, or with tears.

The paperback edition of Leah Hager Cohen's novel **Heart, You Bully, You Punk** has a wonderful cover. What makes it perfect for a book group is that it poses an interesting dilemma: when your head tells you one thing and your heart another, which one should you listen to? The answer to this conundrum will change the lives of the three main characters: a teenage girl, her father, and her math teacher at the private school she attends. One question to begin with is "What does the novelist think about the role of the heart in decision making?"

Barbara Gowdy's **The Romantic** asks us to consider yet another human dilemma—what it means to try to save the person we love best from destroying themselves, while knowing full well that they're hell-bent on making that task impossible for us. Louise, who has loved Abel since both were children, must decide how much responsibility she has for ensuring his well-being when she realizes that Abel is becoming increasingly self-destructive and seems determined to drink himself to death.

Two novels by Anne Ursu make for wonderful discussions. In the first, **Spilling Clarence**, a chemical that causes people to remember everything in their lives infects a city's population—and everyone has a different reaction to being bombarded by their memories.

Some characters are comforted, while others find the return of the past too difficult to bear. The second, **The Disapparation of James**, has an inconclusive and mysterious ending that will drive some readers crazy. Physician Hannah and stay-at-home dad Justin Woodrow take their children—Greta, seven, and James, five—to the circus for Greta's birthday; everyone in the family is thrilled when James is selected to appear on stage as part of the last act of the evening. The magician's final stunt is supposed to make James disappear, but it backfires horribly when James actually does disappear. Ursu takes us inside the lives of all the characters, including the magician, the policeman who is assigned to the case, and of course James's immediate family, offering parallel realities and alternative possibilities of what really happened.

For some good nonfiction selections for your book group, see the "Dewey Deconstructed" section.

MARK SALZMAN: TOO GOOD TO MISS

I usually make it a point not to go to readings by writers I really like, because what if I find them disagreeable or, worse, pretentious? Then, too, after I hear authors read, I can no longer read their books without their voice or public persona coming between me and the words on the page. Horrors! But I have to say that when I interviewed Mark Salzman, I found him to be unaffected, verbally adroit, and very, very funny—all the qualities one looks for in an interviewee. And—it probably goes without saying—he's an awfully good writer of both fiction and nonfiction.

His novels include **The Soloist**, in which former child prodigy Renne Sundheimer comes up against two events that will change his life: he is on a jury considering the murder of a Zen master, and he reluctantly agrees to teach a brilliant child cellist; and **Lying**

Awake, the story of a cloistered nun whose gift of mystical visions comes with a price: severe headaches that seem to be due to a mild form of epilepsy. Should she take a chance on surgery, if its success at easing her pain may also mean that she will never experience that spiritual union with God again?

Salzman's memoirs include Iron & Silk, an account of teaching English in China right after college, and of his classes in the martial arts with one of the leading Chinese teachers; Lost in Place: Growing Up Absurd in Suburbia, a funny, self-deprecating, and totally irresistible story of growing up as the oldest child of three in a middle-class Connecticut family; and True Notebooks: A Writer's Year at Juvenile Hall, about teaching creative writing at a detention center for "high risk" juveniles outside Los Angeles.

SCIENCE 101

Most colleges offer some good science courses aimed specifically at non-scientists ("Physics for Poets" was my own personal favorite). There are also many very readable books written for non-scientists, and even non–science majors. Here's a diverse list of good popular science reading.

Barbara Freese's Coal: A Human History looks at the rise and fall of this black mineral, discussing both its history and related environmental concerns.

Hannah Holmes's The Secret Life of Dust: From the Cosmos to the Kitchen Counter, the Big Consequences of Little Things studies something that most of us brush off as insignificant.

The molecule as hero or villain in various historical events is the subject of Napoleon's Buttons: How 17 Molecules Changed History by Penny LeCouteur and Jay Burreson.

David Foster Wallace considers the two-thousand-year quest to understand infinity in **Everything and More: A Compact History of Infinity**; even though it's compact, it's not always easy reading, but it's certainly fascinating.

Jay Ingram's entertaining **The Science of Everyday Life** covers everything from the creation of the universe to why, when you chew them in the dark, there's a bluish green light emanating from wintergreen-flavored LifeSavers candies.

Donna Shirley describes her childhood as a space-crazy kid, her education as the only woman in the engineering program at the University of Oklahoma, and her management of the Mars Exploration Project at the Jet Propulsion Laboratory, which sent *Pathfinder* and the rover *Sojourner* to Mars, in **Managing Martians**.

Dr. Tatiana (aka evolutionary biologist Olivia Judson) offers answers to all manner of sexual questions from non-human creatures great and small, in **Dr. Tatiana's Sex Advice to All Creation.** Imagine Dr. Ruth answering questions from the likes of sticklebugs and katydids, and you'll have a good picture of this book.

Bill McKibben makes a plea for restraint in **Enough: Staying Human in an Engineered Age**, arguing, "We need to do an unlikely thing: We need to survey the world we now inhabit and proclaim it good. Good enough."

Amir D. Aczel's **Pendulum: Léon Foucault and the Triumph of Science** offers a biography of a brilliant scientist who had almost no formal education, and explains how he proved that the earth actually does rotate on its axis.

CAROL SHIELDS:
TOO GOOD TO MISS

arol Shields won many literary awards over the course of a life cut tragically short (she died in 2003 at age sixty-eight, after a courageous five-year struggle with breast cancer that metastasized to her liver). She is probably best known for **The Stone Diaries**, which won both a Pulitzer Prize and the National Book Critics Circle Award. It's the story of the long life of an ordinary woman, Daisy Stone, seen through a collage of letters, newspaper clippings, and straight narrative told in multiple voices. But my three favorite Shields novels are probably among her lesser known: **The Republic of Love, Larry's Party,** and **Swann** (which I read somewhere was her own favorite of her books).

In **The Republic of Love,** Fay McLeod, a never-married researcher of mermaids in her midthirties, and Tom Avery, the thrice-married (though now single) host of a late-night talk show at a local Winnipeg radio station, fall in love. These two unlikely lovers alternate in telling us the story of their developing relationship.

Larry's Party describes twenty years in the life of Larry Weller—years defined by his liaisons with a variety of women, and his growing interest in designing garden mazes.

Swann is an academic satire—an exploration of the various ways different men and women interpret the work of the mysterious poet Mary Swann, each according to his or her own needs and prejudices.

Shields's other works include her last, **Unless; Happenstance: Two Novels in One about a Marriage in Transition,** also told from the points of view of both halves of a couple; **The Orange Fish; The Box Garden;** and **Small Ceremonies.**

NEVIL SHUTE: TOO GOOD TO MISS

If what you're looking for is a plain old-fashioned good story, well told and with no highfalutin language, you simply can't do better than to hunt up Nevil Shute's novels and immerse yourself in them. James Hilton, author of **Goodbye, Mr. Chips** and no mean storyteller himself, referred to Shute's **No Highway** as "first-rate yarning." The same could be said for all his novels.

Nevil Shute Norway lived from 1899 to 1960, and although he was English born and bred, he moved permanently to Australia, where he set some of the novels that I most enjoy rereading. An infantryman in the British army in World War I and a reservist in World War II, his nonliterary career was in the aerospace industry. (He was probably the first to explore in a novel the then-revolutionary notion that planes suffer from metal fatigue, a phenomenon that is the centerpiece of **No Highway**'s plot). Both his wartime and peacetime experiences show up time and again in his writings. He wrote more than two dozen works of fiction (the first, **Marazan**, was published in 1926, and the last, **Trustee from the Toolroom**, was published posthumously in 1960), but he thought of himself primarily as an engineer. In fact, his auto-biography, **Slide Rule**, is subtitled **The Autobiography of an Engineer**. Although he's probably best known for **On the Beach**, about the last survivors of a global atomic war, my particular favorites—to which I return time and again—include **Requiem for a Wren** and, above all, **A Town Like Alice**.

But here's something about Nevil Shute that I must tell you: His novels, like those of Agatha Christie, Dorothy Sayers, and countless other writers published in the 1930s, '40s, and '50s, include racist language that, while in common usage then, rings uncomfortably in our ears today. So, for instance, despite the fact that Shute's novel **The Chequer Board** is sympathetic to the plight of black soldiers in World War II, and is even supportive of interracial marriages (the

African American character marries a British girl from Cornwall, while the British flyer marries a Burmese woman), the racist language makes for some discomfiting reading.

In addition to the books mentioned above, Shute's books include the following:

Beyond the Black Stump

The Far Country

In the Wet

Landfall: A Channel Story

Lonely Road

Most Secret

An Old Captivity

Pastoral

Pied Piper

The Rainbow and the Rose

Round the Bend

Ruined City *(the American title is* Kindling*)*

So Disdained

Stephen Morris

Vinland the Good

What Happened to the Corbetts *(the American title is* Ordeal*)*

SIBS

Birth order, appearance, talent (or lack thereof), the men and women in their lives (or lack thereof), different interests—all these factors and more can affect the relationships of brothers and sisters. Ideally, of course, siblings look beyond their surface or deep-seated differences, overcome the emotional traumas of growing up, and wind up close friends. Sometimes this happens—and sometimes not, as can be seen from the books below.

David Long has written two wonderful (and very different) novels in which sisters play a major role. When twenty-two-year-old Mark, the main character in **The Falling Boy**, marries Olivia, the third of the four Stavros sisters, he doesn't expect to fall in love with her older sister Linney, but eight years later he does. In **The Daughters of Simon Lamoreaux**, Miles Fanning believes he has recovered from the major traumatic event of his adolescence—his high school girlfriend's disappearance in a case that was never solved—but when her younger sister comes into his life more than two decades after those events, he realizes that the past has never lost its power over him.

In Pete Fromm's first novel, **How All This Started**, Austin Scheer and his older sister Abilene share a love for baseball and Austin's dream of becoming a major league pitcher. But Austin only slowly grows to understand his sister's manic depression and its effects on her personality.

Psychiatrist Jack and his actress-sister Kate lived through the shocking death of their mother when they were children, but when as adults their family home in Ireland is put up for sale, Jack decides it's finally time to go back home and face the ghosts of the past—to reconstruct the truth—in Josephine Hart's elegant **The Reconstructionist**.

Rita Mae Brown's **Six of One** is the first of a series of warm and often humorous novels about the Hunsenmeir sisters, Julia and Louise, living in small-town Maryland. Other good ones in the series are **Bingo** and **Loose Lips**.

Worth searching out is Charles Dickinson's hilarious and touching **The Widows' Adventures**. In an attempt to heal the crevasses in their families' relationships, Helene and Ina, two elderly widowed sisters, take a car trip from Chicago to Los Angeles. This is a journey that is perilous not least because Helene, the driver, is blind and Ina, the navigator, is a little too fond of John Barleycorn.

Shirley Hazzard keeps racking up the accolades of readers and fellow writers alike. She won the 2003 National Book Award for her novel **The Great Fire** and received the National Book Critics Circle Award for fiction in 1981 for **The Transit of Venus**. The latter is the story of orphan sisters Grace (the pretty one) and Caro (the intelligent one), who leave their native Australia to create new lives for themselves in England. One opts for the safety and comfort of marriage, the other for a life filled with unpredictable passion and pain. Yet neither choice is irrevocable, nor does it protect them from what life tosses their way.

Two other sisters who choose different paths are found in Richard B. Wright's **Clara Callan**, which won every major Canadian literary award in 1991, the year it was published. The novel, which spans four years in the 1930s, is told entirely in the journal of Clara (a spinster schoolteacher and closet poet) and the letters she exchanges with her sister, Nora, who left the small Canadian town where they grew up to find fame and fortune as a radio soap opera actress in dangerously seductive New York.

Other good novels about siblings include Richard Yates's **The Easter Parade**, Clare Morrall's **Astonishing Splashes of Colour**, Lan Samantha Chang's Inheritance, Jenny McPhee's No Ordinary Matter, Nancy Reisman's **The First Desire**, and **The True and Outstanding Adventures of the Hunt Sisters** by Elisabeth Robinson.

You might also look at the "Brothers and Sisters" section in *Book Lust*.

SMALL-TOWN LIFE

What are the benefits of setting a novel in a small town? Perhaps one is that you can more fully explore the setting and bring it to life for the reader. And perhaps another is that we tend to think of small towns as bucolic and quaint little villages that are populated with eccentrics. These characters are not only fun to write about, but enjoyable to read about as well.

Pick, Kentucky, is the setting for Lana Witt's **Slow Dancing on Dinosaur Bones**, in which the greed of a coal-mining company comes up against the lives and loves of a variety of quirky characters, including philosophy graduate Tom Jett, auto mechanic Gilman Lee, Gilman's old girlfriend Rosalee Wilson, and his new (and undying) love, Gemma Collett.

". . . And Ladies of the Club" by Helen Hooven Santmyer is a lengthy (more than one thousand pages), multigenerational saga of small-town Ohio life, as experienced by members of a literary society from its 1868 founding through the 1920s. Published in 1982, when the author was in her eighties and living in a nursing home, this was a sensational (and well-deserved) success.

For many years Wendell Berry has been both a farmer (in Henry County, Kentucky) and a writer of poetry, essays, and novels about the joys of the natural world and the importance of community. My favorite of his novels is **Jayber Crow**, which has one of those misfit heroes that so often show up in novels set in small towns. Jayber was a sometime student of the ministry, but he is now Port William's philosopher, gravedigger, most devoted bachelor, and only barber.

Small-town New Hampshire is both the subject and the setting of May Sarton's **Kinds of Love**, which focuses on an elderly couple who, after decades of spending only the summer in the state, decides to move there permanently.

When former folksinger and writer Henry Corvine decides to leave the music business, he goes back to Edson, the foundering mill town where he grew up, and discovers that the past is never quite over, in Bill Morrisey's **Edson**.

John Welter's hilarious and bittersweet **I Want to Buy a Vowel: A Novel of Illegal Alienation** is set in a small town in Texas, where eleven-year-old Eva and her younger sister Ava come to the assistance of illegal alien Alfredo Santayana (who has learned to speak English from watching television).

The Sabbathday River by Jean Hanff Korelitz is part courtroom drama, part morality tale, part examination of the difficulties of being perceived as "different" in a small town, and part hymn of praise to women's friendships. Weaving all these themes together, this novel about a single mother and a murdered infant makes for a compelling and engrossing read.

Love, marriage, and politics in a small New Hampshire town during the early months of the Depression come together in **Sea Glass** by Anita Shreve, definitely a novel with a social conscience.

After leaving the World War II internment camp for Japanese Americans where he spent most of the war years, William Fujita finds his way to widow Margaret Kelly's farm and slowly creates a makeshift family to replace the people he's lost in **What the Scarecrow Said** by Stewart David Ikeda.

Everyone in the small Georgia town where he lives is eager to find banjo-playing peanut pathologist Roger Meadows the perfect wife, but nobody thinks it could possibly be Della, a painter of chickens, in Bailey White's **Quite a Year for Plums**.

Frederick Reiken's **The Odd Sea** describes the effects on a small-town Massachusetts family when teenager Ethan Shumway disappears.

Icy Sparks, the eponymous heroine of Gwyn Hyman Rubio's debut novel, is set apart from the rest of the small Kentucky town where she grows up by her tics and strange behavior, finally diagnosed as Tourette's syndrome.

SOCIAL STUDIES

I'm always interested in books about current or controversial social issues that help me step back from the headlines and really think about the subject. These books all fit the bill perfectly.

Charles Bowden's powerful and moving **Down by the River: Drugs, Money, Murder, and Family** helps us think about the ultimate failure and the moral corruption at the heart of the war on drugs.

Adrian Nicole LeBlanc spent ten years getting to know, gaining the confidence of, and sharing the lives of one extended Latino family in one of the poorest urban areas of the country before writing **Random Family: Love, Drugs, Trouble, and Coming of Age in the Bronx**. Her descriptions of their experiences—teenage pregnancy, friends and relatives in prison, drug-dealing boyfriends, gangsters—are presented from the inside out, giving readers the uncomfortable sensation of being right there.

9 Highland Road: Sane Living for the Mentally Ill is a sensitive portrait of a group of mentally ill people living together in a group home in Glen Cove, New York. Author Michael Winerip also confronts the NIMBY (not in my back yard) syndrome, exploring the problems involved in situating these homes in established neighborhoods.

Cynthia Gorney's **Articles of Faith: A Frontline History of the Abortion Wars** is an amazingly even-handed (and readable) overview of the abortion controversy. Gorney's book will make you think long and hard about your beliefs on this issue, regardless of which side you're on.

Are there any real villains in Anne Fadiman's **The Spirit Catches You and You Fall Down: A Hmong Child, Her American Doctors, and the Collision of Two Cultures**? I don't think so. There's only great sadness at a teenage girl's fate as a result of the collision between the beliefs of her Hmong immigrant family and the American medical establishment.

The Missing Peace: The Inside Story of the Fight for Middle East Peace by Dennis Ross describes the participants and events in the elusive search for stability and acceptance between Israel and the Arab countries in the region. As the chief American negotiator for the Middle East peace process from 1988 to 2000, under the presidencies of George H. W. Bush and Bill Clinton, Ross is well aware of the sticky issues involved: the Palestinian belief in "right of return," Israeli security, the settlement of the West Bank, and the ever-present threat of terror. This is required reading for anyone with the least interest in the topic.

SOUTHERN-FRIED FICTION

From my reading of Southern novels, I've retained many images: the scent of magnolias wafting through the still, hot, moist air; a group of women sitting on a large verandah fanning themselves and drinking large glasses of sweetened iced tea; the honeyed drawl of their voices. These images are balanced, of course, by those from an entirely different sort of Southern novel: the large tobacco and cotton plantations; men and women (usually black) working long hours picking those crops; the painful legacy of slavery and, especially in novels published since the 1960s, the difficult issue of race relations.

The classic Southern novels are by William Faulkner. You'll never know a fictional place as well as you come to know the invented Yoknapatawpha County, where Faulkner set such enduring novels as **The Sound and the Fury; Go Down, Moses;** and **Absalom, Absalom!**

That good black soil of the South has produced a great number of other wonderful novels as well. Try these, which I've grouped by the state in which they're set:

Alabama

Evelyn Couch finds her life rejuvenated when her elderly friend Mrs. Threadgoode tells her the story of Idgie and Ruth, who ran a cafe near Birmingham in the 1930s. Fannie Flagg's most beloved book, **Fried Green Tomatoes at the Whistle Stop Cafe,** tells the story of all these women.

The complicated dynamics of family relationships and long-held secrets are explored in Anne Carroll George's novel **This One and Magic Life,** when after the death of painter Artemus (Artie) Sullivan, her family gathers together to mourn and remember her. (George also wrote a series of mysteries set in Alabama, including **Murder Carries a Torch.**)

A novel that I reread frequently—pure comfort food in print—is Babs H. Deal's **The Walls Came Tumbling Down,** the story of a long hot 1940s Alabama summer in the lives of seven sorority sisters.

Anne Rivers Siddons went on to write many other novels, but her first one, **Heartbreak Hotel,** remains my favorite. It's set in 1956, when the thorny problem of race relations invades a bucolic college town and forever alters the life of beautiful, bright, and talented Maggie Deloach.

Train Whistle Guitar, the first novel in Albert Murray's coming-of-age trilogy (it's followed by The Spyglass Tree and The Seven League Boots), takes place in 1920s Mobile, where Scooter learns about life from a variety of people, including his real mother, his adopted mother, a musician, and the local barber.

Sena Jeter Naslund intersperses her fictional characters with real ones in Four Spirits, as college student Stella Silver joins the civil rights movement in Birmingham and discovers its dangers and its rewards.

In 1961, a family-run hotel in Birmingham becomes the gathering place for freedom riders, reporters, and townspeople, drawn together in the cause of civil rights, in Vicki Covington's The Last Hotel for Women.

Robert McCammon brings a bit of magical realism to Zephyr, Alabama, in Boy's Life, a tale of a father and son who discover a dead man and realize that evil has crept into their once idyllic hometown.

Crazy in Alabama by Mark Childress, which takes place in the 1960s, is filled with wacky characters like Aunt Lucille, who decapitates her husband with a carving knife and then flees to Hollywood in search of fame and fortune (carrying her husband's head in a Tupperware container). Meanwhile, twelve-year-old Peejoe becomes involved in the struggle to integrate a public swimming pool. (Another novel featuring an electric carving knife, although not set in the South, is Peter Lefcourt's Abbreviating Ernie, about a cross-dressing urologist and his wife.)

Sacred Dust by David Hill is about racial violence in Prince George's County, Alabama, and how one woman gathers the courage to defy local members of the Ku Klux Klan, including her own husband.

I enjoyed Tom Franklin's historical mystery **Hell at the Breech**, in which the murder of a politician leads to more mayhem than anyone quite bargained for.

Mississippi

'Sippi by John Oliver Killens (1916–1987) takes place during the civil rights struggles of the 1950s and '60s. Killens, who is unfortunately not much read today, founded the Harlem Writers' Group and taught many of the next generation of African American writers, including Piri Thomas, Ntozake Shange, Nicholasa Mohr, and Thulani Davis. (You might also try Killens's **Youngblood**, which takes place in Georgia.)

Billy by Albert French, set in 1937, is a stunning and painful novel about the execution of a ten-year-old boy who killed a white girl during a racial confrontation.

A lighthearted look at Mississippi (and there aren't many) is James Kaplan's **Pearl's Progress**, about a New Yorker who takes a job at Picket State University and finds himself a fish out of water.

In Rosellen Brown's **Civil Wars**, Jessie and Teddy Carll, who came South to participate in the civil rights movement, find their marriage challenged when they take on the responsibility of raising their orphaned niece and nephew, whose views on race sharply differ with their own.

Bev Marshall's **Right as Rain** also explores the contradictions and paradoxes of race through a story about two black women and the white family they work for.

Other Mississippi novels include Frederick Barthelme's **Bob the Gambler**; Greg Iles's **24 Hours** (and others); Willie Morris's **Taps**, set during the Korean War; all the novels of Steve Yarbrough (including **Visible Spirits, The Oxygen Man**, and **Veneer**); and Elizabeth Spencer's **The Salt Line**.

Virginia

Probably the best-known historical novel set in Virginia is William Styron's **The Confessions of Nat Turner.** This story of a slave uprising two decades before the Civil War won the Pulitzer Prize for fiction in 1968.

Thulani Davis's **1959** and Dennis McFarland's **Prince Edward** deal with the effects of the Supreme Court's landmark *Brown v. Board of Education* ruling in 1954 on the lives of young people, both black and white.

The eccentric residents of Big Stone Gap are sympathetically portrayed in a series of novels by Adriana Trigiani, beginning with **Big Stone Gap,** in which the town's pharmacist (and thirty-five-year-old self-declared spinster), Ave Maria Mulligan, sets out on a quest to discover who her father really was—which results in two marriage proposals. **Big Cherry Holler** and **Milk Glass Moon** complete the trilogy.

Many of Lee Smith's novels are set in Virginia, including **Family Linen,** about a woman whose recovered memories result in the unearthing of long-hidden family secrets; **The Last Day the Dogbushes Bloomed,** told from the viewpoint of a young girl; and my particular favorite, **Black Mountain Breakdown,** the story of Crystal Spangler, who was the most popular girl at Black Rock High, but whose adult life never lives up to the promise of her adolescence.

Jonathan Dee's **Palladio** is set in an artists' colony run by an eccentric millionaire who made his money in the advertising business. The ending of this powerful novel ought to be predictable, but isn't.

I have many guilty pleasures when it comes to books, but none more so than Elswyth Thane's series of historical romances known collectively as "The Williamsburg Novels," which I seem to reread with appalling regularity. As you can infer from the collective title of the series, the family's home is in Virginia, but the action, especially in the later novels, moves away from the sleepy town of

Williamsburg into New York and, especially, London. Each one takes place during a particular war, from the Revolutionary War to World War II. Here they are, in order: **Dawn's Early Light; Yankee Stranger; Ever After; The Light Heart; Kissing Kin; This Was Tomorrow;** and **Homing.**

SPACE OPERAS

I'm sure that many science fiction fans will join me in believing that of all the science fiction subgenres, the one called space operas includes some of the most entertaining books. The term itself probably began as a criticism—describing books that were low in literary qualities and excessively high on drama—similar to the negatives heaped on soap or horse operas. But I use the term as it's now come to be regarded, as a descriptor of exciting adventure novels, often set in an exotic planetary world (or many worlds) far from Earth, with a likable hero who has a worthwhile goal (like saving mankind). Here are some I've thoroughly enjoyed:

The Eleven Million Mile High Dancer by Carol De Chellis Hill, written at the height of the Cold War, is a novel about a feminist astronaut, particle physics, the conundrum of Schrödinger's cat, and a mysterious threat to Earth's security.

Lois McMaster Bujold's thoughtful and swashbuckling series takes place a millennium in the future; the main character is Miles Vorkosigan, who overcomes a difficult childhood to become a spy for his home world, using the cover of a mercenary fighter. The best books are **Shards of Honor, The Vor Game,** and **Barrayar.** (Incidentally, the Vorkosigan novels are great for teenage boys.)

Hyperion by Dan Simmons is set in the twenty-eighth century, in the midst of a galaxy-wide war. Seven pilgrims travel to the planet Hyperion to meet the Shrike, from whom they hope to learn how to save all of humanity from self-destructing. It's followed by the equally strong **The Fall of Hyperion, Endymion,** and **The Rise of Endymion.**

The ultra-imaginative Simmons is also the author of the most enjoyable **Ilium,** a complicated cliffhanger set hundreds of years in the future, in which a group of highly evolved beings—humans, but more than human—use Mars as their staging area to re-create Homer's *Iliad*, casting themselves as the gods and goddesses of the epic poem. (They even import their own Homers, a group of humans from the past who report on the events on and off the battlefield.)

I can't praise Peter F. Hamilton's science fiction opus **Pandora's Star** too much. Hamilton's twenty-fourth-century world is one of thousands of planets connected by wormholes that enable high-speed transportation to occur throughout the galaxy. His characters—from the bad guys to the aliens to the heroes—are entirely three-dimensional. As the plot unfolds—is there some alien being out there who is eager to destroy anything that is not himself?—the tension mounts. This first of a two-part techno-space opera (followed by **Judas Unleashed**) is not to be missed, especially by those who loved Richard K. Morgan's **Altered Carbon.**

Other good space operas include Samuel R. Delany's **Nova; Downbelow Station** by C. J. Cherryh; **The Player of Games** by Iain M. Banks; and **Singularity Sky** and **Iron Sunrise** by Charles Stross.

SRI LANKA: EXOTIC AND TROUBLED

Before Sri Lanka was Sri Lanka, it was Ceylon—a tropical island much coveted for its exotic spices and thus conquered by various European nations from about the fifteenth century on: first the Portuguese, then the Dutch, then the British, who took control of the whole island, something the previous colonial powers had been unable to accomplish. Independence from Britain came in 1948, a year after Britain left India, and within a decade fighting broke out between competing ethnicities—the Sinhalese majority and the Tamil minority, not to mention the European Christians who had lived there for generations. The heaviest fighting took place in the late 1980s and 1990s. Only at the beginning of the twenty-first century did it seem that a lasting peace might be possible. Many novels set here directly address the ongoing, seemingly endless conflict; when it's not the main focus of the plot, it is frequently a subtext, running uneasily throughout the book.

You get a good sense of pre–Sri Lankan Ceylon in the 1930s from Edie Meidav's first novel, **The Far Field**, whose theme is that of the Westerner (in this case, American) come to the mysterious East in order to find spiritual fulfillment.

If you can imagine a novel that seems to be part Agatha Christie and part Kazuo Ishiguro (**The Remains of the Day**) or Chang-rae Lee (**Aloft; A Gesture Life**), then **The Hamilton Case** by Michelle de Kretser is just the book for you. De Kretser, who was born in Sri Lanka and grew up in Australia, sets her novel in Ceylon just prior to its independence from Britain in 1948. The English regard her protagonist, lawyer Sam Obeysekere, as being "other," despite his British schooling and desire to be thought of as English. The

Hamilton case, in which he prosecuted the murderer of a British coffee grower, has defined his career. Only much later in life does Sam begin to think that the conclusions he reached—not only about the case, but also about his own life—might have been terribly wrong. This was a novel I read slowly, in order to savor both the intricacies of the plot and the evocative writing.

In the beautifully written (but painful to read) **Anil's Ghost** by Sri Lankan–born Michael Ondaatje, forensic anthropologist Anil Tissera returns home to Sri Lanka as part of a human rights organization investigating the many religious, ethnic, and political murders that have occurred.

Reef by Romesh Gunesekera is a coming-of-age novel about a young Sinhalese boy who comes to work for Mr. Salgado, an aristocratic marine biologist who teaches young Triton not only how to cook but also how to live. Gunesekera also wrote **The Sandglass** and a collection of stories, **Monkfish Moon**, both of which are also set in Sri Lanka.

Other good novels include Shyam Selvadurai's **Cinnamon Gardens** (set in Ceylon in the late 1920s) and **Funny Boy**, about a young Tamil boy's struggles with his emerging homosexuality during the ethnic violence of the 1970s and 1980s.

Two of my favorite memoirs of this country are Leonard Woolf's **Growing: An Autobiography of the Years 1904 to 1911** and Michael Ondaatje's **Running in the Family**. The five volumes of Woolf's autobiography are consistently interesting, but none more so than **Growing**, in which he recounts his experiences as a British civil servant in Ceylon, from when he was twenty-four until just before he came home to England and married Virginia in 1912. While this book gives a picture of the maturation of a young man in an exotic land, it also depicts (sometimes unconsciously) Woolf's growing misgivings about Britain's role as a colonial power. **Running in the**

Family, Ondaatje's impressionistic memoir of his upper-class family in Ceylon, mixes fact and fiction with great success.

NEAL STEPHENSON: TOO GOOD TO MISS

Brilliant" is the best way to describe Neal Stephenson's writing. Best known as a leader of the cyberpunk subgenre of science fiction, Stephenson is often categorized simply as a genre writer. But in recent years especially, he has shown himself to be conversant with history, science, the history of science, code breaking, computers, human relationships, and languages. His novels just shine with intelligence.

Here are his must-read books. I look forward to many, many more in the years to come.

Snow Crash is the story of Hiro Protagonist, a pizza deliverer in the real world (for Uncle Enzo's CosaNostra Pizza Inc.) and a warrior in the Metaverse world of computer gaming. When a computer virus threatens to bring down both worlds, Hiro is just the person to stop it.

Cryptonomicon is way up on my list of top ten favorite novels. It's a hugely complex and inventive novel about history, computer hacking, men at war, and cryptography, with much of the novel set during World War II at Bletchley Park, home of the British code-breaking men and machinery.

Stephenson's Baroque Cycle series is composed of **Quicksilver, The Confusion,** and **The System of the World.** He may well write something that outdoes this trilogy in the next few years, but for now it's his magnum opus. Each of the novels that make up the trilogy averages more than eight hundred pages; their subject is no less than the history of the seventeenth century in all its confusing glory, and all three novels are filled with high adventure and lots of sly humor. We encounter historical figures such as Isaac Newton, Robert Hooke, and Samuel Pepys, along with the unforgettable invented characters, including Daniel Waterhouse, the son of a murdered Puritan leader (as well as the ancestor of a main character in Stephenson's **Cryptonomicon**); "Half-Cocked" Jack Shaftoe, vagabond and swashbuckler (and ancestor of another major character in **Cryptonomicon**); and Eliza (whom Shaftoe rescues from an Eastern harem), who makes her way carefully to prominence in the newly developing financial centers of a war-torn Europe. These books took me ages to read because I kept putting them down to look up various characters and events in the encyclopedia, but they were worth every moment.

TEENAGE TIMES

In some of my favorite novels, I remember best the teenage characters, even when they're not front and center in the plot. These books are written not for teens themselves, but rather to allow the rest of us a chance to look back on those years with nostalgia, regret, or even anger. Here are some I've most enjoyed:

Teenage Roxanne Fish, the heroine of the humorous novel **The Hallelujah Side** by Rhoda Huffey, tells the story of her eccentric family and their fundamentalist Assemblies of God beliefs, as well as her own spiritual search for truth and her struggle for independence.

The Sleeping Father by Matthew Sharpe tells what happens when the divorced and depressed father of teenagers Chris and Cathy has a stroke (as a result of taking—by accident—two incompatible antidepressants) and falls into a coma, forcing his children to muddle through their lives more or less without him, with mixed results. This quirky novel is sometimes very funny (there's a particularly hilarious scene set at a Thanksgiving dinner) and often very sad. (Not unlike life, really.)

I will be forever grateful to Adam Langer for inventing Michelle Wasserstrom, one of the main teenage characters in **Crossing California**. Langer's novel takes place in 1979–1981 in the primarily Jewish West Rogers Park neighborhood of Chicago, which is bisected by California, a street dividing the upper-middle-class Jewish families on the western side from the primarily middle-class families on the east. Incidentally, for those with short memories or who were too young to remember that time or place, Langer includes a helpful index, with entries ranging from "Kwame Nkrumah" to "Myron and Phil's" to "French Postcards" to "*faygeleh*" and many more.

Chicago, the senior year of high school, and the 1950s are the setting for Ward Just's **An Unfinished Season**, when nineteen-year-old Wils Ravan learns about life and love. (See "Ward Just: Too Good to Miss" in *Book Lust* for more about this author.)

One of my favorite teenage girls is the brave and foolhardy Mattie Jones, true heroine of **True Grit** by Charles Portis. (Even the movie made from this novel is worth seeing, just to appreciate John Wayne as Rooster Cogburn.)

It might be stretching "teenage" a bit to include an eleven-year-old here, but bear with me: **Addie Pray**, the title character of Joe David Brown's picaresque novel, is a delight to read about, as she and the expert con man Long Boy, who may or may not be her father, peddle their special brand of larceny throughout the South in the dark days of the Depression. (The book was made into the film *Paper Moon*, directed by Peter Bogdanovich.)

In **In Country** by Bobbie Ann Mason, seventeen-year-old Sam Hughes mourns for her father, killed in the war in Vietnam, and worries about her uncle, a Vietnam veteran who may be dying from his exposure to Agent Orange.

Other teenagers I've loved include Marian Gilbert and Valerie Boyd in Nora Johnson's **The World of Henry Orient** (the voice of Marian, who tells the story of the two girls' obsession with Henry Orient, is spot-on); Jersey Alitz in Elizabeth Evans's **Carter Clay**; Harley Altmyer in Tawni O'Dell's **Back Roads**; Roberta Rohberson in Lynda Barry's **Cruddy**; Corvus, Alice, and Annabel in Joy Williams's **The Quick & the Dead**; Will Bradford in John E. Keegan's **Clearwater Summer**; Karen Moss in Lowry Pei's **Family Resemblances**; Lucy Diamond in Pete Fromm's **As Cool As I Am**; Nomi Nickel in Miriam Toews's **A Complicated Kindness**; and Josh, the protagonist of Richard Bradford's zany **Red Sky at Morning**.

The sections in *Book Lust* called "Girls Growing Up" and ' Boys Coming of Age" cover this same territory.

TICKLE YOUR FUNNY BONE

Start reading some of these books and you'll find yourself falling off your chair, you'll be laughing so hard. Beware! Right from the dedication of Betty MacDonald's **The Egg and I** ("To my sister Mary who has always believed that I can do anything she puts her mind to"), you know you're in for a lot of fun. This classic memoir, originally published in 1945, tells the story of how the author and her husband (city slickers both) tried (and failed) to make a go of a run-down chicken ranch on Washington's Olympic Peninsula. The book was made into a 1947 movie starring Claudette Colbert and Fred MacMurray (imagine being played by Claudette Colbert!), and was the basis for the ever-popular television series *Ma and Pa Kettle*. (Let me warn you, though, that you may be put off by MacDonald's unenlightened view of American Indians.) MacDonald followed **The Egg and I** with **The Plague and I** (an account of the year she spent in a tuberculosis sanatorium) and **Onions in the Stew**. She is also the author of **Mrs. Piggle-Wiggle** and other humorous books for children about the eponymous character whose child-rearing techniques are somewhat unusual, to say the least, but always seem to work.

Even prior to 1946, when **Mr. Blandings Builds His Dream House** by Eric Hodgins was first published, living in New York was crazy-making. The Blandings are two Manhattanites who discover just how far their lifelong dream of living in an old farmhouse in the country is from the reality of it. This story was filmed twice, first with Cary Grant and Myrna Loy, and again (as *The Money Pit*) with Shelley Long and Tom Hanks.

Jerome K. Jerome's **Three Men in a Boat (To Say Nothing of the Dog!)** was first published in 1889, so it will give you a lovely dose of nostalgia as well as plenty of laughs. The dog is Montmorency, a fox terrier who accompanies George, Harris, and the author on their trip up the Thames. (If you enjoy this—and I've never met anyone who didn't—don't miss **Three Men on the Bummel**. Jerome describes a bummel, in case you're wondering, as "a journey, long or short, without an end"; in this case, it's a cycling trip through the Black Forest, with the same companions as in the earlier book.) Incidentally, the subtitle of Jerome's book—**To Say Nothing of the Dog!**—is, sans exclamation point, also the title of a wonderfully comic science fiction novel by Connie Willis.

Although you probably won't laugh out loud, I guarantee that reading Leo Bruce's **Case for Three Detectives**, a mystery that seems to be written for the express joy of mystery fans everywhere, will elicit a quiet chuckle or two. Three famous British detectives, Simon Plimsoll, Amer Picon, and Monsignor Smith, try to solve the murder of Mrs. Hurston. These detectives are thinly disguised portraits of the well-known fictional detectives Peter Wimsey, Hercule Poirot, and Father Brown. The fun comes in watching as they each go about solving the crime in their own eccentric way, only to find that their (very different) versions of what happened are demolished when the stolid Sergeant Beef listens to their explanations and then lays out the truth.

One of the funniest writers of the 1940s through the 1960s—at least one whose humor hasn't become dated and staid—is H Allen Smith. His work appeared in the major magazines of the time—everywhere from *Playboy* to *Saturday Review*. Whether he's writing about the history of fingers, his boyhood in Indiana, or his neighbor Avery, you'll find yourself guffawing continually. It hardly matters which of his many collections of humorous essays you first pick up (from the library, if you're lucky, or through an Internet search, if necessary), but **To Hell in a Handbasket** is simply spectacularly funny.

Just hearing the names of Stephen Potter's books can give you a good idea of the pleasure you're in for when you read him: **The Theory and Practice of Gamesmanship: Or, the Art of Winning Games Without Actually Cheating; Lifemanship: Or, the Art of Getting Away with It Without Being an Absolute Plonk; One-Upmanship: Being Some Account of the Activities and Teachings of the Lifemanship Correspondence College of One-Upness and Games Lifemastery;** and **Anti-Woo, the First Lifemanship Guide: The Lifeman's Improved Primer for Non-lovers, with Special Chapters on Who Not to Love, Falling Out of Love, Avoidance Gambits, and Coad-Sanderson's Scale of Progressive Rifts.** They're all subversive little instructions for succeeding in life without actually doing anything. I've always felt that Bertie Wooster (of P. G. Wodehouse fame) was familiar with Potter's theories of how to live best in this world.

When newly widowed Julia Piper pulls the emergency brake on her commuter train to save an upended sheep from certain death, she catches the attention of two men: the mild and divorced Sylvester

Wykes and the bird-watching bounder Maurice Benson, in Mary Wesley's **An Imaginative Experience**.

Other books that have made me laugh out loud are George and Weedon Grossmith's **The Diary of a Nobody**, still humorous after more than one hundred years (it was originally published in 1892); Peter DeVries's sexy and very funny **I Hear America Swinging** and **Consenting Adults, or The Duchess Will Be Furious**; William Goldman's **The Princess Bride** (funny and sweet but not cloying); Gerald Durrell's **My Family and Other Animals** and **Birds, Beasts, and Relatives**; and **Poet's Pub** by Eric Linklater, the plot of which includes a failed poet who was a Rowing Blue at Cambridge, the pub of the title, false names, an abduction, thievery, love, and what must be the greatest car chase in literature. (**Poet's Pub** was one of the first ten books reprinted by Penguin in 1935, then a brand-new English paperback publisher. The other nine—some still well known, others far less so—were André Maurois's **Ariel: The Life of Shelley**; Ernest Hemingway's **A Farewell to Arms**; Susan Ertz's **Madame Claire**; Dorothy L. Sayers's **The Unpleasantness at the Bellona Club**; Agatha Christie's **The Mysterious Affair at Styles**; Beverley Nichols's **Twenty-Five**; E. H. Young's **William**; Mary Webb's **Gone to Earth**; and Compton Mackenzie's **Carnival**.)

TIME TRAVEL

Who hasn't thought at one time or another about how exciting it would be to travel through time? And who, following that thought, hasn't come face to face with the contradictions and paradoxes inherent in time travel? Like, if your father dies sometime in his childhood, does that mean you won't be born? Or would you just not be you? Or if one thing in the past is changed—one simple thing, as in Ray Bradbury's remarkable short story "A Sound of Thunder"—is the present altered irrevocably?

Writers have explored these questions ever since H. G. Wells published his classic time-travel novel **The Time Machine** and Mark Twain took his Connecticut Yankee and put him in King Arthur's court, but here are some others you might enjoy as well:

Philip E. Baruth's The X President

Darryl Brock's If I Never Get Back

Octavia Butler's Kindred

Charles Dickinson's A Shortcut in Time

Daphne du Maurier's The House on the Strand

Jack Finney's Time and Again *(I've never met anyone who didn't love this novel)*

Diana Gabaldon's Outlander

Ken Grimwood's Replay

Robert A. Heinlein's Time for the Stars *and* The Door into Summer *(have you ever wondered how Leonardo da Vinci dreamed up ideas that it wouldn't be practical to implement until hundreds of years after his death? Think about a misplaced time traveler named Leonard Vincent. . .)*

Richard Matheson's Somewhere in Time

Audrey Niffenegger's The Time Traveler's Wife

Marge Piercy's Woman on the Edge of Time

John Varley's Millennium

Connie Willis's Doomsday Book *and* To Say Nothing of the Dog

Robert Charles Wilson's The Chronoliths

If short stories are more what you're looking for, don't miss **Time Machines: The Best Time Travel Stories Ever Written**, edited by Bill Adler, Jr., with stories by Jack Finney, Rod Serling, Ray Bradbury, Rudyard Kipling, and contemporary authors such as Larry Niven and Harry Turtledove, master of the alternate-reality genre. Another excellent choice is **The Best Time Travel Stories of the 20th Century**, edited by Harry Turtledove with Martin H. Greenburg, which includes works by Connie Willis, Theodore Sturgeon, Arthur C. Clarke, and Poul Anderson.

TRICKY, TRICKY

There comes a time in each of the following novels when you realize that the author has played a trick on you—employed an elaborate sleight-of-hand so cunning, so daring, that it's hard not to be a bit awestruck, even as you're feeling a little betrayed and annoyed by the deception. And it's a testament to the skill of these writers that despite your dismay, you're still impressed. . . .

> *Ian McEwan's* **Atonement**
> *Anita Shreve's* **The Last Time They Met**
> *Connie Willis's* **Passage**

There's also Agatha Christie's **The Murder of Roger Ackroyd**, the mystery that caused literary critic Edmund Wilson to ask testily in print, "Who cares who killed Roger Ackroyd?" It is perhaps the only mystery ever to be explicated by a French psychoanalyst, Pierre Bayard, who offers an interpretation of the crime that differs from that of Christie's well-known detective, Hercule Poirot, in **Who Killed Roger Ackroyd? The Mystery Behind the Agatha Christie Mystery.**

TRUE ADVENTURES

I f these books won't cause the ordinary reader to become schizophrenic, I don't know what will. After reading them, you'll want to charge out and duplicate the authors' adventures. But at the same time, you'll ask yourself, "Do I really want to risk life and limb, as these men and women did?" It all seemed so simple at first. . . .

Touching My Father's Soul: A Sherpa's Journey to the Top of Everest is written by Jamling Tenzing Norgay, son of Tenzing Norgay, one of the Sherpas who accompanied Sir Edmund Hillary on the first Everest ascent in 1953. The way Norgay weaves together the tragic climbing summer of 1996, memories of his father, and his Buddhist beliefs is unforgettable.

Robert Kurson's Shadow Divers: The True Adventure of Two Americans Who Risked Everything to Solve One of the Last Mysteries of World War II introduces readers to Rich Kohler and John Chatterton, who spent seven years trying to identify the wreckage of a World War II U-boat off the coast of New Jersey, eventually establishing that it was a German boat long thought to have sunk off Gibraltar's coast in the last year of the war. Thrilling, scary, and sad, all at the same time.

In addition to being a darned good adventure story, Shooting the Boh: A Woman's Voyage Down the Wildest River in Borneo by Tracy Johnston can also be read as a cautionary tale about knowing what you're signing up for. Johnston's lost luggage (before the trip even begins) is the least of it.

Borneo is one fascinating place, and in addition to Johnston's book you might try Redmond O'Hanlon's Into the Heart of Borneo.

From its enormously funny first chapter through the actual trip itself, this is a wildly entertaining ride.

In **Facing the Congo: A Modern-Day Journey into the Heart of Darkness,** Jeffrey Tayler attempts to re-create the trip of famed explorer Henry Stanley (yes, he of "Dr. Livingstone, I presume" fame) down the Congo River in the nineteenth century.

Bruce Chatwin's **The Songlines** was his last book before his death at the age of forty-eight. It's an account of his travels across the Australian outback, following the trails of aboriginal culture. If you enjoy this, you'll also want to check out Chatwin's **In Patagonia** and **The Viceroy of Ouidah.**

In Search of King Solomon's Mines is a story told by Tahir Shah, a native Afghani who grew up in England. After a visit to the Middle East, he found himself compelled to locate the mines of the biblical King Solomon. The journey eventually took him across Ethiopia into the (mostly illegal) gold-mining camps as he followed the route of legendary explorer Frank Hayter, who searched for those same mines in the 1920s.

You might also take a look at the "Adventure by the Book: Nonfiction" section in *Book Lust*, which offers many more suggestions for reading in this area.

BARBARA W. TUCHMAN: TOO GOOD TO MISS

If history's your thing, and you aren't acquainted with the writings of Barbara W. Tuchman, you're in for a real treat. Tuchman writes totally readable narrative histories, replete with colorful characters and just enough detail to assure you that she knows what she's talking about but not so much that it reads like an academic treatise. Her ability to evoke time, place, and character has been rewarded by a slew of awards. She won a Pulitzer Prize in 1963 for **The Guns of August**, about the first weeks of World War I, and another in 1972 for **Stilwell and the American Experience in China, 1911–45**, a biography of General Joseph "Vinegar Joe" Stilwell, commander of the U.S. forces and Allied chief of staff to Chiang Kai-shek in 1942–1944. She received the National Book Award for history in 1980 for **A Distant Mirror: The Calamitous Fourteenth Century**, in which she finds many parallels between that century and the twentieth. Tuchman explains her thoughts about her craft in **Practicing History: Selected Essays**.

Other necessary reading for any self-respecting history buff includes the following:

The Zimmermann Telegram is about the telegram from Germany that promised Mexico part of the American Southwest if that country would come into World War I on the side of the Germans—a blunder on Germany's part, since it brought the United States into the war.

The Proud Tower: A Portrait of the World Before the War, 1890–1914 is the story of the events that led, directly and indirectly, to World War I.

In **The March of Folly: From Troy to Vietnam**, Tuchman looks at four mistakes that occurred in the past, and how they changed history: Troy's decision to bring the wooden horse inside their city; the outrageous lives of the Renaissance popes, which helped to bring about Martin Luther's Protestant Reformation; England's intransigent attitudes toward its American colonies; and, finally, America's decision to go to war against North Vietnam.

TWO, OR THREE, ARE BETTER THAN ONE

As I noted in *Book Lust*'s "Companion Reads" section some books simply beg to be read together. Each book seems to reflect and refract the writing of the other(s), making the experience of reading them all greater than that of reading each one separately.

The lives of women are examined:

> Off Keck Road *by Mona Simpson*
>
> Our Kind: A Novel in Stories *by Kate Walbert*
>
> The Easter Parade *by Richard Yates*

The life of a fascinating woman is told in both fiction and her own memoir:

> Fanny: A Fiction *by Edmund White*
>
> Domestic Manners of the Americans *by Fanny Trollope*

Shtetl life in Eastern Europe is described:

> Everything Is Illuminated *by Jonathan Safran Foer*
>
> Your Mouth Is Lovely *by Nancy Richler*

An excellent look at women's roles in the Middle East and India:

> Nine Parts of Desire: The Hidden World of Islamic Women *by Geraldine Brooks*

May You Be the Mother of a Hundred
Sons: A Journey Among the Women of
India *by Elizabeth Bumiller*

Teenage girls' problems with both society and themselves are
described and discussed:

The Body Project: An Intimate History
of American Girls *by Joan Jacobs Brumberg*

Schoolgirls: Young Women, Self-Esteem,
and the Confidence Gap *by Peggy
Orenstein*

Reviving Ophelia: Saving the Selves of
Adolescent Girls *by Mary Pipher*

Queen Bees & Wannabes: Helping
Your Daughter Survive Cliques, Gossip,
Boyfriends, & Other Realities of
Adolescence *by Rosalind Wiseman*

VIRAGOS

In the 1980s Dial Press reprinted a series of British novels under
the general title of Virago Modern Classics. They had distinc-
tive covers (originally black, later dark green backgrounds with
fetching illustrations taken from nineteenth- and twentieth-century
paintings) and thoughtful introductions by a variety of contemporary writers and critics. Most importantly, the series introduced
readers to an exciting selection of mostly unread women novelists
(many of them unknown to all but a few feminist scholars), whose
fictional subjects were the lives of women from the Victorian period
through the 1970s. Here are some of the best.

In the category "The (Book) Lusts of Others," I mentioned how
much I enjoyed Noel Perrin's **A Reader's Delight**, in which he calls
Emily Eden's **The Semi-Attached Couple** the answer to the question of what to read after finishing all of Jane Austen. And of course,

he's right. Published in 1860 but written in the 1830s, when Eden was in India with her brother, the newly named British governor-general there (see also "Central Asia: Crossroads of Empires, Cauldron of War"), this story of a marriage between an eighteen-year-old girl and the man who swept her off her feet is a scrumptious read, filled with a large cast of characters. It's witty, intelligent, and richly sentimental. Not too surprising that it was the first of the Virago series to appear here in the United States.

Antonia White's **Frost in May**, with its young heroine, the Catholic convert Nanda Grey, was first published in the 1930s, but takes place from 1908 to 1912. This ultimately tragic tale of a young and impressionable girl's four years—from age nine to thirteen—at a Catholic boarding school just outside London probes the petty tyrannies and great cruelties that follow any breaking of the rules in the cloistered community.

The life of a gifted and intelligent woman in a Victorian household was not easy, as it was a time and place in which a brilliant woman was not particularly valued; charm and beauty were considered much more important. Such is the plight of the eponymous heroine of **Mary Olivier: A Life** by May Sinclair, who discovers that sacrifice, not intelligence, is the name of the game.

I love Rose Macaulay's **Told by an Idiot**, the story of three generations of the Garden family. Spanning the years of the Victorian era to the 1920s, the novel presents each member of the family as a fully drawn individual, yet one who represents the prevailing social and cultural winds of the times. All of their experiences are watched by the memorable Rome, who participates in nothing save an attempted single great love affair.

Other Virago novels not to miss are E. H. Young's **Miss Mole**; Ada Leverson's **The Little Ottleys**; Barbara Comyns's **Our Spoons Came from Woolworths**; Rebecca West's **The Return of the Soldier** and **Harriet Hume**; Henry Handel Richardson's **The Getting of**

Wisdom; E. Arnot Robertson's **Four Frightened People**; and Margaret Kennedy's **The Ladies of Lyndon.**

VOICE

Along with a book's first few lines, I think it's the narrator's voice that determines whether I'll be drawn into reading a book. Do you remember the dog in the old RCA Victor ads—I think his name was Nipper—whose head was cocked in amazement as he listened to what issued from that phonograph horn? That's just how I feel when I first encounter a true storyteller, someone whose voice is distinct, fresh, and utterly compelling.

The unnamed narrator of Julie Hecht's **Do the Windows Open?** is winsomely neurotic (she's afraid of almost anything you can name, from tall buildings to bus trips to dentists) and devoted to organic food, her friends, and her weirdly cheerful life. Here's a great sample (with my apologies to dentists everywhere): "I went this once to a very mean dentist, who seemed to be a man on the verge of suicide. You've read that dentists have the highest suicide rate? Not high enough, I say."

The hero (antihero, really) of **Karoo** by Steve Tesich, best known for penning the screenplay of the movie *Breaking Away*, is a script doctor who's unable to fix his own life. The self-destructive Saul Karoo is a character you'll never forget. He seems to become a different person with everyone he knows, from his almost-ex-wife, Dianah, to his son, Billy, to Jay Cromwell, the diabolical producer who frequently calls on his writing talents. (My psychologist friend says Karoo is what's known in her field as a "borderline.") Here's how the novel opens, in Karoo's unmistakable voice: "It was the night after Christmas and we were all chatting merrily about the fall of Nicolae Ceausescu."

Two novels that are narrated by a group of people all speaking in one voice are **Our Kind: A Novel in Stories** by Kate Walbert and **The Virgin Suicides** by Jeffrey Eugenides. **Our Kind** is about a group of upper-class women who came of age in the 1950s and are reaping the consequences in the 1990s of their inevitable aging. Here's one example of the narrator's voice: "Years ago we were led down the primrose lane, then abandoned somewhere near the carp pond." The chapter called "Sick Chicks," which describes a book discussion group that meets in a local hospice (in this particular case, they're talking about Virginia Woolf's **Mrs. Dalloway**), is worth the price of the book.

The voice of **The Virgin Suicides** is that of a group of middle-aged men looking back twenty years on the seminal event (and obsession) of their adolescence: the suicides, one after another, of their classmates, the five mysterious and beautiful Lisbon sisters.

I can't understand why more people didn't read and rave about **The Confession of a Child of the Century, by Samuel Heather** by Thomas Rogers when it was first published in 1972. It's a terrifically funny bildungsroman, the story of a son, the narrator Samuel Heather, trying (and consistently failing) to please his father, who happens to be a professional father—the Episcopal bishop of Kansas City. Father and son disagree on every conceivable subject, from sex to the Korean War, from Harry Truman to Karl Marx. Don't miss reading this—among other gems, there's an unforgettable scene of Harry Truman taking a bath at the White House and deciding how to handle the prisoner-of-war issue at the same time.

WAYWARD WIVES

From Nathaniel Hawthorne's Hester Prynne in **The Scarlet Letter** to Gustave Flaubert's and Leo Tolstoy's respective eponymous heroines, **Madame Bovary** and **Anna Karenina**, women in fiction have always fallen in love with men who just happen not to be their husbands. These relationships almost always end in tragedy (especially in novels written before the late twentieth century).

The affair that Laura falls into in Tom Perrotta's **Little Children** frees her from a husband who's addicted to Internet porn, but doesn't in the end bring her much happiness.

When Jane decides to leave her husband and become a nanny, she can't predict the complications that will follow, especially when she falls in love with her employer in **Crane Spreads Wings: A Bigamist's Story** by Susan Trott.

Marian Thurm's **Walking Distance** is about a seemingly happy wife and mother who becomes involved with another man—who just happens to be dying of cancer.

Family Happiness by Laurie Colwin explores the question of whether a successful marriage can be compatible with adultery, as does **The Wedding of the Two-Headed Woman** by Alice Mattison.

Carol Clewlow's **A Woman's Guide to Adultery** chronicles the experiences of four friends as they each embark on a series of affairs.

Other tales of adultery and its consequences include the following:

> **Honeymoon: A Romantic Rampage** *by Amy Jenkins*

Instances of the Number 3 *by Salley Vickers*

Le Divorce *and* Le Mariage *by Diane Johnson*

Love and Friendship *by Alison Lurie*

My Russian *by Deirdre McNamer*

The Road to Lichfield *by Penelope Lively*

The Sex Life of My Aunt *by Mavis Cheek*

She Is Me *by Cathleen Schine*

A Ship Made of Paper *by Scott Spencer*

What Was She Thinking?: Notes on a Scandal *by Zoë Heller*

While I Was Gone *by Sue Miller*

A Widow for One Year *by John Irving (although her husband was the cad first)*

And don't forget Hedda Gabler, the title character of Henrik Ibsen's play, although it's unclear just how unfaithful she's been; and also poor Edna Pontellier, Kate Chopin's unfortunate heroine in **The Awakening**, who doesn't actually *do* anything but suffers the consequences anyway, as does Lady Rice in Fay Weldon's astringent **Splitting**, when her personality splits into four parts after her husband accuses her of adultery (unjustly) and demands a divorce.

JONATHAN WEINER: TOO
GOOD TO MISS

Jonathan Weiner is a non–science major's dream, because he's able to take complicated scientific ideas and theories and make them entirely understandable to the interested lay reader. He's also an intensely compassionate writer, whose affection for the friends he makes while researching and writing his books is eminently evident in the finished product.

His books include **Time, Love, Memory: A Great Biologist and His Quest for the Origins of Behavior** (which won the National Book Critics Circle Award for nonfiction), about Seymour Benzerone, who used fruit flies to test his theories of the relationship between genetics and behavior—now we can blame our parents for the manner in which we laugh; the Pulitzer Prize–winning **The Beak of the Finch: A Story of Evolution in Our Time**, about evolutionary biology as played out on an island in the Galápagos; and **His Brother's Keeper: A Story from the Edge of Medicine**, about the many ethical issues that all of us (including medical professionals) must confront in light of the new gene therapies being developed. How much tinkering with life (and death) should society be allowed to do? Are the risks (and costs) of gene therapy worth it? How much is one human life worth? Should scientists and doctors profit (to the tune of millions of dollars) from their discoveries? And Weiner's own question: How can a writer remain impartial about his subjects when he grows to care for them deeply?

P. G. WODEHOUSE:
TOO GOOD TO MISS

If you can ignore his somewhat rummy behavior during World War II (he did a series of radio broadcasts from Berlin in 1942 after being interned for eleven months by the Germans), you will have to admit that Wodehouse was one of the great humorists of the twentieth century. Of course, ignoring his actions may be hard to do for those, like me, who wonder how rotten-behaving or wrong-thinking people can produce such sublime works (Ezra Pound is another example of that sort of writer).

In any case, it's hard to imagine anyone not marveling at Wodehouse's twisted plots, zany characters, and brilliant use of the English language. Evelyn Waugh, no slouch at writing himself, averred "One has to regard a man as a Master who can produce on average three uniquely brilliant and entirely original similes on each page." Other fans include Anthony Lane, writer and columnist for *The New Yorker* and tens of thousands of readers. You'll want to join them, I know, as you make your way through Wodehouse's ninety-two comic novels and collections of short stories.

Before diving headfirst into Wodehouse's oeuvre, though, you may want to start with Richard Usborne's ultradelightful **Plum Sauce: A P. G. Wodehouse Companion.** He begins his book (after a helpful introduction) with a list of "thirty postulates for relaxed reading of P. G. Wodehouse," including number 13 ("Watch out for girls with two-syllable masculine-sounding shortenings of their Christian names [Bobbie Wickham, Corky Pirbright, Nobby Hopwood, Stiffy Byng]. They get the good man of their choice in the end, but they spread havoc on the way") and number 24 ("Chorus girls are all right and earls [Marshmoreton] and nephews of earls [Ronnie Fish] are very lucky to marry them"). Usborne also includes some prime examples of Wodehouse's writing: "Bingo laughed in an unpleasant, hacking manner as if he were missing one tonsil";"He resembled a frog that had been looking on the dark side since it was a slip of a tadpole"; and "Her face was shining like the seat of a bus-driver's trousers."

I could go on quoting Usborne quoting Wodehouse forever, but it's likely best to get to the books themselves.

These are a few of my top choices—I urge you, if you have any desire to escape from the cares of the world, to read them all.

Books featuring Bertie and Jeeves: These are Wodehouse's best known characters. Bertie is a man about town and Jeeves, his butler, runs his life.

> **Carry on, Jeeves**
>
> **The Inimitable Jeeves**
>
> **Bertie Wooster Sees It Through**
>
> **Jeeves and the Feudal Spirit**
>
> **Aunts Aren't Gentlemen**
>
> **Right Ho, Jeeves** *(The favorite novel of the definitive biography of Wodehouse by Frances Donaldson, called, quite simply, P. G.* **Wodehouse: A Biography.***)*

The Blandings books: Blandings is a castle owned by the Emsworth clan, filled with various servants and hangers-on.

> **Pigs Have Wings**
>
> **Uncle Fred in the Springtime**
>
> **A Pelican at Blandings**

The Psmith Books: Psmith worked as a newspaperman but being incurably lazy, is essentially most fond of sleeping. Note that the "P" is silent.

> **Leave It to Psmith**
>
> **Psmith in the City**

And more:

> Bachelors Anonymous
>
> The Heart of a Goof *(maybe the funniest golf novel ever written—read it before the British Open)*
>
> The Most of P. G. Wodehouse *(a collection of short stories that feature all of Wodehouse's best-known characters, as well as a short novel called* Quick Service, *which was Wodehouse's personal favorite among all his works)*

THE WRITER'S CRAFT

Those interested in writing as a career should read these books, but devoted readers will also appreciate them for the insights they give into literature and the writing life.

Aspects of the Novel, E. M. Forster's classic work, is a collection of a series of lectures he gave at Cambridge University in 1927. In it he defines his topic as "any fictitious prose work over 50,000 words," and in the most welcoming of tones discusses the elements that go into crafting a work of fiction: story, people, plot, fantasy, prophecy, pattern, and rhythm. It's great fun to read because of Forster's candidness and dry sense of humor, *viz:* "Books have to be read (worse luck, for it takes so long a time). It is the only way of discovering what they contain. A few savage tribes eat them, but reading is the only method of assimilation revealed to the West."

In **On Moral Fiction,** John Gardner writes passionately (and controversially) of his belief that literature contains truths about the way we live and ought to live, and that novel writing must not be about the triumph of style over substance. Another book by Gardner about the writer's craft is **The Art of Fiction: Notes on Craft for Young Writers,** in which he reiterates his belief in the validity and seriousness of the writer's craft, offers writing exercises to improve one's writing, and stresses again and again the importance of writers reading the best of literature, past and present.

In Ben Yagoda's **The Sound on the Page: Style and Voice in Writing**, he describes the two historically opposed views of what "style" means in literature. On one hand is the classic view of Strunk and White, who believed that writing with clarity—transparency—was the correct way to write. The opposite view is best demonstrated by the works of writers such as Dave Eggers or Jonathan Franzen. Yagoda suggests combining the two into a "middle style," using the best of both approaches. He intersperses interviews with writers (Cynthia Ozick, Harold Bloom, and Elizabeth McCracken, among others) with a discussion of what makes for good reading.

Since I am a big fan of Janet Burroway's novels (especially **Raw Silk** and **Opening Nights**), I found that her **Writing Fiction: A Guide to Narrative Craft**, although it was aimed at college students and not necessarily the casual reader/writer, offered an excellent approach to issues of craft and style, especially (but not exclusively) in relation to literary fiction.

YOU CAN'T JUDGE A BOOK BY ITS COVER

We're always being told that you can't—or shouldn't—judge a book by its cover, but in fact we all do exactly that. Often the single motivating factor in deciding whether to pick up a particular book is how we respond to the cover. But there are some books—perhaps especially novels—that are so complex and challenging to describe that it's difficult to imagine the right cover for them, one that draws the reader in, hinting at the particular gifts that the book offers. Here are some of my very favorite novels that I'm glad I didn't judge by their covers.

For me, the wickedly leering doll on the cover of Donna Tartt's **The Little Friend** didn't convey the strengths of this coming-of-age novel, which features Harriet Dufresnes, a gutsy twelve-year-old kid on the cusp of adolescence—think Scout Finch of Harper Lee's **To Kill a Mockingbird** or Frankie, the heroine of Carson McCullers's **The Member of the Wedding**—who decides she is going to track down the person who murdered her older brother, Robin, twelve years before.

The cover of **Fool** by Frederick G. Dillen doesn't give much sense of the unexpected treat awaiting readers of this quirky novel about Barnaby Griswold, a middle-aged man who has consistently made all the wrong decisions—in both his public and private lives—and who at last realizes that it's finally time to grow up.

The cover gives little hint of the charms of John Griesemer's **No One Thinks of Greenland**, but this novel about Rudy Spruance, a young army corporal who is sent as punishment to an army base in Greenland (where the six months of winter are known as the "stark, raving dark"), and who finds his loyalties tested when he starts uncovering secrets that his superior officers would rather keep hidden, is a treasure.

In **Front Cover: Great Book Jacket and Cover Design**, Alan Powers reminds us of the power of book jackets to sell books (or, conversely, to influence us not to buy or even borrow and read a book). Although it's decidedly Britishcentric, most of the books whose covers are shown will be recognizable to American readers—William Faulkner's **Light in August**, Norman Mailer's **The Naked and the Dead**, Sylvia Plath's **Ariel**, Philip Roth's **Goodbye, Columbus**, and novels by P. D. James, Agatha Christie, James Baldwin, and Dick Francis, among many others. There's also a picture of the wonderful cover done in England for one of my favorite novels, Colson Whitehead's **The Intuitionist**.

YOUR TAX DOLLARS AT WORK: GOOD READING FROM THE GOVERNMENT (REALLY!)

At one of the Illinois stops on my *Book Lust* tour, a librarian in the audience asked if I had included any government documents. I admitted that I had somehow never thought of "gov docs" (as they're known in Libraryland) as pleasure reading, just as sources of information. But I agreed that if she could come up with some documents that I enjoyed reading, I would include them in *More Book Lust*. She did, and here they are.

United States Army in World War 2, War in the Pacific, Fall of the Philippines *by Louis Morton*

Language of the Land: The Library of Congress Book of Literary Maps *by Martha Hopkins and Michael Buscher*

Mud & Guts: A Look at the Common Soldier of the American Revolution *by Bill Mauldin*

Respectfully Quoted: A Dictionary of Quotations Requested from the Congressional Research Service, *edited by Suzy Platt*

The Openhearted Audience: Ten Authors Talk about Writing for Children, *edited by Virginia Haviland*

Venona: Soviet Espionage and the American Response, 1939–1957, *edited by Robert Louis Benson and Michael Warner*

WRA: A Story of Human Conservation
(the WRA was the War Relocation
Authority, and "human conservation" was
the removal of Japanese Americans from their
homes to internment camps during World
War II)

You can get many of these through the U.S. Government Printing Office, and all of them at any public or academic library that's designated as a federal depository for government documents.

INDEX

A

H

O

R

ABOUT THE AUTHOR

Nancy Pearl has worked as a librarian and bookseller in Detroit, Tulsa, and Seattle. In 1998, she developed the program "If All of Seattle Read the Same Book," which has been replicated in communities around the globe. The former Executive Director of the Washington Center for the Book, Pearl celebrates the written word by speaking at bookstores, community groups, and libraries across the country. She is a regular commentator about books on National Public Radio's "Morning Edition" and NPR affiliate stations KUOW in Seattle and KWGS in Tulsa, and is the model for the Librarian Action Figure.

In 2004, Pearl became the 50th winner of the Women's National Book Association Award for her extraordinary contribution to the world of books. In the moments when Pearl finds herself without a book, she is an avid bicyclist and happy grandmother of two. She lives in Seattle with her husband Joe.